EVALUATING ADMINISTRATIVE
PERSONNEL IN SCHOOL SYSTEMS

Evaluating Administrative Personnel in School Systems

DALE L. BOLTON

Chairman
Educational Administration
College of Education
University of Washington

Teachers College, Columbia University
New York and London 1980

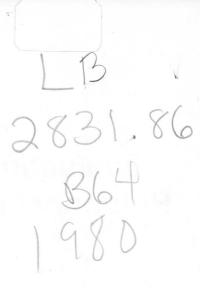
Copyright © 1980 by Teachers College, Columbia University. All rights reserved.
Published by Teachers College Press, 1234 Amsterdam Avenue, New York, NY 10027

Library of Congress Cataloging in Publication Data

Bolton, Dale L   1927–
    Evaluating administrative personnel in school systems.

    Bibliography: p.
    Includes index.
    1. School administrators, Rating of.   I.   Title.
LB2831.86.B64   1980   371.2′01   79-21121
ISBN 0-8077-2572-2

Designed by Romeo M. Enriquez
10 9 8 7 6 5 4 3 2 1   89 88 87 86 85 84 83 82 81 80
Manufactured in the U.S.A.

CONTENTS

1 Introduction to Evaluation 1

2 Phase I: Planning for Evaluation 39

3 Phase II: Collecting Information 79

Phase III: Using Information   91

Assessment of the Evaluation Process   113

6 **Applications and Examples   136**

LIST OF FORMS

Forms Showing Various Scales for Measurement   195

Summary Forms and Documents   204

Checklists and Forms for Planning   213

FOREWORD

When contemplating the massive perplexities of personnel evaluation in education, one might understandably conclude that the process consists of attempting to do the impossible by measuring the unmeasurable in situations that are uncontrollable, resulting in plans that are unworkable and decisions that are untenable. Because the evaluation of administrative personnel is undoubtedly even more difficult to accomplish defensibly than is the evaluation of teachers, it would be easy to be skeptical when a book appears with a title such as this one bears.

The instruments and processes that have been so typical of personnel evaluation in schools have not been such as to inspire much confidence. All too often, personnel evaluation is viewed as a process in which an evaluator, who usually possesses very little organized information that is relevant, analyzed, and interpreted, checks items on a rating scale. The scale categories are usually a conglomeration of criterion- and norm-referenced terms (e.g., "acceptable" and "average"), which are not necessarily based on hard data and do not provide much helpful guidance for improvement efforts. The behaviors or characteristics that the evaluator rates are seldom well defined (e.g., what is meant by "common sense" or "emotional stability"?); they are often combined into confusing mixtures of disparate entities lumped into one category (e.g., this little gem, found in a teacher rating scale used in a respected urban school system: "Exemplifies personal integrity that reflects high moral standards and refinement; shows enthusiasm for work, evidences creative ability and perseverance; is loyal, consistent, and sincere"); and there are numerous illusions such as "voice modulation" that are unimportant or irrelevant, even if they could be assessed reliably. The users of such scales almost always declare that the improvement of performance is the primary purpose of the evaluation process, and yet the accomplishment of such a purpose through these scales would be fortuitous, indeed.

Bolton offers no quick and easy how-to-do-it nostrums for the ills of administrator evaluation. Instead, he systematically proceeds from a general consideration of personnel evaluation and the problems it entails to a discussion of the essential steps in the process. He sets forth a convincing case for the individualization of evaluation through management by objectives, and he shows the reader how to make MBO work in a real-life situation. He includes a chapter on the assessment of the evaluation process itself, an often neglected aspect of evaluation.

This is not an esoteric, jargon-laden, pie-in-the-sky treatment of a tough problem. School boards and administrators who are looking for a practical guide to action will find material here that is understandable and right to the point. The final chapter presents an impressive collection of examples to illustrate the author's points, and the examples are described and categorized in order to make them maximally useful.

A sound system for evaluating administrative personnel will never be an easy one to implement. Bolton makes it a manageable process—and that is no small accomplishment. Professors of educational administration and practitioners alike should find in this book the kind of help they have been seeking.

—Kenneth E. McIntyre
Department of Educational Administration
University of Texas, Austin

PREFACE

The story has been told about a man who was asked how to determine whether a school administrator was good or not. His reply was "Can he eat? Can he sleep? Can he laugh?" The implication was that if the administrator had a hearty appetite (or did not have ulcers because of worry about the job), did not allow the stress of the day to affect his sleep, and still had a sense of humor after working with the problems of the day—then he was a good administrator. All this may very well be related to good administration if in fact it is important for an administrator to be capable of handling stressful situations without exhibiting stress symptoms. However, adjusting to stressful situations is not sufficient to being a good administrator. If one wants to identify good administrators, one must examine administrative behaviors that develop conditions conducive to eating, sleeping, and laughing. Indeed, if one thinks that the capability to eat, sleep, and laugh are unrelated to whether the job is being done well, it may be that the person simply does not understand the complexity of the administrator's job.

Analysis of this story hints at the necessity of examining both the characteristics and behaviors of administrators, and herein lies some of the complexity of the task of evaluating administrators. The complexity of evaluation and the significance of the job being done by the administrator are what make the evaluation problem so fascinating.

During the time that I have been involved in educational administration, I have become more and more concerned about clear specification of the purpose of administrators. Many of them consider themselves "generalists," yet I maintain that they are as much "specialists" as any other member of the educational organization. It seems to me that their specialty is related to the goals and direction of the organization that they are charged to administer. If the organizational goals are not clear to them, and if they cannot articulate them to clients, students, teachers, and noncertificated personnel, when questions and problems arise they are likely to exert leadership solely on the basis of their authority—i.e., on the basis of the position they hold. This behavior causes problems because the real basis of their leadership is their capacity to develop and articulate the goals of the organization in such a fashion that specific plans may be made for implementing these goals.

In exercising this leadership, educational administrators must focus on two things: (1) maximizing productivity and (2) maximizing morale of the organization. Note the emphasis on *maximizing*. Unless they focus on this, the tyranny of the urgent has a very strong tendency to drive out the important. In order to maximize productivity, administrators must take into consideration both effectiveness and efficiency. This means that the administrators must help members of the organization to determine *what* should be done as well as *how* it should be done. At no time should administrators slip into a pattern of being satisfied with ordinary results or mediocre morale; satisfying is not an acceptable substitute for maximizing.

If administrators are interested in maximizing productivity, they have three approaches available: (1) change personal administrative behavior, (2) change the working conditions of subordinates, or (3) change the behavior of subordinates. The first two of these are much easier to manage than the third, but to be done well all three should be based on evaluative data.

When an administrator wants to bring about change in others, the major strategy is to set goals via a planning process. In order to *sustain* the highest level of productivity, the administrator should provide feedback. These two processes (goal setting and feedback) are the administrator's means for initiating change in the behavior of others (or self, for that matter) and for sustaining that change. A common error is for the administrator to expect the positive feedback to bring about a higher level of productivity, but this misses the point of providing feedback.

It should be noted that both goal setting and feedback are parts of the evaluation process. Therefore, evaluation contributes significantly to increasing the productivity of an organization. It requires little insight to see that the manner in which evaluation occurs has a great deal to do with the morale of the individuals in the organization. Therefore, we have two major reasons for the importance of evaluation: it contributes to the productivity as well as to the morale of the members of the organization.

In addition to these motivational factors for writing about the evaluation of educational administrators, I have been concerned about two other aspects of evaluation. First, because of its very nature, evaluation allows one to plan systematically for changes in the organization. Because administrators are in key positions, the evaluation of them provides considerable leverage for bringing about change in the organization by allowing the school system to become more sensitive to clients and society and to initiate as well as to respond to change. Second, evaluation allows one to correct errors that may creep into the system. Again, because of administrators' positions in the system, errors that creep into their behavior can have a particularly dysfunctional effect on the school organization.

Because I am interested in the training of administrators as well as their continuing development, I have included some research findings and theoretical background as well as some applicatory materials. Chapter 1 provides a perspective concerning the environment within which the administrator works followed by some views of the administrator and the evaluation system. Chapters 2, 3, and 4 then discuss in detail the phases of the evaluation process and how evaluation can be used. Examples are provided that should be of assistance in implementing an evaluation system. Chapter 5 explores the assessment of the evaluation process, an activity which is essential in detecting any errors in the evaluation system itself. Suggestions are given for the training of evaluators of administrators, which is usually required for proper implementation of the evaluation process. Finally, Chapter 6 gives a set of guidelines, examples, and forms that can be used to develop procedures and materials in a given school district. Although Chapter 6 can be read independently of the other chapters and the materials may be used without attending to the ideas in the early chapters, I think the optimum use of the examples and forms in Chapter 6 will be obtained by relating them to the prior chapters. One might even read Chapter 6 first, but I would encourage the reader to go back to the prior chapters in order to understand fully why the examples and forms are included.

In writing a book, one is always indebted to numerous people, including other authors who provide ideas that stimulate and encourage. In addition, I have been assisted by students in my university courses and by participants in workshops. The stimulation provided by these two groups is different from each other in that students have divergent views and one must work to convince them of the adequacy of models and concepts, while practitioners require that ideas be applicable to their situations. Because of the nature of the interaction with these two groups, it is often impossible to identify sources of many of the ideas. However, feedback from both groups has aided me in developing the ideas presented here.

Finally, this book is a natural outgrowth of my work in the evaluation of teachers. I have often said that the evaluation of teachers will never be done very well until administrators are evaluated on how they evaluate teachers. Therefore, I think a book on the evaluation of administrators will eventually be beneficial in the evaluation of teachers, which in turn will benefit the education of children and youth. It is my hope that some administrators will find this book useful in this effort.

Dale L. Bolton
Seattle, Washington
August 1979

EVALUATING ADMINISTRATIVE PERSONNEL IN SCHOOL SYSTEMS

1

INTRODUCTION TO EVALUATION

As one contemplates the problems involved in designing and implementing a system of evaluation for administrators of schools and school systems, there is a strong tendency to revert to the history of personnel evaluation. However, this may be a mistake, or at best of little significance, inasmuch as the rural agrarian environment where personal independence was a major value has been replaced by a densely populated, industrialized environment where interdependence is a necessity for survival and well-being. To examine personnel evaluation practices of the past twenty-five years makes some sense, but contributions of earlier periods would not be practical.

It should come as a surprise to nobody that the administration of school systems has changed in recent years. The whole milieu in which schools exist has changed. Not only is the technology, the substance, the student body, and the methodology of education changing but also the environment and the clients. As a result, school systems and their administrators are being bombarded on all sides by demands to satisfy the expectations of parents, students, school boards, government agencies, to name only a few. The fact that many of these expectations are conflicting by nature adds to the complexity of the administrator's task.

The state of education was not always so. In many communities in the past, the expectations were straightforward, relatively uniform, and well known. When administrators and teachers fulfilled these expectations, they were respected by the community and their judgments were trusted. Often parents were well acquainted with teachers and administrators with the result that communication encouraged similarity of viewpoints. Since both the parents and the professionals were thinking along similar lines in relation to desired outcomes and necessary procedures, parents willingly delegated this decision making to teachers and administrators. Even where differences of opinion occurred, many parents were of the view that the professionals knew what was best for their children.

However, an increased level of education of the general public, larger schools and school systems, increased mobility of the population (including teachers and administrators), a more complex body of knowledge and work technology, and decreased assumption of responsibility by the home and church (and even the individual) for the growth and development of youth have produced some interesting concomitant responses:

1. Schools are expected to be responsible for problems of behavior, motivation, and attitudes of youth—in spite of the fact that there is little unanimity among parents in any of these matters. This makes it difficult to provide social stimuli that promote behaviors, motivations, and attitudes acceptable to diverse clients.
2. Decisions that are made by professionals (even when parents consider the decisions within the professionals' prerogative) are being questioned by parents and taxpayers. There is less trust of school officials' decisions now than pre-Watergate; many no longer think that most public officials are committed to making decisions that are designed to "benefit the total population."
3. Many people are of the view that public officials are responsive only to pressure; consequently, there is an increase in the number and type of manipulative procedures being used to pressure administrators into making desired decisions. Fewer people use personal acquaintance with the administrator as a means of facilitating communication and problem solving.

Environment of Administration

Although one may be aware of these views regarding the environment of the administrator, she or he may not be aware that there are some general characteristics of this environment that contribute to an understanding of the need for evaluation of administrators and are pertinent to the details of a system of evaluation. First, let us examine some of the general characteristics of the environment and then turn to some that are more specifically related to the evaluation of administrators.

UNCERTAIN

Guthrie and Willower describe the social setting within which teachers and administrators function:

> As a social organization, the public school is characterized by political vulnerability, a sometimes unwilling clientele bound to the organization by law rather than by choice, prominent logistical problems in serving its student clients in a crowded setting reminiscent of an Oriental market, a quasi-professional staff that must process people but in diverse styles uninformed by a widely celebrated work technology and goals that are often vague and varied and not amenable to ready assessment (1973:284).

The statement appears merely accurate and descriptive with the first reading, and one might pass it by as obvious. However, note the elements of uncertainty that permeate the social setting for administration of the school system. First, it is politically vulnerable. The budget is subject to annual review[1] by local groups or individuals who have a variety of vested interests, which makes it relatively unique in the political arena of the United States, since other municipalities invoke less interest, and state legislatures and the Congress are much less accessible to taxpayers. In addition, subjects of heated public political activities have included the nature of the curriculum, provisions for minority interests, methods teachers use, disciplinary procedures used, sports programs developed, attendance boundaries, hiring procedures, school calendar, decentralization and desegregation, busing, school closures, teacher negotiations and strikes, and release of personnel. The vulnerability of the school system is directly related to the intensity of the activity, which varies from district to district according to the issues involved.

Second, the school has some unwilling clients. Some students, especially after reaching a certain age, do not see the relevancy of the school for their lives—at any time in the future, but especially at the present. Because of this there is an uncertainty involved in their behavior from day to day. The rebelliousness is not uncertain, but it is sometimes more active than at other times; when it will be active and when passive is unpredictable.

The logistical problems are not uncertain in themselves, except when the students are mobile, shifting from one school to another. However, the diverse styles of teachers and the lack of an accepted set of practices to defer to introduces considerable uncertainty. This is particularly evident where teachers have become more independent—some pleading that they desire to "do their own thing," others appealing to academic freedom, and still others making a case for an expression of professionalism. Under such circumstances, varying degrees of uncertainty prevail on the part of parents and school officials regarding what reactions are appropriate.

Last, the uncertainty of goals probably contributes to the other uncertainties. For example, the vagueness of goals probably contributes to the political vulnerability of the budget and the curriculum; people may be quite reluctant to invest in vague goals that are difficult to measure. Yet, at the same time, it may be very difficult to reach agreement on specific goals—so the very fact that a consensus is needed in order to pass a budget may cause the goals to be stated in vague and general terms. Specific goals may be desirable for obtaining commitment from some members of the community, yet general goals may be needed in order to reach agreement. Therefore, considerable uncertainty exists regarding what the general goals mean and even more uncertainty regarding how measurement should be done.

---

[1]In order to obtain an adequate budget for operations, most schools in the State of Washington have been required to pass an operating budget annually with a 60 percent majority; in addition, at least 40 percent of those voting in the immediately preceding election must vote in order for the vote to be valid. In an election immediately following a presidential election, it has been difficult in some districts to validate elections; in many it has been difficult to obtain a 60 percent majority.

Levinson (1968:8) expresses the predicament in these terms:

> If he (the manager) demands that people produce, he is exploitative. If he treats them with beneficence, he is paternalistic. If he is unconcerned about their worries, he is rejecting. If he opposes what he believes to be irrational, he is hostile. If he gives in, he is weak. He no longer knows with the certainty of his predecessors which way to turn.

So, one characteristic of the environment within which an educational administrator operates is uncertainty. He may choose to cope with it or to ignore it, but it is there.

COMPLEX

A contributing factor to the feelings of uncertainty in the administrator's role is the *complexity* of the task and the environment within which administrative tasks are performed. Raia (1974:7) describes these conditions in the following terms:

> The manager's job, then, is both complex and changing. He is faced with the task of continuously redefining his role and activities in the light of changing circumstances. His responsibilities are diverse, but his authority is fuzzy and unclear. The claims on his time and energy are severe. He can no longer respond to all of the demands and pressures placed upon him. Unless he has a clear idea of where he is going and how he plans to get there, frustration is inevitable. He can ill afford to stand around waiting for something to happen or for someone to tell him what to do.

As Raia points out, the complexity of the task interacts with its changing and uncertain expectations, and this displays itself in the form of a lack of goal clarity. It is easy to have clear and agreed-upon goals in a simple and static situation, but not many such conditions exist for educational administrators today.

Gaynor (1977:42—43) indicates that a part of the complexity of the environment is due to the multiple expectations placed on administrators. A school principal, for example, must be very sensitive to the expectations of citizens, teachers, and upper administrators; in many school systems, these expectations may contain substantial differences. Not only may there be differences between such groups, but differences within the groups may be sufficient to precipitate conflicts. On issues of any consequence, such conflict is evidence of forces that can have considerable impact on how the administrator behaves.

Levinson discusses the world of the executive in terms of simultaneous forces acting upon the potential performance of the administrator. Four of the five forces (public, sources of finance, management controls, competitors, and employees) that impinge on business executives also affect educational administrators.[2] He indicates that these forces are interrelated and always being dealt with simultaneously by a leader. Levinson (1968:7) hints at the complexity when he states:

> The way in which these sources of power are managed by the leader depends on the

---

[2]In a strict sense, education is not considered a competitive enterprise, except in the sense that it competes with other governmental services for funds.

strength of any one of the forces, the competence of the leader, and the cumulative effects of their acting in concert and acting upon each other.

Since each of these acts as multiple sources of power rather than single forces, the complexity of the world of the administrator is considerable.

PROBLEMATICAL

A third way of describing the environment of administrators is that it is problematical. Not only must administrators contend with the disruptions due to unexpected events, but they must also deal with obstacles that occur as a result of attitudes among those with whom they work.

Gross and Herriott (1966:68) note that one such obstacle is the claim of subordinates to professional status. Such an attitude sometimes exhibits itself in the form of resistances to leadership efforts—on the basis that efforts to influence or help are basically an invasion of professional territorial rights. They say that, "in short, the fact that subordinates have a claim to professional status could lead them to resist any efforts on the part of their administrators to serve as their leaders."

Posner, Allen, and Wortman (1975) describe a more pervasive attitude of the mid '70s that may not have existed on such a large scale during the time of Gross and Herriott's research, viz., a new attitude toward work. This new attitude is based on the view that work should provide much more than a means of livelihood. Since much time is spent in a work setting, there should be opportunity for personal growth and achievement, independence, activity, and responsibility. Within such an ethic, problems of motivation, sphere of control, planning, and implementation of work can arise—especially when conflicting views of attitudes toward work prevail between administrators and those they supervise.

Another obstacle to the administrator is the heavy demand on time made by routine clerical and administrative duties (Gross & Herriott, 1966:68). This demand is complicated by the fact that when administrators spend a good deal of their time performing such routine duties (or other activities which do not bring them into contact with those they supervise), the actual activities are incongruent with the major role perceived by clients—a helping relationship to them (Estosito, Smith, & Burbank, 1975:63). This role-activity incongruity becomes an obstacle to initiating leadership or maintaining harmonious relationships with others.

Under conditions where many problems exist, administrators must be aware of the limitations of the role they have and be careful not to try to do too much. Levinson (1968:8) has stated the problem in this way:

> The head of an organization unwittingly assumes the responsibility of being all things to all men who are related to the organization. He must revere the past, predict and succeed in the future, make a profit, carry the burdens of people and operations no longer efficient, and enjoy himself besides.

Anyone who has held an administrative position recognizes the internal problem of adopting an omnipotent posture, but the problem exists because of the nature of the position and the nature of people. The position allows one to help others, to provide answers, to make decisions, to have authority and power; the nature of man is to be self-serving. Under such circumstances, problems occur easily. Perhaps it is wise to remember words attributed to Lord Halifax, "The vanity of teaching often tempteth me to forget what a fool I am." If one recognizes that the opportunity for vanity in administration is magnified in comparison with teaching, then he should heed the implicit warning.

CHANGING

It may hardly seem necessary to discuss the changing aspect of the administrator's environment after the prior discussion of its uncertain, complex, and problematical nature. However, certain aspects may be worth pointing out.

For example, the national climate for education has changed in the past twenty years. The immediate post-Sputnic era saw a heavy commitment to general education in the form of academic achievement. The mid-'60s and early '70s brought the promise of increased commitment to social good (implying an even heavier commitment to education) if the Vietnam war could be ended; but by the mid-'70s it became apparent that education was perceived less favorably as an agent for bringing about socially desirable goals than it had been in the mid-'60s. A climate of economic "belt-tightening" mixed itself with skepticism regarding whether education could produce what it promised.

Such changes, of course, engendered changes in the roles of educational administrators. Gaynor (1977:43) presents the view that changes in the national climate for education, legal and fiscal supports for and demands on the school, the nature of students in a given locale, and composition of the faculty can change so drastically over time that not only will priorities change, but the need for a dramatic change in the style of leadership will be evident.

And while external pressures quite often provide the impetus for change, there are some evidences that certain internal factors make it difficult for an educational leader to initiate change. One of these factors is the diversity that exists within the teaching faculty. Since openness of organizational climate in school faculties has been shown to facilitate educational change, one might reasonably assume that dogmatism would impede change. However, Brown and Anderson (1967) report that it is not the *amount* (mean level) of dogmatism that is related to openness of school climate but the *variance*. This means that it is not whether a faculty is close-minded or open-minded that is important in relation to school climate but whether they are homogeneously so. Therefore, if a school is relatively homogeneous on a measure of dogmatism, it is likely to be open in climate. The problems arise if the faculty is diverse in dogmatism. When this is the case, the climate is likely to be more closed, with the result that it may be very difficult to initiate educational change. One might hypothesize that similar conditions would hold for external populations, but empirical evidence is not available in this dimension.

ACCOUNTABLE

The trend toward accountability in recent years has not escaped any segment of public enterprise. If one has any doubt regarding the desire of the public to make governmental agencies and personnel accountable, he or she surely has not been reading newspapers and news magazines. The trend has permeated much of our life, to the extent that many people believe they need very little expertise to evaluate whether others are doing their job. The following is taken from a newspaper article titled "Dentists Pulling Too Many Teeth?":

> Harrisburg, Pa.—(AP)—Six million teeth are pulled unnecessarily each year, Herbert Denenberg, state insurance commissioner, said today in issuing "32 rules on how to keep your 32 teeth—or however many you have left." . . . At least 15 per cent of all dentists are incompetent or dishonest, said Denenberg, who was criticized by doctors for a similar statement he made when issuing "A Shopper's Guide to Surgery" (*Seattle Times,* 1973:A9).

Notice who was attempting to hold the dentists accountable for their activities. When conditions are such that insurance commissioners feel they can evaluate dentists and surgeons, surely there are many who think they have the expertise to suggest the means for making educational administrators accountable for their actions. After all, almost everyone has gone through high school, encountering at least three principals along the route. Seeing them function in certain aspects of their job (which did not look nearly as technical as that of the dentist or physician) developed a certain familiarity and "feel" for how the job should be done.

Interestingly enough, the increase in concern for accountability in education occurred concomitantly with development of management by objectives (MBO) procedures within administration. Although one may not have precipitated the other, they certainly are perceived as being related. MBO was initiated (or originally discussed by industry) during the mid-'50s, and its primary impetus was a concern for product or output. There was very little initial concern for monitoring procedures used to accomplish objectives, but considerable leeway was given if managers were able to produce what was expected of them. However, in education, we have seen much concern for both process and product (Bolton, 1974), and the tendency is for the public to hold administrators accountable for both.

The public's desire for accountability often expresses itself in its concern about increasing costs. However, the public is becoming more and more sophisticated economically. Their concern is related not only to an increase in absolute cost of education but also to the increased cost in relation to the quality of the product obtained. Much of the public is very aware of the fact that increases in wages without increases in productivity contribute directly to inflation. In effect, if workers obtain a 10 percent increase in wages while their productivity rises only 6 percent, there is a 4 percent contribution to an inflationary trend. With our recent history of double-digit inflation, the public is justifiably interested in the cost/quality relationship in education. Many are willing to pay increased salaries for educational personnel, but they expect those involved to be held accountable for increased productivity when that occurs.[3]

In addition, the public wants to hold the profession accountable for incompetent or ineffective members. There are some, undoubtedly, who can be classified in these categories; their number and identification will vary with the individual doing the classification. In a suspicious climate when public officials' images are not high, there is an increased clamor for accountability.

The last two concerns, i.e., for cost/quality examination and for ridding the profession of incompetent and ineffective members, appear to be directly related to the increased power of professional organizations. That is, the needs have grown at the same time that power has increased. When these concerns are expressed to organizations that are feeling this increased sense of power, the potential is great for conflict within the environment of the educational administrator.

Another element of accountability that has emerged in the past five years is related to the reduced enrollment in some school districts. Because of reduced enrollments, reduction in force (RIF) procedures have been initiated in order to adjust staff size to the enrollment. In many cases the strong accountability forces in these communities have asked that program needs and seniority not be the only criteria for reducing the force. In effect, they would like for personnel evaluation to be the means of holding officials accountable for efficient and effective use of funds.

In spite of the considerable amount of discussion and writing regarding accountability, many are still unclear as to how the term is used. There seem to be some who interchange the term *accountability* with the term *evaluation*. Perhaps it would be well to differentiate between the two. *Accountability* has to do with responsibility for taking action of a particular sort. It has to do with whether the following conditions have been met:

- Action was taken with the intent of accomplishing organizational goals.
- Action that was irrelevant to organizational goals was not taken.
- At the time the action was taken, and in light of the facts known, the action appeared to be sufficient to accomplish the organizational goals.
- Steps were taken to determine if the results were satisfactory and if modifications should be made in the actions taken.

On the other hand, *evaluation* has to do with making judgments regarding the set of events, behaviors, and/or results of behavior in light of predetermined and well-understood objectives. Therefore, evaluation is a control mechanism that allows one to correct errors and plan changes, whereas, accountability allows one to determine whether a person (or organization) carries out responsible actions. In a nondeterministic domain such as education, accountability is for actions (procedures) only;

---

[3]For a discussion of one way of allocating funds for salary purposes to educational personnel, see Bolton, 1965.

therefore, one must evaluate processes in order to determine if one is accountable. But part of the action all professionals are accountable for is evaluation to determine if additional or different actions are needed. Therefore, evaluation contributes to the accountability process by becoming one of the actions for which everyone is responsible. Evaluation is necessary for making accountability statements, but it also may contribute to making other types of statements (e.g., those that help to correct errors that creep into the system).

LEGALISTIC

The environment in which schools are administered is also legalistic. This is evident by the number of differences and conflicts handled through court actions. Many school districts of medium size have full-time legal counsel, and larger districts sometimes have a retinue of lawyers providing advice and dealing with legal settlements.

Laws pertaining to education are becoming more numerous and complex. Recent laws regarding evaluation of personnel have increased the need for more detailed information of a high quality. Not only have many states passed laws requiring an annual evaluation of all certificated personnel, but some have specified the minimum amount of time administrators must spend in classroom observations.[4] Some laws are so specific and detailed in delineating an administrator's responsibility that they place considerable constraint on use of his time.

The reasons for the establishment of laws regarding evaluation of personnel (and programs, in some states) are closely allied to the concern for accountability in relation to effectiveness of personnel. The public wants evidence that personnel are effective in their jobs and, if they are not, that efforts are being made either to improve their performance or release them from their positions. If they can improve, evaluation should provide information for designing supervision processes that will be instrumental in bringing about improvement; but if they show evidence that they cannot correct deficiencies, then evaluation should provide the basis for release. This interest in accountability is only partially concerned with economics; another part is related to protection of children from incompetent teachers and administrators.

Although the public is insisting upon accountability for economic reasons and protection of children, professional organizations want to be assured of protection and due process for members of the profession. They want to be sure that teachers will not be released without adequate evaluation procedures. Their concern is that the laws regarding evaluation of personnel might create a situation where an overzealous, capricious, or incompetent administrator would make adverse decisions

---

[4]One state, Washington, requires that principals make at least two observational visits per year to each teacher, taking at least sixty minutes in total duration, followed by conferences with the teachers. Failure of the principal to follow the procedures specified by law can become a basis for his release.

without providing appropriate information and assistance. If a teacher is released without having been provided information about deficiencies and how these deficiencies can be corrected, then that teacher has been denied due process according to law. Consequently, teacher organizations are keeping close watch over the details of laws that require certain processes to provide protections to their members.

SYSTEMATIZED

In any organization where tasks are repeated, there is the tendency to attempt to systematize them. This is true of educational organizations as well as organizations and individuals who interact with school systems. However, in recent years, systematization has gone beyond the mere routinization of tasks. An entire methodology has developed around the area of systems analysis. At times the methodology has leaned heavily on mathematics; at other times it has used generalized problem solving and analytical skills. The approach has incorporated the use of computers, the visual display of models, and the simulation of real world phenomena. But the attempts have all incorporated a common element, the viewing of a total system by examining the parts of the system carefully and analyzing the interrelationships of these parts. The attempt has been to avoid the isolated examination of subsystems and to emphasize an examination of their interrelatedness.

This trend toward systems analysis in organizations has permeated much of management in business and industry and governmental agencies; more recently it has infiltrated education and has had considerable impact on some school agencies. Specifically, it has caused examination of interrelationships among the personnel subsystems of selection, supervision and in-service training, and evaluation (Bolton, 1973:133−134; 1974:184−185).

As a subsystem, selection is basically a *prediction* decision—i.e., an attempt is made to predict how a person will behave in a particular situation and what will result from such behavior. Based on such predictions, a choice is made among various applicants. At the time the choice is made, however, another often neglected decision should be made. Since the person who is hired is placed in a position or assignment where certain tasks are to be done, and since the person will be supervised with relation to those tasks, there should be a determination at the point of hiring regarding what type of supervision is appropriate. If the person has had experience in a position of similar nature, the supervision would be somewhat different from that of an inexperienced person. Based on the information obtained in the selection process, the supervision and in-service program is then designed.

The supervision and in-service training program is basically a *treatment* process rather than a prediction process. It provides conditions that help the person do the tasks most effectively and efficiently. For some people, activities within the organization may be appropriate, e.g., special assignments, participation in special meetings or workshops, committee memberships, visits to other locations where similar tasks are being performed. For others, it may be helpful if they engage in activities outside the organization, e.g., seminars and workshops, university courses, reading programs, participation in selected professional programs, collaborative research projects. Regardless of what treatments or conditions are selected for an individual, the information obtained from both the selection and the evaluation processes should be used if the supervision process is to be individualized. To design the supervision process without thought of its interrelationship with the other two subsystems would lead to dysfunctional or trivial activities.

The evaluation subsystem, in addition to providing information to the supervision and in-service subsystem, also provides information to the selection process. In fact, it allows one to validate the selection process. Because it provides basic information to the other two subsystems, it is viewed primarily as a *feedback mechanism* rather than either a prediction process or a treatment process. It provides feedback that allows one to know whether selections have been made properly and whether supervision and in-service programs should be modified in order to increase effectiveness of personnel. Without this feedback, errors can creep into the system undetected; when this happens, the deviations that are occurring tend to amplify themselves, things get worse, and major crises arise. Evaluation many times allows detection before major problems come about.

Two General Characteristics of the Successful Administrator

It is not the intention of this section to provide another of many armchair descriptions of the successful administrator; rather, it is to examine some pertinent ideas in the literature about the topic.

First, it is difficult to acquire empirical research that identifies administrator characteristics that can be generalized to a variety of situations, which could therefore be considered as necessary to a successful administrator. In general, research indicates that there is much variability in how a person can function and still be successful as an administrator. This is probably due to the compensating nature of many of the variables under consideration (e.g., hard work sometimes compensates for lack of brilliance, and vice versa), or perhaps because of the way in which the immediate environment adapts to the characteristics and behaviors of the administrator.

However, in a study done with Sears managers (Bentz, 1967:177), it was found that "successful performance in specialized areas is distinguished by the same kinds of psychological characteristics as is successful executive performance in nonspecialized assignments." It should be noted that this study was conducted within the boundaries of a single company that placed its managers in a given set of constraints.

Because of the lack of generalizability of personality characteristics across various situations, there has been a tendency to move entirely to the practice of evaluating only "objective" behaviors or outcomes. However, Kavanaugh (1971:654) argues that there is not sufficient empirical evidence to accept the "objective traits only" view and to abandon the evaluation of a worker's personality traits. He emphasizes the rather practical approach of including personality traits when they appear to be relevant to a particular situation or job performance.

Because of this long history in the research literature of difficulty in ascertaining generalizable characteristics, I am very hesitant to identify any which I think generalize. However, it is quite evident that two characteristics *are* generalizable; they therefore are considered as necessary for successful administrators.

PURPOSEFULNESS

Hughes (1968:38) states that "an effective manager is one who accomplishes the organization's goals." This appears to be definitional at first rather than descriptive. However, Hughes points out that if goals have not been set in the past, they cannot be used for evaluating job performance. In addition, when an organization does not have clear goals, it is difficult to expect members of the organization to be goal-seeking or purposeful. So, it appears that one of the characteristics of the effective manager is purposefulness in attitude and behavior. This characteristic is one that can be modeled for each member of the organization.

In relation to being purposeful and accomplishing the goals of an organization, Odiorne (1969:184) indicates two needs: setting good goals and making right choices once the goals have been set. His discussion of these two elements makes it appear that they are both necessary and sufficient for success in management, and indeed this does seem reasonable. If one can establish "good" goals and then follow this goal setting with a sequence of impeccable choices in all circumstances that follow, then surely success will be attained. There must not be any quarrel with such a formula, but certainly the second element would bear more detailed description before it would be very useful.[5] However, there is value in continuing to emphasize the necessity for setting clear goals and directing effort toward those goals.

A good administrator's activity *ought* to be purposeful. One can be efficient without clear goals, but one never knows whether effectiveness is achieved without goal specification. Even if considerable emphasis is placed on the possibility of serendipitous events making real contributions to the organization, there is no reason to believe that such events will occur more often for a person working without clear goals than for a person who has specified precise ones. The difference in meaningful productivity is still likely to be due to effort directed toward prespecified goals.

DISCERNMENT

Perhaps one of the characteristics contributing to a manager's setting good goals or making right choices is *discernment*. This can be thought of in a variety of ways. In one sense it is the ability to differentiate among a multitude of cues, or to

---

[5] It appears very similar to a formula that says behavior is a function of two factors, i.e., $B = f(P,I)$, where $B = $ Behavior, $P = $ Personality and $I = $ all of those Intervening variables that interact with personality.

reduce such cues to meaningful wholes, or to screen out nonrelevant information. He has to perceive what is a "good" goal for an organization at any point in time. For example, there are times in an organization when considerable change is needed— e.g., in organizational structure, motivational factors, emphasis on staff training, or strategies for decision making. At other times, it may be very beneficial if the consolidation and maintenance of recent gains are emphasized. The perception of the immediate needs and the vision for long-term thrust are part of discernment.

In another sense, discernment is the ability to be aware of various forces that impinge on the operation of the organization. Tannenbaum and Schmidt (1973:180) state it this way:

> . . . the successful leader is one who is keenly aware of those forces which are most relevant to his behavior at any given time. He accurately understands himself, the individuals and group he is dealing with and the company and broader social environment in which he operates. And certainly he is able to assess the present readiness for growth of his subordinates.

They further point out that success hinges on the ability to behave appropriately in light of the discernment of the situation. Where direction is needed, it is given; if participative freedom seems appropriate, it is provided.

Thus, the successful administrator is one who is flexible enough to behave in various ways and who has reasonable discernment in assessing the forces that determine appropriate behavior at a given time. As Tannenbaum and Schmidt (1973:180) point out, "being both insightful and flexible, he is less likely to see the problems of leadership as a dilemma."

A consequence of being both purposeful and discerning is that the executive will be able to perform an evaluative function more adequately. Landau (1973) suggests the necessity of preventing and correcting errors. If one is not purposeful, having set goals and initiated activities to accomplish those goals, errors will not be recognized. However, neither would they be recognized without discernment. Preventing and correcting errors related to prespecified goals allows an administrator to manage on the desirable basis of information rather than by rituals and authoritative posture.

Need for Evaluation

Generally, the need for evaluation (of either program or personnel) is justified on a basis similar to Landau's suggestion, viz., to prevent and correct error. A slightly different perspective is that the planning necessary to ensure good evaluation allows one to plan for change. At the same time, the planning and carrying out of evaluation procedures permits errors to be corrected.

The need to evaluate administrators has a similar basis, i.e., the need to plan efficiently and to correct errors. However, in planning a system of evaluation for administrators, it is imperative that errors made in systems for evaluating teachers not be repeated. For example:

> Teacher evaluation has been prostituted until it neither improves instruction nor eliminates the incompetent. What it did with a high degree of success was harass both the evaluator and evaluatee into a mutual state of distrust. We can no longer afford to allow administrative evaluation to succumb to this trap (Carvell, 1972:32).

The point seems well taken. If administrator evaluation systems are not designed so that performance is improved and selection errors are corrected, we will not have profited from the years of trial and error involved with teacher evaluation.

Bentz (1967:197) makes the point that it is easier to establish a personnel system[6] that reinforces what *is* occurring that it is to create new molds. This emphasizes the fact that there is a strong tendency to design evaluation procedures in terms of administrators who are operating effectively at present without consideration of how they *should* be functioning in an ideal situation. This is an overemphasis on the empirical at the expense of a deductive analysis of the system or an examination of future needs. Basically, most evaluation models are based on past performance, couched in terms of the value system which previously prevailed rather than in terms of what is likely to be of value and produce good results in the future. Therefore, it is important to include both the empirical and the deductive processes when attempting to determine what is desired in terms of processes or attributes or outcomes of administrators.

A consideration of the need for evaluation should not be made separately from the overall mission of the school system *in the particular locale*. Too often the evaluation system is viewed as something entirely separate from the mission of the organization (Olds, 1977:47), and such a perspective gives no direction whatsoever to evaluation. Unless the evaluation system contributes directly to accomplishing the major goals of the organization, it will be viewed as a necessary evil at best or a useless appendage at worst. Therefore, the evaluation of administrators must be an integral part of the management system in order to accomplish the mission of the school district; without this, it will be endured or ignored.

Once the idea is accepted that administrator evaluation is an integral part of the total management strategy, there is a normal tendency to search for a means of accomplishing the evaluation. Since economy is uppermost in most administrators' minds, there is a strong urge to acquire a new evaluation *form*. The thought is that the form is the heart of the evaluation system, and a great deal of time has been wasted searching the country for the "perfect" evaluation form (Olds, 1977:19). If, indeed, such a perfect form existed, it would take very little time to find it—because many would recognize it, and it would be distributed widely. However, there is ample experience to indicate that (a) the form used to record summary evaluation

---

[6]Bentz's comment is in relation to selection procedures rather than to evaluation procedures, but the comment is relevant to both.

information may be a necessary element for most evaluation systems, but it certainly is not sufficient for optimum success; (b) the way in which one implements a total evaluation system, the criteria one uses, and the soundness of the data collected are also extremely important; and (c) the forms and systems used in one organization may not be satisfactory in another system due to differences in requirements and values of the two organizations. Therefore, one should resist the urge to search first for forms; rather, careful consideration should be given to the uniqueness of the organization (including its special values and mission) and how the evaluation system can contribute to the overall managerial strategy to be used.

Management by Objectives

Among recent trends in evaluation of administrators—open record systems; concern for effectiveness as expressed by desire for productivity, accountability, and performance-based evaluation; systems analysis; concern for efficiency as expressed by the desire that appropriate processes be used and that self-evaluation occur; examination of process/product relationships; and management of information regarding evaluation[7]—perhaps the one trend that has had the most impact on evaluation systems and managerial strategies in general is management by objectives. Although some may consider MBO as a fad, its extensive use and prolific treatment in educational literature seem to indicate that its demise is not imminent.

One of the attractive elements of MBO is that, properly used, it imposes few working restraints once clear goals have been established. In addition, during the goal-setting process there is an underlying assurance of school district approval. No one need be in doubt about what is to be done or the reasons for doing it under an MBO system, and also freedom is allowed for accomplishing the work.

The major emphasis of MBO is on production rather than procedures. This is true in the sense that major decisions in planning are related to outcomes desired and how measurement will occur in relation to these outcomes. Although procedures are discussed (and the evaluator may provide considerable assistance in helping the evaluatee to decide on procedures), the evaluator's major function is not to tell the specialist what procedures to use but rather to make sure that the outcomes are compatible with school district goals and that procedures used will not undermine organizational goals.

Odiorne (1969) indicates that the essential element in continuity of organizational management is comparison of actual results with statements of expectations prepared prior to taking any sort of action. In essence, he describes MBO as a two-step process of comparing results to objectives:

1. The individual manager operates under self-control and provides his own instantaneous feedback of results against goals.

---

[7]A similar listing and discussion of trends in teacher evaluation procedures is provided in Bolton, *Selection and Evaluation of Teachers*, 1973:131—150.

2. The superior provides information of a cumulative or periodic nature to the subordinate to confirm or correct this observation of his own performance (Odiorne, 1969:114—115).

Odiorne has pinpointed the responsibility for both self- and external evaluation in the MBO process. The superior has responsibility to regularly collect information and arrange for a systematic feedback to the evaluatee; the evaluatee has responsibility to continuously collect and use information for making corrections and new plans.

There has been some resistance to use of MBO in education because of the difficulty of measuring some of the results of administrative behavior. However, this is also true in many areas of teaching where considerable progress has been made in recent years. Kelber (1972:572) answers this objection as follows:

> The fact that the output is difficult to evaluate should not be used as an excuse for not managing that output. MBO is desirable because it is a means for directing management attention to purpose, instead of letting it wander to activity.

Although lists of rules or guidelines for the successful use of MBO abound in the literature, Kelber (1972:575) provides three ideas that need to be considered in education.

> First, an MBO approach can be begun at any level of management in an organization. But it works best if started at the top.
>
> Second, MBO is a motivational system of management. A manager's deep personal commitment to his objectives is achieved only if he is personally involved in setting these objectives. An authoritarian style of leadership is out of step with the thrust of management by objectives.
>
> Third, management of output is strengthened if an organization's systems of rewards and performance appraisal are objectives-oriented.

These three ideas are particularly pertinent to education for the following reasons. First, the idea that the MBO process should be begun at the top appears to contradict some of the literature of the fifties that suggested that most activities should be begun from the lower levels of an organization in order to maintain a democratic atmosphere. This democratic tradition in educational administration is long standing and justified, but some of the prior writing appeared to assume that there is an inherent conflict between providing direction for an organization and being democratic. Actually no such conflict exists. Democratic operation does not preclude administrators devising ways of managing that include initiative on their part to clarify goals and establish procedures for assuring that those goals are met. In fact, goal specification and role clarification are generally considered to be among the most significant of the administrators' responsibilities.

Kelber's second idea concerned with the motivational aspects of MBO emphasizes the linkage between MBO and the style of leadership. Some people have misperceived MBO as being a "hard-line management" point of view that says that the role of supervisors is to lay out the work for the subordinate and then see that it's done in a prescribed manner. However, the actual use (and its initial intent) has not been to bolster and facilitate autocratic behavior. In fact, collaborative methods and team management are quite compatible with MBO (see French & Hollman, 1975). In addition, Kelber's second point emphasizes that MBO is not simply a gimmick to be added to a management system already established; it is aimed at the more complex aspects of motivation of personnel.

The third point has to do with integrating the management of output and the system of rewards. For reasons that are varied and complex, this has seldom been attempted in education; and when it has been attempted, there has been little or no evaluation of the results. However, it does seem that a system of rewards, whether it is monetary, modified assignment, recognition, etc., should be integrated with the output of an individual rather than with some random variable or a capricious evaluator's value system. Kelber's idea needs serious consideration among educational administrators as they design their own evaluation systems; no longer should it be dismissed because of some bias acquired early in one's career.

Some school systems are tying the MBO evaluation process to salary improvement (see Ritchie, 1976:36). In such a system, a simple "contract" with the administrator has the following four steps, as described by Ritchie (1976:34):

I. A precise description of the project, process, skill, etc., to be evaluated in this agreement. This should include (to the degree that is possible at the initial conference): A. Intent of what is to be done. B. Outcomes to be expected. C. Procedures to be used.

II. A description of who will do the monitoring and evaluation of #I, i.e., one or several people.

III. A description of any materials, resources, other aids *not readily available* but needed to properly execute this agreement and *who will see that this is provided* (and how).

IV. How often will the evaluator/evaluatee meet to *officially* review progress.

Although these goals may be modified during the year, they must be mutually agreed upon by the administrator and his evaluator. In addition to the MBO process, administrators are also evaluated on regular or routine responsibilities. Ritchie reports that where the evaluation system has been tried, linking monetary rewards to job performance, it has proved to be a salutary element of the total management strategy.

General Elements of an Evaluation System

The foregoing discussion of MBO certainly does not exhaust the description of an evaluation system. If MBO does not characterize all of the qualities of an evaluation system, how may it be described? If the evaluation system is designed to answer such basic questions as, "How well are we doing and how do we know?" "How can we do better—specifically?" (Olds, 1977:64), what does the system look like? Conceptually, of course, evaluation may be viewed in a variety of ways. The ideas that follow are presented with the thought that they will form the basis for making decisions regarding the actual policies and procedures that a school district may desire to establish.[8]

EVALUATION AS A CYCLICAL PROCESS

Evaluation as a cyclical process of planning, collecting information, and using information is based on the view that information is needed in order to evaluate, i.e., that one needs to collect information in order to make any kinds of judgments regarding whether objectives are attained. However, there are things that must be done both before and after the collection of information; therefore, there are the three phases of planning, collecting information, and using information (Bolton, 1974:171−177). In addition, the process is cyclical and continuous rather than linear and terminal. This means that once information is used, one begins again to plan for the collection of additional information. Since the process is continuous rather than spasmodic, one may go through the process several times during a given school or calendar year. In fact, there is research evidence that frequency of performance review is related to many positive managerial attitudes and to higher performance of administrators (Carroll & Tosi, 1973:48). This means that the "normal" annual (or less often) review of performance with no intermediate reviews to supplement it may not accomplish the *purposes* of the evaluation system.

I emphasize purpos*es* because arguments are sometimes initiated over the "only" or the "primary" purpose—such arguments are either facetious or misinformed. Of course, most systems are developed for the purpose of assisting people to improve their performance, but to claim that this is the only purpose is to ignore the full scope of the environment in which schools exist and in which administrators work. I have reviewed purposes for evaluating teachers elsewhere (Bolton, *Selection and Evaluation of Teachers,* 1973:26−28, 98−102), and many of the purposes for evaluating administrators parallel those for evaluating teachers. Recently there has been considerable concern over whether evaluation systems *can* accomplish certain multiple goals simultaneously, e.g., increasing job performance and justifying salary decisions (Pyron, 1968:4). Despite the concern, there is some research evidence that multiple purposes are not only possible, but also that those who are involved in evaluation systems that have such goals become advocates for them (Cummings, 1973).

There is not much doubt that the way in which the evaluation system is planned and administered has an impact on the interrelationship between the evaluator and the evaluatee (Arikado & Musella, 1975:15). It can reduce trust and communication or it can increase them. Many claim that evaluation breaks down the trust level

---

[8]This section leans heavily on prior work (Bolton, 1974:170−195), although it is viewed now from a more general perspective.

between teacher and evaluator. However, Lindemann (1970:207) found "that teachers who perceived that they were being evaluated by their supervisors communicated more frequently with their supervisors than teachers who perceived that they were not being evaluated by their supervisors." Further, he found, "The more formal the evaluation, the greater the trust. The greater the trust, the more frequent teacher-supervisor interaction, . . . " (p. 208). Although one should take care in generalizing these results to populations other than teachers, one might hypothesize that results with administrators would be more likely to be similar to Lindemann's than opposite to them. Also, since Lindemann's study was not an experiment, it is difficult to know whether greater trust precipitates more teacher-supervisor interaction or whether more teacher-supervisor interaction precipitates greater trust. It may be that the direction of the causality is dependent on circumstances and changes from one situation to another.

Since there is this impact on the interrelationship between evaluator and evaluatee, one should recognize it as a part of the reality being dealt with and not try to ignore it. There are tensions involved in evaluating others and in being evaluated. However, Ingle points out that one probably should not try to produce an evaluation plan that is completely tension free. Ingle (1977:240) makes his case in this way:

> The concern of the evaluator should be to generate an evaluation plan that will be carried out in an atmosphere of trust. Trust here refers to knowledge on the part of those being evaluated that data will be collected in an unbiased manner, that only data that bears some demonstrable relationship to their job functioning will be gathered, that they will have an opportunity to examine the data and explain or refute as necessary, and that they will have an appeal route which may be used if necessary. Note that the notion of carrying out an evaluation in an atmosphere of trust is quite different from the notion of carrying out an evaluation in a threat-free atmosphere.

The point seems to be well taken; when combined with Lindemann's findings, it appears that one should attempt to establish trust by means of repeated evaluation sessions of a more formal nature. By building the review sessions into the formal process, the nature of the interactions would be about the task at hand. Under such circumstances, the subordinate would begin to trust the professional judgment of the evaluator rather than simply to interact with her or him on a personal or social level.

One point should be emphasized regarding the relationship of this continuous cyclical process to the development of a trust relationship. During the planning phase, the evaluatee should help to determine the criteria on which he or she will be evaluated (Pyron, 1968). Two aspects of this point are important: (a) each individual will know the criteria, rather than being surprised at a later time, and (b) helping to determine the criteria will more likely bring about commitment to them in the form of effort to accomplish objectives. In addition, it should be noted that criteria may include both procedures to be completed and results or outcomes expected. When either is included, the evaluatee should be involved in determining the means whereby they will be measured.

INPUT, PROCESS, AND OUTPUT

Regardless of whether one is discussing programs or personnel, there is no question but that evaluation will occur. Evaluation will always occur; that is not at issue. The real issue is how systematic the evaluation will be. And if one wants to be systematic, an application of systems analysis procedures will indicate that attention should be given to input, process, and output. The input stage is critical in terms of determining standards for both processes and output; the process stage is crucial because of the need to maintain standards for the procedures chosen; and the output stage is important because it provides a comparison of actual accomplishment with desired output—and clues regarding what the next steps should be (Bolton, 1974:178-181).

Both situational factors and values within the school system should be used for determining what standards are appropriate at the input stage. That is, the major input variables to consider for determining outcomes desired are those which adequately describe the values that are influential during the period of evaluation.

In order to determine the most appropriate procedures to be used, however, different input variables need to be considered. Here, one should do a logical analysis of the functions and tasks performed by the administrators to be evaluated and also examine what ''good'' administrators have done in similar situations. Consideration of these two factors meshes the practical experience of people in similar situations with the logic which a specialist (e.g., in curriculum or personnel) might apply to a situation to determine what processes might be used. It cannot be overemphasized that this procedure is considerably different from many procedures used in the development of numerous so-called competency based training programs, where the error is often made of asking all practitioners (regardless of how well they perform or whether they are in similar situations) their views on the efficacy of particular processes or functions. The summation of such data will arrive at the lowest common denominator of current practices. It will not accentuate the practices used by those who are more successful; it will provide very little by way of deductive analysis, and it will contribute nothing to the understanding of future needs. Its biggest contribution appears to be toward a uniform mediocrity.

PROCESSES AND PRODUCTS OF SEVERAL PEOPLE

Although the mission of a school system is concerned with the learning of students, the procedures of administrators are generally only indirectly related to student outcomes. Some administrators, e.g., principals, are more closely allied with the processes that precipitate student learning, but even their processes are not directly responsible for student output (Bolton, 1974:181—183). Although the principals are responsible for monitoring the teacher process-product relationship in such a manner that they know whether teacher behavior is producing student changes that have been agreed upon, this monitoring simply provides data that will help them to identify what outcomes (in terms of teacher behaviors or procedures) and processes they should be using in order to assist teachers in changing their behavior. In essence, the principals should focus on outcomes that they can effect directly and not assume the responsibility that others have for working directly with students. In effect, the heart of the argument is inherent in the question, "If the principal can be held directly accountable for student learning, what can the teachers be held accountable for?" (Ingle, 1977:242). For administrators who have the responsibility for supervising building administrators, the same principle holds: identify outcomes you are willing to be responsible for accomplishing (e.g., assisting the building principal to function more effectively in some particular area) and identify appropriate procedures for accomplishing those outcomes. Do not assume responsibility for improving teacher behavior through supervisory procedures that should be assumed by the principal and do not assume the responsibility for student learning.

The significance of such a principle as this regarding processes and products is that it assists in determining the tasks and responsibilities for which different individuals are responsible. Unless each administrator in an organization identifies major responsibilities in terms of outcomes desired, almost any activity in which a given administrator is engaged can be justified as contributing to the mission of the organization. Yet, certain tasks may be ignored and others may have too many people working on them.

For example, there is a common tendency for one to persevere in performing tasks learned on a given job even when promoted to a higher level. Principals have a tendency to continue a teaching relationship with students even after they have left the classroom—because they know how to teach and because they enjoy it. In addition, they may not have developed as many skills in supervision of teachers as they have in teaching of children; therefore, they tend to do those things which they do well and enjoy. After they have been a principal for a number of years, they may develop considerable skill in working with teachers. When promoted to a central office position where they have responsibility for supervising principals, they may have a strong tendency again to do those things which they like to do, viz., work directly with teachers. When they do, they deprive the principals they are supervising of the responsibility for doing the job they are supposed to be doing—and in the process fail to develop the principals properly (which is their responsibility).

INTERRELATED SUBSYSTEMS

The system used for evaluating administrators must be considered as a subsystem of the total personnel system; as such it is related to teacher evaluation, supervision and management development program of administrators, and selection of administrators. It interacts with the teacher evaluation subsystem in that the products of certain administrators are the processes of teachers. It is related to the selection of administrators in that it provides the feedback necessary to validate the selection process. And it is related to the supervision and management development program of administrators in that it provides much of the information needed to individualize that program.[9]

In addition, the system has an impact on the managerial system, and in turn the managerial system has an impact on it. For one thing, the system is an integral part of the control mechanisms built into a managerial cycle (planning, implementing, maintaining, and evaluating), which is a natural outgrowth of cybernetic concepts and the use of feedback mechanisms for controlling organizations. Control here is used in the sense of a process of establishing dynamic equilibrium in the organization through reduction of deviation amplification; in effect, the development of stability by finding and eliminating errors that creep into the system.

Another impact that evaluation has on the managerial system is related to both *intermediate decisions* (e.g., it answers such questions as, Were the goals met? Are the goals still considered reasonable? Did we implement the procedures as planned? and Should the procedures be changed?) and *terminal decisions* (Was the accomplishment of goals sufficient to warrant promotion and salary adjustments? Should specific supervisory treatments be initiated? and Were the deficiencies in performance sufficient to justify probation, modification of assignment, or release?). Many times these terminal decisions are neglected because they produce tension and anxiety for both the evaluator and the evaluatee. Olds (1977:62) states that dismissal steps are rarely taken, not because of a lack of legal guidelines but because of the lack of a sound and defensible evaluation program, one which genuinely is focused on the correction of inadequate performance as well as the improvement of the adequate and good.

In designing a program that will facilitate the decision-making process, attention should be paid to the manner in which purposes of evaluation are specified. Clear purposes of the evaluation system will provide direction for the evaluation and managerial systems. In addition, both the evaluation and the managerial systems will need to be concerned with (a) taking action based on reliable data, (b) monitoring processes so that both intermediate and terminal decisions can be made, and (c) providing support for the processes (Bolton, 1974:185–187). A breakdown in acquisition of needed resources or providing support during the action must be considered a contributing factor if there is a discrepancy between actual outcomes and the goals and objectives established.

Several advantages occur when the evaluation subsystem is integrated properly with the total management system. For one thing, individuals are able to identify with the success of the organization; they are able to see that their own success is interrelated with the success of the school district (Olds, 1977:54). When this occurs, there is a commitment on the part of the individual to certain responsibilities

---

[9]See Bolton (1974:183–185) and Bolton, *Selection and Evaluation of Teachers* (1973:133–137) for a discussion related to this section; see Gray (1975) and Gray (1977:97–98) for an emphasis on the individualized aspect of this function.

and tasks that will help to achieve the common objectives of the entire school district; both the individual and the evaluator understand how the results will be measured in relation to these tasks (Odiorne, 1969:144). Without such commitment and understanding of measurement, authentic relationships among professional personnel never emerge. In fact, the relationships become absurd.

Odiorne (1969:141–144) discusses absurd relationships at some length. He indicates that the absurd exists when the logic of the system developed for two problems is each perfectly executed—and the two actions cancel one another. This can also happen when one subsystem asks that certain actions be executed (e.g., for the evaluation subsystem) and this action is ignored or not supported by another subsystem (e.g., the managerial subsystem). Odiorne emphasizes that such lack of authentic relationships (indeed absurd relationships) should be dealt with in the planning process.

> To put it more personally, unless you and your boss are now jointly committed to a set of specific projects for the coming six months or year, you have less than necessary commitment and a significant portion of your relationship is in the realm of the absurd (1969:144).

One can avoid the absurd by communicating regarding objectives and how these objectives are being accomplished.

This is not a "game-playing" activity. It involves true participation in the determination of goals and activities necessary to achieve those goals, not a dictating of either by a superior to a subordinate. When such participation occurs, there is a redistribution of power and influence in the organization; without such, the activity may lack relevance. Tosi and Carroll contend that, "The subordinate must be given the opportunity to participate. The superior must be willing to relinquish some influence. If this redistribution does not occur, participation will not work" (1968:425). At a later date these same two authors make an even stronger statement regarding participation:

> To have any impact, participation in goal setting must be part of a more general overall managerial style consistent with mutual goal setting. The subordinate must be given the opportunity to participate meaningfully in more than setting goals (Carroll & Tosi, 1973:43).

Integration of the evaluation subsystem with the total managerial style of operation can have benefits other than commitment to organizational goals. Cummings (1973) found that changes that incorporated increased involvement of subordinates in decision making related to the appraisal system generated positive shifts in appraisal attitudes. In this case, the increased involvement included a decentralization of authority regarding how decisions were to be made as well as allowing lower level supervisors to make decisions regarding pay. Zand (1972) found that groups that expected trusting relationships among their members (as compared with groups that did not expect such trust) were found to be more effective in clarification of goals, exchanging information, broadening the scope of search for solutions to problems, and commitment to implementation of solutions. Evidently, shared trust is a significant determinant of managerial problem-solving effectiveness.

SELF-EVALUATION AND EVALUATION BY OTHERS

Self-evaluation has a tendency to focus on the process needed to accomplish objectives rather than on the outcomes produced. This often has been justified on the basis that the outcomes of education are so long-range that it is difficult to attribute causality to any process-product relationship. However, this primary emphasis on process has been criticized in that very few benefits are obtained from evaluating behavior in isolation from the outcomes.

The real advantage of self-evaluation is that it tends to reduce the threat of an external evaluator and at the same time increases the potential for creativity and motivation. The disadvantages are that the individual being evaluated may choose to ignore district goals, establish goals incompatible with district goals, examine behaviors in isolation from outcomes, or interpret data in a biased fashion because of prejudice or lack of framework for interpretation (Bolton, 1974:187).

A program for administrator evaluation should attempt to take advantage of the creativity and motivation that comes from self-evaluation. At the same time, care should be taken to use external evaluators so that individuals do not operate on their own criteria only, with the concomitant tendency for everyone to be going in different directions according to one's own whims and interests. Under such circumstances, individuals tend to serve themselves rather than the organization they are hired to serve. Drucker makes the point (1968:43) that "managing the enterprise's social impacts has importance because no organ can survive the body which it serves; and the enterprise is an organ of society and community." Drucker was referring to a business enterprise; how much more true this must be of a school system that exists as part of and as a creation of the larger society. When a particular type of society dies, then we can expect that organ—in that form, at least—to die. Therefore, to live means the organ must adapt to the body. One might even assume that the school system is a transplanted organ that has the function of continuously adapting to the larger society. Even if one were to presume that the school system should be causing the larger society to adapt to it, it would still be necessary to acknowledge an interdependence between the two elements, i.e., that one cannot function without recognition of the other.

ASSESSING COMMON AND SPECIFIC OBJECTIVES AND PROCESSES

Job descriptions designed to illustrate common elements of similar or identical postions (e.g., elementary school principalships) may be of considerable benefit to a school district. The general job description identifies common and routine responsibilities and helps to define the role of incumbents. This is beneficial for orienting new principals and for evaluating common elements. Since all situations are not homogeneous, it is usually necessary to describe those elements of a given position that are unique or are related to one-of-a-kind projects. The unique elements of a situation are often taken care of via MBO procedures or under some very general responsibility category. It appears much more defensible to use the MBO procedure to deal with projects, but a detailed and unique job description may be used to form the basis for evaluating routine or ordinary responsibilities; both are preferable to a common general category that may be misunderstood by many.

It may even be beneficial to have a summary report device by job category, rather than a single form for all administrators. Using a common report form may reduce the amount of paperwork for the evaluator, but accomplishing the purposes of the evaluation system must precede the reduction of paperwork. Obviously, completion of a general form that answers one question would reduce paperwork to a minimum, but it is doubtful that it would aid much in improving performance or making administrative decisions over a long-term period. Since there are both common and unique objectives for each position, the general principle appears to be: *use common reporting forms and job descriptions for efficiency where possible; use unique job descriptions and MBO procedures for effectiveness where needed.*

MONITORING THE EVALUATION SYSTEM

It should be emphasized at this point that one of the reasons for having an administrator evaluation system is to allow and stimulate the administrator to do his job better. This means that the evaluator and the evaluatee should profit from the evaluation system; both should know what their job is and how the evaluation system contributes to it. Both are involved in providing service to an organization and to individuals within that organization. They should be providing these services in such a way that the job is satisfying to them as individuals. Harkin (1970:340–341) points out that "both the organization and the individual profit from an arrangement which permits organizational goals to be met with behavior that is satisfying to the needs of the individual." Facilitating communication through interaction (which can provide a means of self-determination) and providing avenues of growth for individuals so that their role will increase with their competence are both particularly helpful in achieving congruence between task demands and personal desires. The first of these can be achieved as one plans for evaluation and as data are analyzed and interpreted in the decision-making process; the decisions that are made can, of course, contribute to the latter.

The evaluation system should be monitored to determine whether it is accomplishing what it is designed to accomplish. Monitoring the evaluation system should be specified as a given person's responsibility, but it cannot be done effectively without the support and backing of the top administrators. A personnel director can be given major responsibility for monitoring and evaluating the system of administrator evaluation, but his or her efforts can be completely nullified by a higher administrator who does not see the benefits of the evaluation personally or to the organization.

This monitoring should be systematized for two reasons. First, it should provide a means through which problems can be taken care of as they arise—rather than waiting for a given checkpoint. Second, prespecified checkpoints should be initiated so that information can be collected regarding whether the system is functioning as it should, whether changes should be made, or whether the system should be abandoned and new procedures devised.

Resistances to Evaluation

When two people confront each other with evaluative data, there is a possibility that one or the other will need to change behaviors in order to accomplish objectives or meet organizational standards. The evaluatee may need to change processes in order to produce desired results; the evaluator may need to change the nature of assistance provided. In either case, each is vulnerable to change, sometimes a major change in style of operation and at other times a minor change. When viewed as major, it can be traumatic for either individual and considerable resistance can occur. In many cases overcoming resistance "requires clear organizational goals, resources adequate for training evaluators, provision of adequate time for them to perform the tasks required, and a clear relationship of the organizational goals to the task of the evaluator (Bolton, *Selection and Evaluation of Teachers,* 1973:96).

One of the reasons *evaluatees* feel vulnerable (and therefore resist evaluation in spite of its potential benefits) is that many systems of evaluation use categorization schemes. For example, rating scales that classify people into general categories, such as *superior, above average, average, below average,* are reacted to emotionally rather than cognitively. Even when a person is classified as superior, he has a tendency to resist the scheme of categorization because of the possibility of being placed in one of the more inferior categories. Since this classification system is reacted to emotionally, it is evident that some type of psychological support system is required if the category system is necessary. The support system needed is one that develops a strong trust relationship built on honesty between the evaluator and the evaluatee; usually honesty cannot develop unless considerable information is analyzed and discussed prior to a determination of what category is appropriate. Also, the organization should examine its categories very carefully and determine the function of the various categories. For example, unless superior is attached in some manner to a reward system, it may be better to omit it and stick with categories that are functionally related to decisions. For instance, *retain, consider for release* both pertain to decisions, but *above average* may not.

Another reason that evaluatees resist deing evaluated may be a desire for complete autonomy, based on their belief that self-evaluation is sufficient for trained professionals. They may think that prior training and admission to the profession make them adequate for the task of determining their own needs.

A closely related reason for resistance to evaluation is that many evaluators are untrained or inept, and evaluatees feel that their own ability or point of view is as good as or better than that of the evaluator. They may feel that a part of the ineptness of the evaluator is his tendency to focus on fault finding rather than providing genuine help, an inability to diagnose problems or suggest new strategies of managing, or the inability to manage time in such a way that data are collected under diverse and appropriate circumstances and then shared with the evaluatee.

According to Bolton (*Selection and Evaluation of Teachers,* 1973:96), resistances to evaluation by *evaluators* include the following:

(a) A general lack of certainty regarding criteria, measurement process, and procedures for analysis and interpretation of data.
(b) The evaluator's dislike of being in a position to manipulate or adversely affect other people's lives.
(c) A fear of precipitating an unpleasant reaction on the part of the person being evaluated. This reaction then prevents a relationship conducive to helping the individual improve.
(d) A lack of ability to cope with the weaknesses of the individual in terms of organizational needs and his ability to improve. This is sometimes linked with a failure to communicate to the individual the necessity of dealing with both individual and organizational problems.
(e) A failure to see the relationship of evaluation of others to the purposes of the evaluator.
(f) An inability to organize time so that adequate observations can be made.

This list of six resistances by evaluators was made after a series of structured interviews with administrators in schools, businesses and industries, and governmental agencies. Since that time, I have had the opportunity for numerous unstructured conversations with many educational administrators in classes, workshops, and consulting and research relationships. The following list of resistances by evaluators was compiled from these conversations:

1. A feeling that the planning of activities will prevent spontaneous response to opportunities that arise. If this should happen, it would reduce the possibility for use of creative skills.
2. A fear of being held to a commitment (in the form of an objective) that will not be as important as day-to-day operation activities. Since the normal activities will be required, the additional commitment will have to be done *above and beyond* the normal and probably will require additional time. This attitude many times springs from a belief that the evaluation process is not an integral part of the managerial style.
3. An unwillingness to change style of management from one of daily problem solving (which some describe as management by crisis) to one of planning in relation to major goals and acquiring feedback regarding outcomes. Sometimes this is not an attitudinal problem but one of lack of information or skills.
4. A lack of support from higher levels of the organization. Work done on evaluation is not valued, is ignored, or discouraged. Sometimes this occurs when the organization is harried by external pressures and needs to provide quick responses to

problems, but at other times it is an attitudinal or skill problem of the top management.

5. A lack of conviction that the time needed to do the evaluation will provide as much payoff, in terms of productivity, as the equivalent time spent in other activities. Sometimes this is a rationalization, since individuals who give this reason have very little information about how their present activities contribute to the productivity of the organization.

6. A fear of becoming insensitive to needs of people. Many administrators are people oriented, and some feel that an emphasis on productivity might reduce their sensitivity to people. In effect, they perceive a conflict between a concern for productivity and a concern for people and either do not understand (or do not have the skills to cope with) how the two needs can be satisfied concurrently.

Obviously, from among these two lists one could find several reasons for resisting evaluation in almost any given situation. However, the intent is not to bolster an unwillingness to evaluate administrators but to provide an understanding and recognition of these resistances so that administrators of a school district can design an evaluation system that will reduce or eliminate them.

Problems and Issues Regarding Evaluation

From among the many problems and issues that could be discussed regarding the evaluation of administrators, a few significant ones have been chosen. These have to do with problems of a general nature; planning, organizing, and controlling; expectations for performance; adjustments to situations; and changing others.

GENERAL PROBLEMS

One of the more basic problems regarding evaluation of administrators is how one defines and perceives evaluation. For our purposes here, evaluation is defined as the process of making judgments regarding the value or *goodness* of certain events, behaviors, or results of behaviors in light of certain agreed upon or well-understood and predetermined objectives. Notice that there are several implications of such a definition.

First, it is dynamic or involves movement, as indicated by the term *process*. This movement is continuous and cyclical, allowing one to provide feedback in an iterative fashion. Such feedback stimulates correction before major damage is done and allows new plans to be made.

Second, it provides direction, in the form of predetermined objectives. The underlying assumption of this part of the definition is that the organization is purposeful and that specifying purposes is beneficial to the organization.

Third, the value system for making judgments regarding events, behavior, or results of behavior is open and available rather than hidden. This openness is provided by the predetermined objectives that are either agreed upon or at least well understood by those involved. No surprises should occur when such a definition is in operation.

Fourth, there is an interest in situations, processes, and outcomes. To evaluate one of these without the other two will not allow decisions to be made about adjustments in goals, implementation, or procedures.

Fifth, the making of judgments occurs late in the process. Unless adequate measurement, analysis, and interpretation occur prior to making value judgments, there will be errors and poor results. Snap judgments made on inadequate information or hearsay may give one a tremendous sense of importance or a feeling that intuitive processes are working adequately, but such activities are not permitted by this definition.

But why is the definition of the term evaluation a problem? For one thing, some people misuse the term; they interchange it with *measurement,* or they mistakenly think of a *rating* system as the only means for making judgments, or they view it as the act of making a *summary statement* about an individual's performance for a specified year. Any of these perceptions of evaluation is inadequate and will lead to deficient practices.

Measurement is merely the quantification or quasiquantification of events, behaviors, or results of behavior; as such, it does not incorporate any judgment making or require any value system to be applied. It is a prerequisite to evaluation, but it is not evaluation. When a person uses a structured observation guide to record data regarding another person's behavior, measurement is occurring. But this can be done independently of any judgment about whether objectives have been accomplished.

The *rating* of characteristics or traits on either normative or criterion-based scales can be of value as a part of a total evaluation system, provided the items on which the person is being rated have some direct pertinence to the organizational goals and provided that adequate means have been taken to acquire information regarding these characteristics. However, when used independently of specific, current organizational goals and with no other means for dealing with unique individual situations, ratings are insufficient for total evaluation purposes. Likewise, in the past, they have been done with very little backup information, and sometimes they have not been communicated to the evaluatee. Under such conditions, they provide little benefit to anyone.

A *summary statement* may well be required in an evaluation system, but it should not be considered as synonymous with evaluation. When it is, other parts of the evaluation process are ignored. The summary statement may indeed be a record of the value judgments made at the end of the year. But value judgments made during the third, fifth, or eleventh week of the year are just as important as any value judgments made at the end of the year. Likewise, early value judgments on which decisions were made to modify procedures or to establish new goals are also part of evaluation. To pick out one part of the total evaluation process and consider it only as evaluation is to misunderstand the need to study and develop skills in the total process. Unless it is continuous and cyclical, designed to correct errors as they arise and facilitate plans for change, it falls short of its potential. Some people do many of the tasks involved in evaluation on a day-to-day basis as part of their regular duties but do not consider them a part of the evaluative process. Conscious inclusion of these duties as a part of evaluation would improve the evaluation system and their proficiency in using it.

A second problem of a general nature concerns the political nature of the educational administrator's task. This is especially true in large city systems, where survival in a job may depend more on circumstances than on the capability of the administrator. Griffiths (1977:3) believes that only the most astute school principals survive through a finely attuned political acumen. Further, he believes that "the superintendency, at least in major cities, has been rendered virtually untenable." One reason Griffiths considers this area so important is that there is a need for new theories regarding concepts such as *authority* that will provide guidance to administrators under circumstances where people do not really want to be governed. He says:

> It is clear that the faculties of universities really do not want presidents and deans, that public school teachers do not want principals or superintendents, but that these administrators are necessary if the institutions are going to operate (Griffiths, 1977:3).

Levinson (1968:8), along this same line, states that, "the head of an organization's law is often treated as if it were whim, for few people want to recognize a law other than their own."

When these problems exist regarding governance and authority, surely a process such as evaluation (designed as a control mechanism for the organization and the individual) can expect difficulties. Warnings of the type just mentioned emphasize the need to examine with all members of the organization the mutual benefits to be derived from carefully implemented evaluation processes.

A third problem relates to measurement difficulties that complicate the evaluation process. Kelber (1972) identifies education as one of the six hardest areas to manage by objectives and one of the major reasons is the difficulty of measuring outcomes. However, Latham, Wexley, and Pursell (1975) provide experimental evidence that training in workshop situations helps to prevent errors of measurement such as similarity (to oneself), contrast, halo, and first impression errors. In addition, group discussion helps to prevent all except first impression errors. Also Campbell et al. (1970:155) indicate ways that data can be combined to reduce rater errors.

A final problem or issue of a general nature has to do with one's perception of motivation. What causes a given individual to act and another not to act? Some of the procedures for evaluation of administrators depend on what might be described as a cognitive theory of motivation. This theory places emphasis on individuals' *knowing* what they want, *knowing* the approximate effort that will be needed to acquire what they want and to overcome obstacles along the way, and *knowing* the values that will be attached to the outcomes of their efforts. Under these circumstances, individuals can make decisions about their own actions; therefore, they will be motivated to do certain things. Ivancevich, Donnelly, and Lyon (1970:140) state that "to the extent that an individual makes clear plans, is guided by his expectations and the risks involved, and moves steadfastly toward his goals, he is motivated by his cognitions." Some people reject this view of motivation; they reject the detailed planning and goal setting required by MBO type of procedures. Because of this, they reject many of the evaluation procedures that rely on predetermination of direction, relying instead on making judgments on the "goodness" of outcomes on the basis of values determined at the time of the outcomes rather than at the initiation of the action. To use an analogy, once the rifle has been fired and an object hit, you go and examine the object to determine if it was worth hitting—or if you struck the object you now think you should have been shooting at. This view of evaluation provides very little help in designing methods for firing a rifle, much less in knowing which direction to aim it.

PLANNING, ORGANIZING, CONTROLLING

In any organization, there exists what some people call *the tyranny of the urgent*. The urgent, and sometimes the trivial, tends to take precedence over other activities that may be more long-range and significant. This is especially true when an administrator neglects planning.

> The manager who does not plan or plans poorly, soon finds himself engaged in "management by crisis." Most of his time is spent fighting fires and dealing with problems which might otherwise have been avoided. He has precious little time left for creating opportunities which contribute to the growth and development of his organization (Raia, 1974:7).

Although one type of problem occurs when planning is ignored, another occurs when the wrong starting point is chosen. Drucker points out that any analysis of work situations requires that one start with the question, What do we want to produce? One proceeds from this question to questions regarding what types of activities will accomplish such a product and eventually to consider what will be most efficient and effective. As Drucker (1968:201) says, "to start with the task rather than with the end product may result, however, in beautiful engineering of work that should not be done at all." The significance of this point of view is that many educators tend to begin with activities or processes rather than products or outcomes. The enjoyable part of teaching or administering tends to be in the creative act of designing new activities or procedures. Because this is true, the arduous task of determining what is important to do (which eventually determines what is to be omitted because it is less important) may well be postponed until it is too late to do anything about it.

At least as important as planning new projects are plans to abandon old activities that no longer are productive in terms of the organization's goals. In some ways, this is a more difficult problem than initiating new activities because there are often emotional attachments that make parting painful. Drucker maintains that it is more difficult to abandon yesterday's success than it is to reappraise failure.

> Success breeds its own hubris. It creates emotional attachment, habits of mind and action, and, above all, false self-confidence. A success that has outlived its usefulness may, in the end, be more damaging than failure (Drucker, 1968:159).

In order to plan so as to abandon obsolete activities or projects, Drucker (1968:126) suggests asking, "If we were not committed to this today, would we go into it?" If the answer is no, one then asks, "How can we get out—fast?" This procedure appears to have considerable worth in ridding a school district of activities that tend to persevere and become traditional even though the purpose for which they were created is no longer central to the life of the school district.

Problems of organizing time, people, resources, and tasks are closely related to problems of planning. Raia (1974:7) indicates that organization is primarily concerned with establishing effective relationships between tasks and people, involving such things as: (a) determining the major functions or activities that must be done to meet planned goals (indicating that the establishment of goals is in the planning stage rather than a part of the organization task); (b) dividing these activities into manageable positions or tasks, which may involve grouping and relating the activities in some logical manner, and (c) selecting appropriate people to do the work. In addition, the sequencing of the activities and allocation of time to the tasks (along with deadlines to be met) are sometimes included in the organizing of the work.

Once work has been planned and organized, there is the additional problem of control so that the output desired is actually produced. The primary control mechanism within the evaluation process is the feedback provided to the person doing the work. Odiorne emphasizes that the feedback itself is not sufficient to control the action—"It is the action which is taken by the person receiving the feedback which turns the organization about in its tracks and starts the action back into proper channels once more" (1969:115–116). This underscores the necessity of obtaining compliance of the individuals responsible for actions in order for evaluation to function as it should in relation to controlling actions in the direction of desired goals. In modern school systems this compliance is not something demanded or coerced; rather, the evaluation system is designed in such a way that all who are affected by it are integrally involved in its development. When this happens, compliance and the subsequent controls are effected.

Drucker (1968:217–218) also emphasizes that controlling the work process is not a matter of controlling the worker but of controlling the work. Because of this, control is a tool rather than an end in itself or the master of the worker; as such, it should never become an impediment to working. One should always be reminded, Drucker says, that "control is a principle of economy and not of morality. The purpose of control is to make the process go smoothly and properly, and according to high standards" (1968:218). The problem that some people find in evaluation is in this area of control, when evaluation does at times become a matter of morality rather than a means of accomplishing what is desired.

One of the more basic characteristics of a control mechanism, whether it is a thermostat, an automatic pilot on an airplane, or an evaluation procedure in a school system, is that it must be preset. There not only has to be a specification of the desired outcome (and/or performance), but there also should be a specification of the permissible deviation from this desire. And the presetting is often a source of problems. For example, the level of the thermostat and the deviations allowed can become a source for a quarrel in the home; the goals to be accomplished and how they should be accomplished become a source of contention in the school district. In each case, there is likely to be a problem over *who* makes the determinations. However, once permissible deviations are determined, control may be only by "exception," allowing only significant deviation from the norm to trigger the control (Drucker, 1968:219). When this happens, no action is required as long as the process operates within the preset standards. When this is applied to evaluation, the problem is not only in the establishment of the goals and the permissible deviations but also in collecting adequate data to determine if exceptions occur.

Without adequate planning, organizing, and controlling, an organization such as a school district will not function as effectively or efficiently as it should. Relating evaluation to each of these tasks should make it a more integral part of the total managerial strategy and, therefore, more functional to a school district.

EXPECTATIONS FOR PERFORMANCE

One reason that evaluation has potential for raising an individual's level of performance is due to feedback and the adjustments that individuals can make in response to it. However, another potential is due to the expectations that are set for individuals in the planning process. Korman (1971) reports on five studies, all of which support the general proposition that high expectancies of competence by others are positively related to performance. In two field studies it was found that performance increased as a direct result of supervisors' communicating a higher level of expectation; the higher the level of expectation communicated, the higher the level of performance (Korman:218).

Further, the findings generalized to expectations expressed by individuals other than superiors and applied to a wide variety of workers. Korman concludes that, "Apparently, we use whatever we can, authority figure or not, intelligent or not, to define ourselves vis-à-vis a given situation, and then we behave in a way consistent with such a definition" (1971:220—221). The issue taken with such findings is in relation to who establishes the expectations for individuals and work groups within the educational administration setting. The answer is not simple because the educational administrator is influenced by a variety of individuals and groups; teachers, parents, students, fellow administrators, supervisors, and citizens all attempt to set expectations for administrators. When some of these are in conflict with each other, an administrator may need to have some sort of clarification before the expectation becomes part of the social reality which affects performance. The formal leadership of a school district should recognize that peer group norms and administrator group values may be stronger for setting expectations of a given administrator than the formal leadership. Therefore, the planning for evaluation of administrators may well occur with groups as well as individuals; to ignore the group esprit may well eliminate powerful motivating forces for some of the members.

ADJUSTMENTS TO SITUATIONS

For some time it has been evident that the style of leadership used by an individual varies with the situations faced. Problems have arisen in attempting to determine precisely what leadership behavior is appropriate for what type of situation. Bass (1967:118) describes a model based on relationships between requisite leadership and the extent to which there is agreement about an organization's means and ends.

ENDS

		Agree	Disagree
	Agree	Bureaucratic skill	Negotiating skill
MEANS	Disagree	Expertise	Charisma

Bass's hypothesis is that where there is considerable agreement regarding both means and ends, bureaucratic skill is required; where there is disagreement on ends (outcomes), but agreement on means or processes to be used, negotiating skill is required; where there is agreement on ends but disagreement on means, one needs to be an expert who can convince others of the procedures needed; where there is disagreement on both means and ends, there is the need for a charismatic leader. Bass points out the implications of such a model for personality characteristics of a would-be leader:

> Persistence, methodicalness, and administrative knowledge would seem most relevant in the bureaucracy; intelligence and intellectual skills most appropriate for the expert; dominance and Machiavellianism for the negotiator; status and self-esteem for the charismatic leader (119—120).

Where little information of an empirical nature is known regarding a particular situation, such a model as this may be helpful in establishing some of the characteristics pertinent to that situation. It also may be beneficial in analyzing a particular situation.

One of the adjustments supervisors and evaluators must make to situations concerns the amount of permissiveness to allow. Every supervisor must make decisions about how much leeway to allow subordinates in the performance of their work. Bass (1967:122) reports on some research that showed that permissive approaches to supervision correlated with productivity. Yet the evidence fails to answer whether permissiveness produces productivity or productivity produces permissiveness. Bass concluded, ''It may be that only the supervisor who has a productive department can afford to be permissive.'' The problem is not resolved via the research; results should be observed in a local situation to determine whether productivity would warrant additional permissiveness. It would appear to involve less risk to become more permissive after high productivity than to use permissiveness to try to produce more.

Some supervisors have proposed that there should be a certain amount of ''social distance'' between supervisor and subordinate, maintaining that too much familiarity and communication somehow reduces commitment to productivity. However, this too may depend considerably on the nature of the workers and the situation in which they work. Bass's (1967:124) findings indicated that in a research laboratory where scientists were working frequent interaction yielded high productivity but only if the scientists were treated permissively. Productivity was lower with the same permissive treatment when scientists contacted their chief infrequently. ''The amount of interaction between chief and subordinates,'' Bass states, ''was a modifying variable, affecting the question of whether or not permissiveness was desirable.''

This complicates the entire matter of permissiveness in relation to particular situations and would lead one to hypothesize that with educational administrators, one might well: (a) clarify with some degree of certainty the expectations of the administrator, (b) provide considerable leeway in regard to procedures to be used for accomplishing the outcomes expected, (c) not annoy the administrator with relation to progress being made, and yet (d) provide a lot of opportunity for interaction and, if desired, daily contact with supervisor. Such a hypothesis would seem to be compatible with findings reported by French and Hollman (1975:20) indicating that managers' perceptions of the supportiveness of the organizational climate was significantly related to the attitudes of the managers—specifically, the attitudes of the managers in relation to how effective they thought MBO procedures to be and their overall satisfaction with MBO as it related to their jobs.

Blanchard and Hersey (1970) discuss situational factors in terms of the maturity of individuals and groups. In effect, leadership style should be chosen in terms of the maturation level of the people interacting with the leader. The theory of leadership proposed by Blanchard and Hersey suggests that varying amounts of initiating structure and consideration are used to interact effectively with an individual. As subjects are found to be more mature, the leader would move from (a) high structure and low consideration, to (b) high structure and high consideration, to (c) high consideration and low structure, to (d) low consideration and low structure. This is compatible with Bass's views, and one would anticipate that more mature individuals would be more productive (as a result of being committed to organizational goals) and thereby would move in the direction of less structure and eventually fewer consideration needs. Carroll and Tosi (1973:41) found results which were related in that their data show that "difficult goals are more positively received by the more confident, more mature, more career-oriented manager."

Although it is generally recognized that a supportive style of management is related to higher levels of job satisfaction, Thompson (1971) found that self-perception mediated that relationship. He found that individuals with high favorable self-perception were less likely to perceive the style of the supervisor as supportive and also less likely to have high job satisfaction. It may be that such individuals are frustrated managers themselves and, therefore, more critical of their supervisors; or, they may be more discerning or feel more confident in expressing views regarding the nature of the support provided. At any rate, the self-perceptions of administrators is something which should be considered when making adjustments to local situations.

CHANGING OTHERS

One problem which must be faced in devising and implementing an evaluation system for administrators is whether analysis of the situation or evaluative information regarding administrators should be used to try to effect changes in the administrator's views, knowledge, and skills regarding his job and environment, or whether such information should be used to try to change the environment and the task in such a way that it coincides more adequately with the views and skills of the administrator. Etzioni (1972:47) found that

> persons have deep-seated preferences in their work behavior that are very difficult to change, and we concluded that it may be unethical to try to change them . . . , especially if we are correct in suggesting that people's existing preferences can be readily analyzed so that they can be helped to choose jobs compatible with their personalities.

He also argues that it is much less costly to test and assist people than it is to train and mold them, and that the total-change approach, which has been effective with some groups, has worked primarily with such groups as addicts, mental patients, prison inmates, and others who do not volunteer to join; therefore, such an approach is less applicable to social problems than some would lead us to believe. Because of this, one generally makes one of two assumptions regarding the group with which he works: (a) people can be taught to change their habits—they can learn to remember and they can will to act in a particular way, or (b) people need not, or will not, change and instead choose to alter their environment so that goals can be accomplished. It may be that some type of interaction needs to occur between these two positions, i.e., a supervisory treatment should be chosen which interacts with the situation and the personality variables so that adjustments are made in both the environment and the behavior of the individual.

Summary

This introductory chapter has several themes running through it. One is that the environment within which educational administration occurs is extremely important. Administrators function differently in different locations and situations, and a consideration of these differences certainly affects how one evaluates educational administrators. A brief description of some of the more salient elements of the administrator's environment was provided at the beginning of the chapter. There is little doubt that the current environment is uncertain, complex, problematical, changing, accountable, legalistic, and systematized. The relationship of this environment to various aspects of evaluation was discussed.

There was no attempt to establish criteria for evaluating administrators in this chapter, but two characteristics of the successful administrator, namely, purposefulness and discernment, were discussed. To be oriented toward accomplishment of goals and to have the ability to perceive good goals and good means of accomplishing them appear to be necessary requisites of a good administrator.

The need for evaluation is evident; it helps to plan for change and to prevent and correct errors. In planning for evaluation, one should be cognizant of good practices in the current system; there also should be a recognition of the need to plan for a future which is different from the present. One is cautioned that the need to change an evaluation *system* may mean much more than merely changing some *form* used for making a summary report.

Management by objectives was recognized and discussed as one of the strongest trends in recent years in the sense of having an impact on organizations and of having some permanency in the repertoire of administrators. Its attractiveness stems from its emphasis on outcomes and its considerable leeway for administrators to proceed without stifling interference to accomplishment of their goals. The emphasis is on production, but the application of MBO to education does not ignore procedures. MBO is best implemented by starting at the top; it has an impact on the motivation of administrators and functions best when integrated with the organization's system of rewards.

The general elements of an evaluation system are

1. It is a continuous and cyclical process.
2. It includes examination of input, process, and output.
3. It involves consideration of processes and products of several people.
4. It is a subsystem interrelated with other subsystems in the school organization.
5. It involves self-evaluation plus evaluation by outsiders.
6. It includes the assessment of common objectives and unique objectives.
7. It should be monitored to determine its effectiveness.

People resist the evaluation process for a number of reasons, most of which have to do with anxiety in confronting others with one's own perceptions of reality and change. Categorization schemes cause people to feel vulnerable, and any evaluation system requiring categorization of administrators should also develop means of providing strong psychological support through developing trust relationships. Evaluators also resist evaluation on several bases, including: (a) a general lack of certainty regarding criteria, measurement process, and the procedures for analysis and interpretation of data; (b) a fear of precipitating an unpleasant reaction on the part of the person being evaluated; (c) a failure to see the relationship of evaluation of others to the purposes of the evaluator; (d) an inability to organize time so that adequate observations can be made; (e) an unwillingness to change style of management to the point that evaluation becomes an integral part of it; and (f) a fear of becoming insensitive to the needs of people.

Several problems and issues regarding evaluation are of considerable importance in relation to the evaluation of administrators. For example, how one defines evaluation is particularly pertinent because definitions provide guidance to action. Evaluation was defined as the process of making judgments regarding the value or "goodness" of certain events, behaviors, or results of behaviors in light of certain agreed-upon or well-understood and predetermined objectives.

It is important that an administrator plan well to avoid becoming engaged in management by crisis. A starting point for planning is in relation to outcomes desired rather than procedures needed, since the latter may lead to unnecessary or dysfunctional action. Systematically planning to abandon obsolete procedures is as important as planning new ones.

Controlling work rather than workers is a problem which needs consideration. Control should always aid the worker and prevent the enlargement of error—rather than repress behavior. Presetting goals and permissible deviations is an important concept in relation to control mechanisms and can become a source of problems.

Expectations supervisors have for administrators has an impact on performance; the higher the expectation, the higher the performance one can anticipate. Work groups also have expectations for administrators, and potential conflicts exist in relation to expectations.

Style of leadership must be adapted to varying situations. One should consider the extent of agreement on means and ends of the school system, the level of productivity of teachers and administrators, and the maturity and self-concept of those being supervised.

Finally, evaluation should be used judiciously when considering whether working conditions should be changed to fit the administrator or whether there should be an attempt to change the individual because of the requirements of the job. The latter is expensive and difficult to effect. In many cases, adjustments should be made in both the job and the individual if maximum results are desired.

2 PHASE I: PLANNING FOR EVALUATION

All administrators are evaluated. Regardless of the amount and type of information collected, or how often formal reports are written, or when interim decisions are made, administrators are evaluated—and rather often. They are evaluated primarily by teachers, those who supervise them, and parents; but students, peers, and taxpayers also evaluate them. Since evaluating administrators cannot be avoided, it is a question of how systematic the evaluation process should be in order for the system of evaluation to be most effective in terms of how much it assists the school district in effecting its goals and objectives.

In the last chapter, evaluation was defined as the process of making judgments regarding the value or goodness of certain events, behaviors, or results of behaviors in light of certain agreed-upon or well-understood and predetermined objectives. It was emphasized that evaluation is not an activity that occurs at a single point in time by simply completing a summary report device but that it consists of multiple phases that are sequential, cyclical, and repetitive, building on information and activities of the prior cycle. Evaluation must be based on information; planning must occur for the information to be useful; and the information collected must be used and applied to achieve meaningful purposes. Therefore, the three main phases of evaluation are:

1. *Planning for evaluation,* which involves analysis of a specific situation, establishment of purposes for evaluation, setting of goals and specific objectives, and deciding on means for measuring the processes used and the eventual outcomes.
2. *Collecting information,* which involves monitoring and measuring the activities planned and the outcomes that result from the activities.
3. *Using information,* which includes communication regarding the analysis and interpretation of information as well as making decisions about the next steps to be taken.

The information analyzed during the third phase provides the basis for reviewing the situation and resetting goals and objectives; therefore, it becomes a natural prelude to the first phase, allowing the cycle to be repeated. The process is illustrated in figure 2.1.

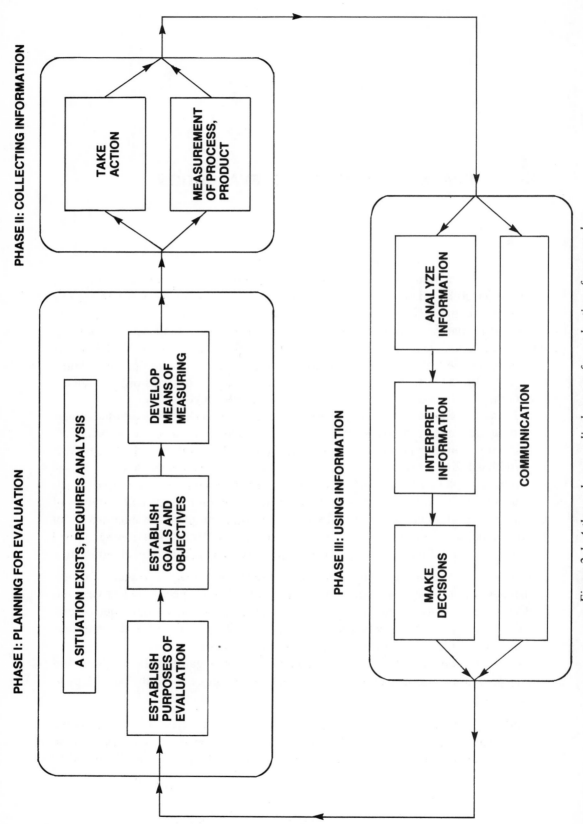

Figure 2.1: A three-phase, cyclical process for evaluation of personnel

Analysis of the Situation

In Phase I, examination and analysis of the specific situation within which a given set of administrators is to be evaluated provides the basis for determining the purposes of evaluation, establishing suitable goals and objectives, and specifying the appropriate type of measurement. Therefore, situational variables, the nature of job descriptions and general areas of responsbility, and the expectations of others for administrators must be considered.

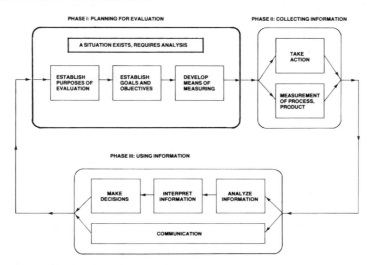

NEED FOR CONSIDERING SITUATIONAL VARIABLES

The tendency is to examine carefully only the internal factors of the organization. However, Pfeffer (1973) emphasizes the idea that studies of organizational behavior must account for influences of the environment as well as internal factors in attempting to analyze performance and effectiveness within the organization. Gaynor (1977:42) also points out that the environment is a significant source of variation in the principal's role, suggesting that individuals and groups upon whose commitment and support the school organization depends are particularly important. This is compatible with the concept of accountability, which posits that individuals should not be held accountable for those forces over which they have no control. One type of force over which administrators may have very little control is forces external to the organization. These should be carefully analyzed to determine if they function as constraints on the behavior of the administrator. If these external forces differ from one attendance area to another (or from one administrative unit to another within a larger school district), it may affect the leadership style of the administrator. House, Filley, and Gujarati (1971:429) found that leadership style measures were differentially intercorrelated from organization to organization, suggesting the importance of the situational factors to the leadership role.

An internal variable that has drawn considerable attention over a period of time is the span of control. For some time, it has been known that situational differences relate to the number of individuals who can be supervised by a given administrator (e.g., if the individuals do not interact much with each other, or if the actions of one individual do not depend on the actions of another), and Blanchard and Hersey (1970:310) indicate that the span of control may depend more on the maturity of the subordinates than on other factors. They state that ''the more independent, able to take responsibility, and achievement-motivated one's subordinates are, the more people a manager can supervise.'' This variable of maturity would not only affect the span of control possible, but it also would affect the role of the administrator (which, of course, would affect the criteria for evaluation of a given administrator). If subordinates reach a level of maturity where they are self-motivated, then it would appear that the role of the administrator would move away from organizing, direct-ing, motivating, and controlling the group more to one of planning, acquiring, and controlling. In essence, the administrator would become more of a representative for the group in the next higher level of the organization (Blanchard & Hersey, 1970:309).

Since higher-level administrators ordinarily work with more mature people, it would be reasonable to deduce that skills learned early in one's career may not be as useful in a later stage. In fact, it may be that quite different cognitive qualities are necessary for effective decision making at higher and lower levels of administration in an organization, a conclusion suggested by Campbell et al. (1970:97). If this is the case, it would be extremely important to study each position in a school district to determine the precise nature and limits of the decision making expected, so that all levels of the system would not be judged by criteria that were wholly inappropriate. In essence, the vice principal of a school should not be judged on the same evidence for decision making as the deputy superintendent; nor should they both be expected to exhibit the same behavior in relation to other aspects of their duties.

Frederiksen, a person well known for his research in administration, indicated that one of the methodological difficulties in studying administration is that we lack a satisfactory classification of situations (1972:115). This lack of classification schemes has prevented rapid progress in studying the role of situations in determin-ing behavior of administrators. However, Frederiksen (1972:122) used a three-mode factor analysis for demonstrating that person-factors and person-by-situation interac-tions do exist.[1] For example, one such factor described what one might call a *systematic supervisor* as the type of person who deals with short-range, day-to-day operational problems, tending to be orderly and to work through subordinates in solving problems of personnel and problems with other organizations. The signifi-cance of Frederiksen's work is that it opens the door for work with groups rather than

---

[1]An early collaborator of Frederiksen's, John Hemphill (1960), factor analyzed 575 items responded to by ninety-three business executives from five companies and three management levels and five functional areas of business. He found ten factors which provided a claim for specifying the dimensions of working conditions for executives, but the final 191 items and the scoring procedure appear to be somewhat cumbersome—perhaps contributing to lack of follow-up to this work.

individuals in making predictions about behavior, making placements as far as positions are concerned, and making supervisory treatment decisions.

Levinson (1968:58) contributes two ideas pertinent to analyzing the situation within which administrators work. First, "the larger the organization, the more control people must exert over their feelings, the more they must abide by formal and informal codes of conduct, the more middle-class values govern." Perhaps this indicates that certain people may have difficulty adjusting to large organizations, or that more radical changes in their own behavior may need to occur, or that greater changes are needed in large organizations if they want to blend diverse types into the organization. Second, the leader "must understand the values and expectations of his followers. Unless he does, he will be unable to win their consent. Without consent, he cannot lead."

Since the research literature does not provide definitive answers regarding what variables must be examined in order to determine purposes for evaluation and goals and objectives, one might conclude that deductive procedures and consensus of those involved most intimately should be the major determinants of importance. In effect, if a group of administrators in a given situation indicate that they think it would be important to consider the age and experience of the faculty as background to determining major projects on which the building principal should be evaluated, then that probably makes sense.

In addition, one might conclude that the following variables should be considered: (a) the number of individuals and groups that have an impact on the commitment and support of schools who interact with the administrator or are within the domain of the administrator's influence; (b) the maturity level of the people being supervised by the administrator; (c) the nature of the decisions to be made and the cognitive tasks to be performed by the administrator; (d) the size of the organization (and perhaps of the subgroup within which the administrator works); and (e) the value system and expectations of those with whom the administrator works.

JOB DESCRIPTIONS AND GENERAL AREAS OF RESPONSIBILITY

Companies and school organizations depend to varying degrees on job descriptions in their management and evaluation practices. Likewise, the substance of the job descriptions varies from organization to organization. Odiorne (1969:124) and Kelber (1972:571−572) both argue for inclusion of three areas of responsibility as substance for dialogue in the evaluation process: (a) performance of regular and/or routine responsibilities, (b) achieving satisfactory solutions to problems (i.e., correcting things that have gone wrong), and (c) completing new and innovative projects. It appears that the regular duties and problem-solving capabilities are more appropriate than the new projects category for inclusion in the normal job description. Since the new project is likely to change more often than the job description, it may be handled better by MBO procedures than by the job description. In effect, the job description has a semipermanency to it that may be related to a contract; the new project comes under the category of "performs any other duties assigned by or agreed to by the supervisor."

Although the job description is a beneficial tool in managing an organization, Hughes (1968:40−41) believes that, since it is basically static and non-motivating, an administrator can expect too much from it. He says,

> Job descriptions are intentionally written in general terms, and they are static abstractions rather than dynamic documentation of the important business to be accomplished by a person. It is the job that motivates, not the job description. Responsibility for establishing plans and controls in one's work forms the basis for motivation and also provides meaningful criteria for the assessment of performance.

Reddin (1970:6) also warns about job descriptions, indicating that they tend to cause individuals to think in terms of maintenance and efficiency rather than in terms of initiation and effectiveness. For example, he points out that job descriptions tend to lead to the kind of thinking shown in the left column below, while effectiveness standards lead to that shown on the right:

do things right	do right things
solve problems	produce creative alternatives
safeguard resources	optimize resource utilization
follow duties	obtain results
lower costs	increase profit

These appear to be fair warnings and lead one to believe that if a job description is desired it should be used as a basis for discussion about priorities, significant elements of the job, and elements which have changed since prior discussions. Used in such a way, it will serve as a reminder of the comprehensiveness of the job and of the limitations within which an individual works.

Campbell appears to agree with this point of view. He says that

> . . . a measure of any given manager's effectiveness should be based on a careful definition of the total domain of his job responsibilities along with statements of critical behaviors believed to be necessary for using available and potential resources in the best possible way (1970:107).

Campbell's view of the total evaluation of administrators is very comprehensive in that he argues that to examine the effectiveness of executives, one needs to consider personal traits, behavior, results of managing, and organizational environments. He specifies that the question which should be asked is, What are the varieties of combinations of organizational circumstances, personal characteristics, and behavior patterns that are likely to be perceived as effective managing? If one were to follow his advice and incorporate all of these elements in a job description, it would be wise for the administrators involved to review all of these elements periodically to determine their pertinency. In addition, it would be mandatory to be selective in each of the four categories because an exhaustive list of the variables would become too cumbersome to be useful.

Carroll and Tosi (1973:84) advise that measurement of routine duties should be of concern only as performance falls below acceptable levels. They propose that minimum performance levels be set for routine activities and that only performance that falls below these minimums be noted in any evaluation discussion or report. This allows evaluation of routine goals to be done by exception, or when standards are not met. It would seem that minimum standards should become a part of the job description under such circumstances.

Concrete examples of all of these ideas in school districts are not plentiful. However, Ritchie (1976) does describe a school district in which the individual administrator is rated on a total composite rating composed of 70 percent weighing on the objectives set (in MBO style) and 30 percent on "givens" of the job description. In this case the contract for the objectives set is based on what Odiorne and Kelber call the innovations to be programmed or attempted. The implication is that the 30 percent deals with the regular or routine responsibilities. It is unclear whether the "problems to be solved" discussed by Odiorne and Kelber would fall in the objectives set or in the "givens"; it seems more probable that it would be in the job description.

EXPECTATIONS OF OTHERS FOR ADMINISTRATORS

Considerable interest has been evidenced in recent years in the expectations that others have for the administrator. Some have gone in the direction of attempting to "validate" roles and responsibilities for given positions by asking various groups to react to statements of tasks and responsibilities. For example, project ROME (Results Oriented Management in Education) has been engaged in identifying a set of principal-competency statements classified by functional areas of responsibility by asking practitioners to react to statements; this has been followed by factor analysis of the statements (Ellett, 1976). The hope is to identify administrative performances that will be related to or make a difference in the effective operation of a school. The major problems with much of this type of research are that (a) the initial statements of performance are generally obtained from a group of practitioners of unknown proficiency, so their statements of what is important are suspect; (b) reactions to the questions suffer from the same malady in that nothing is known about the proficiency of the practitioners who react to either the frequency of practice or the importance of the practice; and (c) the validity of the competency statements is based on a relationship between respondents' perceptions of the frequency and the importance of the statements (regardless of the experience, expertise, or training of the respondent). Needless to say, simply the fact that a group of people perceive a given task to be done often and well by an administrator does not mean his behavior has an impact on a school; very little research is available to suggest which administrator behaviors have a real impact on schools.

However, research indicates what people like in an administrator, or what type of behavior causes people to be most satisfied. Brown and Anderson (1967) found that faculty consensus with respect to satisfaction with all aspects of the teaching situation turned out as predicted—greater in schools where principals exhibit person-oriented rather than system-oriented leader behavior. However, these results are correlational rather than experimental, and as such, it is difficult to determine whether the principals who were person-oriented felt they could exhibit such behavior because the faculty were already task-oriented. Without such information, it is difficult to know whether one should be task-oriented until productivity is high and then become more people-oriented or be people-oriented with the hope that satisfaction with this orientation will lead to high productivity.

Another point to remember is that satisfaction may be more complex than simple orientation toward people or system. Campbell et al. (1970) reported on research in industry which found that the effectiveness level of department heads was directly related to their definitions and expectations for job behavior of their subordinates (who were supervisors). For example, it was found that an intelligence test was the best predictor of success among the more effective department heads, but for the less effective department heads a clerical aptitude test was the best predictor. This appears to be saying that more effective department heads place greater value on intelligence; less effective ones value clerical skills. The results are difficult to generalize, but it may be that people are attracted to people who are similar to themselves. If such is the case, clerically oriented department heads may like similar subordinates, and vice versa. It may be that highly intelligent superintendents of schools like intelligent principals, and vice versa. If one desires to predict subordinate satisfaction with a work situation, it appears that he or she should consider not only the people and task orientation of the supervisor but also the match of supervisor-subordinate on characteristics such as intelligence. Since research does not provide definitive answers regarding these variables in school system settings, it may be very beneficial to identify locally the characteristics and behaviors that are valued by subordinates of administrators. Empirical evidence of this kind may be more beneficial than tangential research data of questionable generalizability.

Inclusion of subordinates in decision making may affect both their satisfaction and productivity. Although the evidence is not conclusive, the views relating to this are based on experiences of administrators and on deductions related to the ideas involved. Tannenbaum and Schmidt (1973) classify the possible leadership behavior available to a manager as existing on a continuum ranging from "the manager makes the decision and announces it" (boss centered) to "the manager permits the group to make decisions within prescribed limits" (subordinate centered). Central to their classification system is a focus on the way a leader includes others in the decision processes. It is probable that the expectation of others in this domain would significantly affect the leader's capacity to perform.

People's expectations regarding such things as age of the administrator may have an impact on ability to lead. It may be that there is an optimum age when people expect the style of leadership desired, and this age may vary with the nature of the organization and the type of community. Lehman (1942) listed the ages at which presidents of universities assumed their duties and how long they served. If such information were available for various leadership positions in school systems (perhaps by geographical region and size of district), it might be helpful, from a common practice standpoint, in assessing when people may well expect to attain positions of leadership. In addition, it might assist in analyzing situations in which administrators serve and are evaluated.

In some school districts administrators are merely expected to comply with the routine directives of the organization; in others they are expected to influence the organization to do things which go beyond present attainment. Katz and Kahn (1966:302) consider this ''incremental influence'' to be the essence of organization leadership, with the result that the expectation for such influence should be considered in analyzing the situation. However, House, Filley, and Gujarati (1971:428) indicate that an extreme amount of influence may not be the most desirable quality. They report:

> These findings suggest that low influence serves little or no purpose in enhancing the effects of leader decisiveness, that high influence may have dysfunctional consequences, and that there is a midrange in which influence is optimal for leadership purposes.

It may be that high influence is dysfunctional because the individuals serving the organization do not expect such behavior. However, if high influence is expected, even midrange influence may be regarded as weak leadership. Again, the need for specific local information is evident.

Establishing Purposes of Evaluation

If the local school situation has been thoroughly analyzed and all seemingly pertinent variables examined, the next step is to establish the purposes for evaluating administrators. If the evaluation system is to be successful, these purposes must be

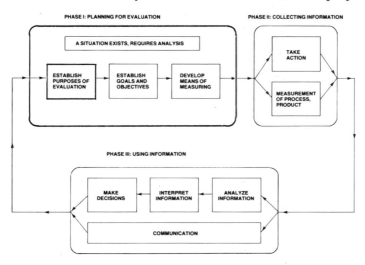

identified, discussed, and agreed upon by all who are involved in the process. This is important so that the additional phases of the process will be given direction and a reason for existence. Without purpose, activities have a tendency to be generated or omitted on the whim of those involved.

Some statements of purposes for evaluating administrators include a philosophical statement, indicating what the adopting body believes to be true about such things as behavior, the nature of man in general, the way adults learn, and motivational factors for adult behavior (Bolton, 1977:72). Also, assumptions are sometimes stated regarding such things as whether individuals desire change in themselves, what constitutes fairness among employees, or what productivity a person can be responsible for. At other times, these must simply be inferred from procedures and criteria described; but it is helpful if these values and assumptions are explicitly stated and discussed.

The real problem in stating all purposes is that the group involved tends to become embroiled in meaningless arguments or discussions over whether one purpose is primary or more basic than another. Yet, the key question is not whether one is more important than another, but whether a system can be designed that will allow all purposes which are important to the individuals and the organization to be accomplished. Another problem is in stating the underlying assumptions and value system of the evaluation process without becoming so ponderous and/or so general that the statements become meaningless to anyone except the initial author. In providing background information for the statement of purposes, it would be helpful to state what assumptions are made about the need to restrict the administrator's behavior and whether one is to assume that each administrator in the organization desires to improve her or his performance.

There appear to be differences among people regarding whether the evaluation system should function as a major source of motivation for administrators. Pharis (1973:37) adovcates that evaluation programs be designed around basic motivators for human behavior. However, if the evaluation system is primarily a feedback mechanism to determine if one is "on course," then it would not necessarily be designed for the purpose of reward or award. Indeed, motivation would have to come from another source if this were the case. This issue cannot be decided from outside an organization but must depend on the value system of those who have responsibility for design and implementation of the system.

Sometimes conflicts are generated when evaluation systems are designed around multiple purposes, especially when a reasonable balance is not maintained between purposes designed to help the administrator and other purposes designed to maintain standards of the school system. Gaynor discusses the need to keep in focus the principal's behavior in relation to organizational complexities.

> Mainly, the intent of evaluation should be to help the principal to understand better the complexities of the bureaucratic, cultural-political, legal, and fiscal environment of the school and to mirror for the principal her/his behavior in relation to that environment. The prime focus should be upon helping the principal to determine what changes in

task priority and administrative style are likely to work better, to help the principal to gain the knowledge and skills necessary to make those changes, and to provide formative feedback on the process over time (1977:46).

Since the purposes for evaluation are multiple and must be determined for specific local situations, a list which fits all situations cannot be recommended. However, Bolton (1974:172) believes that consideration should be given at least to the following:

- changing goals or objectives
- modifying procedures
- determining new ways of implementing procedures
- improving performance of individuals
- supplying information for modification of assignments
- protecting individuals or the school system
- rewarding superior performance
- providing a basis for career planning and individual growth and development
- validating the selection process
- facilitating self-evaluation

CHANGING GOALS OR OBJECTIVES

There are times when it is not obvious that direction should be changed, or that sights should be raised or lowered. It is at these times that systematic evaluation can assist in making decisions about change of goals or objectives. Sometimes administrators will set goals that are too ambitious, considering the reality of the situation and the constraints in effect. When this happens, they may become discouraged, frustrated, or even give up and reduce their activities. An examination of data in light of the objectives may cause them to reassess the situation within which they are working and agree on more reasonable goals. Also, goals may be revised upward when evaluation of results warrants it. As significant as adjusting one's objectives either upward or downward is the dropping of them altogether. This is a matter of periodically examining objectives in light of the situation in which one is functioning and determining whether objectives are still as appropriate as they were when initially written. Although this is a very simple matter to do, it may easily be overlooked if evaluation does not occur.

MODIFYING PROCEDURES

Sometimes there are resistances to modification of procedures when an administrator has been involved in designing those procedures. For example, the administrator who has been involved in designing a new scheduling procedure for students may resist a suggestion that it be changed. However, if data are gathered to show how well the procedure is functioning, how well it is liked by parents and students, and how teachers think it affects their jobs, the administrator may well be encouraged to consider alternative scheduling procedures. Without evaluation of the specific results or outcomes, procedures used by administrators may acquire an unwarranted momentum and permanency.

DETERMINING NEW WAYS OF IMPLEMENTING PROCEDURES

There are times when a procedure is not faulty but simply implemented inappropriately. If such is the case, the procedure should not be rejected; the implementation should be controlled more precisely. The key to evaluation in relation to implementation is a careful examination of the exact nature of the processes used (as opposed to those planned). It may be that inadequate resources were used, or that support from higher levels of the school district were lacking, or that there were breakdowns in communication. There may be a variety of reasons that a good procedure was not properly implemented, but the correction for poor implementation is considerably different from correction of a faulty procedure. For example, a faulty scheduling procedure may be replaced or drastically modified; but if it has never been implemented fully, one should not conclude that such action is warranted.

IMPROVING INDIVIDUAL PERFORMANCE

The first three purposes cited above are concerned with ways of changing the environment within which an administrator works, but this purpose is concerned with providing information that will allow the indiviual to change. Evaluation provides the information base; supervision procedures or self-teaching provides the mechanism for change. The information acquired for this task should indicate the relationship between the processes used by the administrator and the results (products) of these processes. Precise knowledge of the process-product relationship should provide clues to the nature of actions that need to be taken to correct outcomes. If new skills are needed, either the supervisor or the administrator should be in a position to know what these are and how they may be acquired.

SUPPLYING INFORMATION FOR MODIFICATION OF ASSIGNMENT

There are times when a given assignment is not suitable for a particular administrator or when the administrator would be better suited for another assignment. Evaluation can play an important role in helping to make decisions in such cases. Modifications may include a change in load (by increasing or decreasing the tasks required), a shifting to another building or level of the organization, changes in those being supervised, promotions, demotions, change in type of assignment (e.g., from a personnel job to one involving curriculum or finance), or release. While these decisions must be made in all organizations, morale tends to suffer if the procedures for determining such decisions are not systematic and if the emphasis is on elimination of the weak and ineffective. Consequently, the negative emphasis should be avoided. When dismissal or demotion procedures are necessary, they should be orderly, systematic, and understood by all in the organization.

PROTECTING INDIVIDUALS OR THE SCHOOL SYSTEM

Administrators and the school districts they represent are particularly vulnerable to criticism, some of which may be unjust. At the same time, they are held accountable for establishing and maintaining a system of education that accomplishes goals established by the board of education. Since school boards have the right to establish the kind of school system they want, as long as it remains within constitutional limits (Howsam, 1963; Heald & Moore, 1968), including the prerogative of setting up any form of evaluation they desire, the evaluation of administrators' actions and results can portect both the school boards and administrators from being criticized unjustly. Arguments about factual information are unprofitable; criticism of systematically evaluated individuals, when they are performing in accordance with agreed-upon goals, will largely go unheeded. If unjustified and disruptive elements pursue legal means for accomplishing their purposes, systematic evaluation procedures will provide protection of either the individuals involved or the school system.

REWARDING SUPERIOR PERFORMANCE

Rewarding superior performance financially has generally been resisted by the teaching profession; however, there probably is less resistance among administrators than among teachers. Regardless of the extent of acceptance of practices for differentially paying administrators according to performance, there is an almost universal concern that any such practice should rely on precise measurements and open systems of communication regarding expectations. With increasing pressures from people outside the schools to pay for services in accordance with quality and quantity of performance, there are likely to be more school systems accepting the purpose of rewarding superior performance with increased salaries.

Other types of rewards for superior performance should be considered, also. If, indeed, the underlying motive for reward systems is to provide an incentive to the individual to produce more, then perhaps a school system should look beyond the monetary. For example, feelings of accomplishment, satisfaction with nature of work, professional growth, recognition, responsibility, and advancement are all considered to be true motivators (Herzberg, Mausner, & Snyderman, 1959; Herzberg, 1968), whereas pay, benefits, and working conditions are considered to be sources of dissatisfaction if withheld rather than motivators when provided. If motivation is really what is being sought, school districts should seek creative means of using evaluation procedures for helping administrators to recognize their achievements and analyze means for achieving more.

PROVIDING A BASIS FOR CAREER PLANNING AND INDIVIDUAL GROWTH AND DEVELOPMENT

One evidence of a good administrator is that she or he develops the talents of the individuals being supervised. If this is to be done effectively and if one assumes that each administrator desires to improve, evaluation becomes the information basis for development of talent. Development and growth should occur within the context of the long-range career goals of the administrator in order to be meaningful. In addition, it should be beneficial to the school district to know of the ambitions and desires of its administrators. Diagnosis and interpretation of evaluation information will help administrators view themselves realistically; this may or may not cause the long-range plans to be adjusted. When evaluation is done properly, in a spirit of guidance and sincere desire for the well-being of the administrator, there should be opportunity for growth, meshing of long-range goals with reality of performance and capabilities, and a harmony of individual aspirations with the goals of the organization. These results are not likely to occur unless the system of evaluation explicitly incorporates this purpose.

VALIDATING THE SELECTION PROCESS

Here is another purpose of the evaluation system that is often overlooked. Not only should the criteria used for the selection of administrators be consistent with those used to evaluate administrators, but the evaluation of administrators selected should provide the feedback necessary to analyze whether selection information (e.g. that obtained from examinations, placement papers, and other written documents, interviews, and assessment centers) was beneficial in making decisions. Evaluation.information can also be helpful in determining whether certain interviewers are effective, whether decision strategies being used are appropriate, and whether certain information tends to be overlooked or stressed too much in the selection process. If evaluation information is not used to validate the selection process, there is a tendency to evaluate selection decisions at the time they are made; this is analogous to determining whether one made a good decision in the purchase of a house at the time of buying the house rather than after living in it for a while.

In addtiion, there is a need for all who are involved in administrator evaluation to understand the relationship of evaluation to selection. When administrators are involved in both selection and evaluation of those whom they supervise, they see the necessity of selecting someone who will respond to the type of supervision provided. In addition, they are more likely to feel responsible for the individual when they see how the feedback provides information to the selection procedures. This does not necessarily mean that supervisors should make the final decisions regarding the selection of administrators, but their intimate involvement in the determination of criteria and attributes should help the selection process and at the same time contribute to their own understanding of the interrelationship of selection and evaluation.

FACILITATING SELF-EVALUATION

One of the functions of external evaluation is to facilitate self-evaluation. The value of self-evaluation, of course, is that it allows administrators to continuously diagnose what is happening and to make minute adjustments in terms of the information available. The better the external evaluator, the more sensitive administrators will become to surroundings and the more willing they will be to view events realistically. Both sensitivity and realism are beneficial to making judgments about actions to be taken in the day-to-day activities.

In conclusion, then, it can be said that *all* purposes for evaluation of administrators should be discussed openly and clarified in writing so that all who are involved may understand the bases for the evaluation program. Such discussion and writing should help to alleviate any unknowns that would lead to fear, hostility, resistances, and low morale and should promote commitment of administrators to the activities involved. In essence, evaluation programs that have written statements of purposes that are clear, precise, and complete are more likely to produce a sound basis for open communication and cooperative relationships than programs designed around ambiguous or unwritten purposes (Bolton, *Selection and Evaluation of Teachers,* 1973:26).

Establishing Goals and Specific Objectives

Surely one of the more important aspects of administrator evaluation, and one that captures the attention of most people, is determining *what* should be evaluated. Various headings are used for this, including establishing goals and objectives, setting targets, specifying standards of performance, and determining criteria. Regardless of what one calls it, there is the necessity to determine a standard against which comparisons can be made. Certainly this task precipitates the largest number of differences among people who are intimately involved, including differences as to perceptions of role expectations, how goal statements should be written, the setting of priorities, and the determination of variables to be considered.

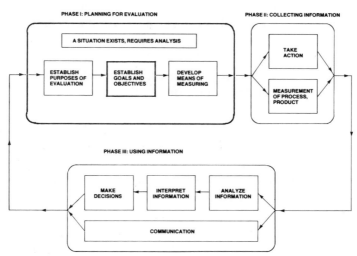

ROLE SPECIFICATION

Role theory may not be as popular today as it was in the sixties. For example, Griffiths indicates other approaches may be more valuable. He says:

I submit that the concept of role as *the* set of expectations held for a position has little value in today's complex organizations. We would be better off if we described behaviors and perceptions and dropped the role spectacles (1977:7).

However, Beer and Ruh (1976:60−61) think that it is valuable to consider the triple role of managers in dealing with subordinates: as *managers,* they are responsible for achieving organizational goals; as *judges,* they must evaluate performance and make decisions about salaries; and as *helpers,* they must develop subordinates into more effective and promotable employees. In many cases the judge role (in the sense of affecting salary) is eliminated from the role of educational administrators, and the helper role is paid lip service only. This leaves the managerial role, where many times the precise definition of achievement is left to one's imagination rather than put in writing.

If educational administrators are expected to be involved in all three of these roles, there should be clear recognition that sometimes one of the roles interferes with another. For example, the judge role may interfere with the helper role. In addition, it should be made clear precisely what is expected in each of these roles. If this is put in writing in the form of general goals or specific objectives, and if communication is open and authentic between an administrator and the evaluator, then the potential conflict between these roles may be alleviated somewhat.

WRITING OBJECTIVES

Goals or purposes are rather general outcomes that one desires to accomplish. For example, a personnel director may want to establish a new teacher evaluation process. This is a general outcome, but there may be no time specification connected with the goal at the initial statement of it. As one begins planning for the goal, there may be several parts of it that can be specified in the form of objectives. These objectives are much more specific than the general goal and include deadlines for accomplishment. Two general criteria are important when considering objectives: they should be worth doing (in terms of the organizational goals), and they should be well written.

If an objective is worth doing, it is because someone has conceived it and someone has approved it. Usually the conceptualization of the objective is the responsibility of the person who also must see that the objective is accomplished (in the major part); but the approval is the responsibility of the person supervising the administrator who initially conceived the objective. For example, the personnel director may have conceived the general goal of establishing a new teacher evaluation process. She or he may have several objectives in mind in relation to this goal, but the supervisor of the personnel director is the person who must make the judgment regarding whether this set of objectives is worthwhile in relation to other needs of the school district and the demands on the personnel director's time. In making this judgment, the supervisor may lean heavily on the expertise of the personnel director, but she or he may also obtain information (or ask that the personnel director obtain it) from teachers, department chairpersons, curriculum specialists, principals, and the budget division. Research information may be sought as well regarding the benefits of evaluation for improved performance.

It appears obvious that if an objective is judged to be worthwhile, the administrators have given considerable thought to what their true mission is, what will be the cost to them and their division in order to accomplish the objective, and what the results are likely to be. Otherwise, administrators may simply compile a list of routine activities that they plan to pursue (McConkey, 1972). In essence, one should first focus on the results desired and then begin writing objectives.

Sometimes administrators begin with a rather hazy idea and take this idea to a group of people for discussion and consensus regarding initiation of it. A problem with this procedure is that it may be easy to obtain consensus on the vaguely stated objective without having a clear idea of the implications in terms of commitment of time and energy. In addition, an eclectic collection of activities may result rather than a set of actions based on clear theory of what one is attempting to do (Lawrence, 1974:300). The value of consensus procedures is that a true discussion of the idea may lead to an understanding of diverse views regarding the idea and an acceptance of both the objectives and the underlying theory base. The choice of whether one uses such a procedure may depend on the nature of the objective and the stake which the discussants have in the outcome. Use of consensus procedures does not mean that there has been fuzzy thinking on the part of the leader, however. Clear thinking of the details and the underlying theory may be done prior to a meeting in order to help clarify the thinking of the group during the consensus process.

Development of consensus related to objectives is similar to the involvement of other administrators in the development of objectives. In their discussion of collaborative MBO procedures, French and Hollman (1975:15) suggest there is a need for this kind of involvement but very little evidence of it among the companies they studied:

> Eight of the nine companies (four British, five American) require that forms be filled out in the MBO programs, but in only one company's form is there any space for the manager to specify the extent to which his objectives require involvement of other managers.

Any necessary support and involvement of other personnel should be taken into account by an administrator during the planning phase. For example, if the personnel director needs the cooperation and assistance of the principals in order to implement a new teacher evaluation process, then it will be beneficial to specify this on the form that states the objective. This will allow the supervisor of the personnel director to know more about whether to approve the objective.

Another technique an administrator may find beneficial is to do some type of task structure breakdown. For example, Keegan (1975:37) suggests the following sequence for developing performance objectives:

1. Identify purpose or reasons for evaluation of administrators, keeping the number to a minimum

2. Identify the characteristics or job functions that relate to the position being evaluated
3. Identify the "indicators" or "tasks" that are necessary to carry out in order for the job function (characteristic) to operate smoothly
4. State the indicators (tasks) in performance terms

It should be noted that this is a hierarchy and that the eventual indicators could be written after forming a breakdown of characteristics or job functions, which are themselves a breakdown of the purpose chosen. The number of eventual indicators would depend on the number of functions, and the number of functions would depend on the number of purposes.

Raia (1974:65–66) provides us with a set of guidelines that relate directly to whether an objective is worth doing:

1. It should be realistic and attainable.
2. It should be both relevant and important.
3. It should be challenging.
4. It should be consistent with organization plans, policies, and procedures.

Each of these guidelines is worth examining prior to making any judgment regarding whether an objective should be accepted.

In addition, an objective should be well written so that all who are being asked to commit themselves to it will understand what is to be done. The following are criteria for a well-written objective:

1. It should be clearly written, avoiding such relative terms as "adequate, sufficient, reasonable," since they lead to countless misunderstandings and make measuring practically impossible.
2. It should focus on an identifiable outcome or result as a target.
3. It should specify the action to be taken, the activities to be engaged in.
4. It should specify who should accomplish the objective.
5. It should be time limited, specifying not only when it is to be accomplished but also any time constraints.
6. It should specify cost, in terms of all resources needed.
7. It should be stated so that it is verifiable.[2]

Raia (1974:65) suggests that any statement of "why" or "how" should be omitted from the goal-setting process and included, instead, in a separate statement of rationale. This would mean that a separate "action plan" would need to be devised that would include a discussion of the advantages and disadvantages of various alternatives for accomplishing the stated objective. There are advantages and disadvantages to the procedure proposed by Raia. It may work best for an administrator

---

[2]The following sources all discuss guidelines or criteria for writing objectives: Arikado and Musella, 1975; Campbell et al., 1970:107–108; Carroll and Tosi, 1973:40; McConkey, 1972:16; and Raia, 1974:65–66.

who has the habit of hastily choosing an alternative without considering a complete analysis of the situation. On the other hand, for more mature and responsible administrators, the action plan may simply be discussed in the goal-setting conference (or conferences) and only the process to be used may be written. The choice appears to be one that should be individualized on the basis of the behavior pattern of the administrator.

SETTING PRIORITIES

There may be times when an administrator sets a group of goals, each of which in turn has a group of objectives involving a variety of activities. At the same time, the supervisor may identify one or more objectives that have been overlooked by the administrator. Or perhaps the administrator may simply identify too many objectives to be accomplished in a given period of time. Under such circumstances, it is necessary to establish priorities in order to reduce objectives to a manageable number. Unless this is done, frustration will result because of not being able to accomplish all that is written down.

In calculating the time needed to accomplish certain objectives, it may be beneficial to have both the administrator and the supervisor estimate minimum and maximum times. This may give a better idea of the real time needed. In addition, one should allow enough leeway in the total time schedule for emergencies and discretionary time, since the complete scheduling of one's time can be another source of frustration when emergencies occur.

Another reason for setting priorities is to establish which objectives are to be met first in case some cannot be accomplished. Thus the administrator and the supervisor may identify those areas where extra resources may be used in order to complete a project and to specify what will be set aside if it becomes apparent that what was originally planned cannot be finished (Keegan, 1975:38). Ritchie emphasizes that it is important for both the administrator and the evaluator to be willing to modify objectives during the school year, but that this must be done by mutual agreement in order to assure successful operation of the administrator's unit (1976:34). Such modification, of course, allows flexibility for adjustment of the priorities of both the administrator and the supervisor as it becomes apparent that problems that were unimportant or unapparent at the beginning of the year have suddenly become more pressing because of either internal or external changing conditions.

VARIABLES TO CONSIDER

Various types of criteria can be described, and there is a general lack of agreement in the profession regarding the relative significance of each type. For example, it is generally recognized that the following can be evaluated: (a) characteristics or personal qualities of administrators (such as emotional stability, appearance, and sociability), (b) functions performed (such as implementation or maintenance), (c) procedures used by administrators (such as conducting in-service programs for teachers, planning with Parent Teacher Student Association (PTSA) groups, or initiating a change in some aspect of the curriculum), and (d) results of behavior (such as changes in teacher behavior, or changes in school climate or parental satisfaction). It is important to keep in mind that any one of these variables may be expressed as a general goal or a specific objective to be attained, but considerable confusion occurs when goal expectations are not clarified.

In addition, problems arise in relation to the amount of detail to be specified in any statement of performance standards (Bolton, 1977:74). Because of the almost unlimited number of behaviors and results of behaviors that might be specified, it is difficult to determine a level of generality that is likely to be most helpful to evaluator and evaluatee. Statements should be specific enough to give direction and allow judgments regarding excellence and progress to be made. However, one should be wary of too much detail; it may become cumbersome paperwork, cause a lack of attention to important tasks, and tend to stifle creative, assertive people while attracting only the passive and conforming.

One further statement of warning may be necessary regarding determination of what should be evaluated. One should not confuse the following:

1. The mission of the school system as a whole (e.g., to maximize the learning of all students attending school, considering their interests and abilities as well as societal needs)
2. The purpose of the evaluation system (e.g., to improve the performance of all administrators in the school system)
3. The specific objective of a particular administrator (e.g., to use an individualized supervision and evaluation system that will cause each teacher being supervised to initiate at least two new projects during an academic year)

The total school system should be designed to accomplish the mission of the district, and the administrators' actions should be taken on the basis of goals and objectives designed to facilitate this mission, but *not* to accomplish it directly. If the mission of the school district or the purposes of the evaluation system are not being accomplished, the administrator may or may not be effective. Certainly there may be problems in the school system, but an examination of the integral parts of the system is needed; an administrator should be held responsible for individual objectives rather than for the more general overall mission to which many contribute.

What is the significance of the discussion thus far in regard to establishing goals and objectives?

1. Each individual administrator has a responsibility for establishing objectives that are compatible with and contribute to the overall mission and goals of the school district. It is not the responsibility of the supervisor of an administrator to establish objectives that are unique to the given administrator, even though the school district may establish some which are common to a given group of administrators.
2. The objectives of the individual administrator are not synonymous with the goals

of the district or the objectives of teachers. The processes and products of the administrator are unique to the role of the particular administrator being evaluated.

3. The supervisor of each administrator has the responsibility for approval of the objectives; when this occurs, it is presumed that the objectives are compatible with organizational goals.

4. Establishment of objectives by the administrator means commitment of time and effort; acceptance by the supervisor means approval and support via school district resources.

The emphasis of the writing thus far has been on individualizing the evaluation process by analyzing the individual situation and specifying goals and objectives in terms of the uniqueness of the situation. This is in alignment with much of the literature regarding administrative behavior and with the experiences of administrators in varying assignments. It runs counter to making global assessments based on limited information. Campbell et al. (1970:124) indicate that global estimates of administrator effectiveness have little utility, especially in providing knowledge of specific problems or areas of effectiveness. They emphasize that people often make decisions about effectiveness on the basis of global impressions "formed from job-irrelevant factors reflecting society's stereotypes of success" rather than on the basis of factors directly pertinent to organizational goals. The same authors also specify that effective administrative behavior must be tested in specific situations rather than devised in speculative armchair fashion. They say:

> We firmly believe we cannot overemphasize the essential inadequacy of opinions, hunches, speculations, and expertise as a basis for prescriptions concerning the prediction of effective executive behavior (Campbell et al. 1970:10).

In addition, research indicates that no single criterion can be considered as supreme or sufficient. Dunnette, for example, says:

> I would argue that as we talk about managerial effectiveness, we must continue to ask for and investigate many criteria, rather than seek any single elegant, "ultimate," or composite criterion. I do not believe that there is or can be such a thing as a single best criterion of managerial effectiveness (1967:12).

With these dangers in mind, it should be pointed out that the following variables must be considered locally—rather than used regardless of the values and constraints of a given situation. In addition the variables to be examined take into account more than merely the *what* and the *how* (i.e., the process and the product) of the role of educational administrators.[3] A number of the variables have to do with the

---

[3]Gaynor's position is more limiting than the one presented here. He says, "The role of the school principal, like any role, can be conceptualized in terms of two primary components. The task component of the role defines *what* the principal is expected to do. The style component of the role defines *how* the principal is expected to perform those tasks in a social context. Evaluation designs will probably need to facilitate description and analysis of role behavior on both of these dimensions" (1977:34—35).

characteristics of administrators, while others deal with the functions and tasks of administrators. These latter variables are among the less frequently discussed; consequently, they are not found on some of the summary evaluation forms in use at the present time. This discussion, then, is intended as a supplement to the forms and examples provided in Chapter Six and should provide assistance in the eventual decisions regarding what should be evaluated.

Cognitive Complexity.   This is one of the characteristics of administrators that should be evaluated. Cognitive complexity is directly related to the ability to process information and is necessary to decision making in a complex organization. In general, the integration of behavior with situation is a function of information; there is an increase of integration with increasing information load until an optimum performance is reached, beyond which the amount of integration decreases with further increasing information load. This can be visualized as an inverted U-shaped curve relating load of information to performance. However, differences in conceptual structure of individuals result in different levels of this inverted U-shaped function (Streufert & Schroder, 1965). This means that the optimum level of information processing varies from individual to individual, depending on the cognitive structure of the individual. Studies done by Streufert and Schroder indicate that the more flexible, integrative, complex and/or "abstract" the structure of the group members, the higher the level of integration involved in performance. This suggests that there is a need to select and/or train individuals who are high not only in ability to deal with concrete ideas but also with abstract concepts.

Silver (1975:62) found that principals with more abstract conceptual structures were more person-oriented in their leadership style. If cognitive complexity is desirable, Silver specifies that the following competencies are important:

- ability to search a broad range of information before making decisions
- skill in perceiving the relevance of broadly diversified information to given problems or situations
- ability to defer closure on decisions so as to remain receptive to new information
- competence to view each situation from numerous alternative perspectives
- techniques for creating diversity, divergence, and ambiguity in situations over which the individual has some control (1975:63-64)

How significant this variable is depends on the role expected of an administrator in a specific situation. Where the organization is not very complex or where maintenance or stability is extremely important, this variable is reduced in significance. In a complex school system where creativity is valued, an administrator's cognitive complexity should most probably be evaluated.

Awareness.   Awareness is not discussed much in the literature regarding administrator evaluation. Perhaps it is implied or taken for granted in relation to other characteristics or behavior. For example, it seems evident that it would be very important in relationships with people. Levinson (1968:253−254) attests to the importance of this variable, when he says, "In contemporary innovative organizations, the most successful executive is high in achievement motivation, low in power motivation, and keenly aware of himself, his employees, and the market." Being aware of oneself and having an awareness of one's employees contribute to healthy human relations, and having an awareness of the market (in business organizations) indicates a real concern for productivity of the organization.

Levinson provides a cue as to how this awareness can contribute to the success of a leader in an organization. He indicates that motivation studies show

> . . . that a good superior gives recognition to his subordinates, helps them grow in the job, represents their interests to higher management, looks out for their interests, corrects them justly and in private, and does not exploit them for his own gain. In this country the major objective of parents is to help their children grow to independent responsibility. The executive implicitly is expected to do the same in the course of fulfilling the objectives and goals of the organization (1968:18−19).

This parent figure concept of leadership (where the leader shows awareness of needs of subordinates) is different from paternalism, however, in that a paternalistic leader actually acts as if he really were the parent. Under such circumstances, the paternalistic leader provides things for the subordinates that they might better do themselves, e.g., recreation programs. Awareness that leads to consideration and good human relations, but stops short of paternalistic smothering, appears to warrant evaluation.

Decisiveness. My interest in this variable has persevered since the time of an earlier study in which I found that the measure of certainty an administrator experienced in making teacher selection decisions was a function of the format of the information provided. In the experiment conducted, there was significantly more certainty expressed with audiovisual than with audio interview information (Bolton, 1968:36). In effect, administrators choosing teachers after interviewing them via telephone would be less certain of their decisions than when they interviewed them in person. The certainty variable was included in the experiment because it was assumed that uncertainty can lead to indecision, vacillation, and wasted motion. It is interesting that House, Filley, and Gujarati (1971:431) came to a similar conclusion. They report that:

> . . . decisiveness emerges as an important variable with both a high degree of pervasiveness and generality. Surprisingly, little attention is or has been given to decisiveness as an independent variable in organization theory or studies concerning leadership behavior.

It seems that this variable would be most significant in situations where there is pressure of time and heavy work loads. It may be valued as a personal quality in other circumstances but it would affect outcomes of the organization most where time and work loads require speed of operation.

Personality.   Certainly this variable has precipitated considerable discussion. Many consider it as important but are wary of it because of the problems of measurement. It may be helpful to examine some of the more measurable qualities or behaviors which are a part of personality.

Consideration.   A concern for and interest in those with whom one is working is generally thought to be desirable in a leader and has been analyzed and measured in a number of studies. It is a valuable quality without regard to other variables, but it is also thought to interact in a favorable way with certain other variables. For example, Cummins (1971) found that the impact of initiating structure on the part of leaders was moderated by consideration, i.e., initiating structure did not have as much impact unless accompanied by consideration. However, he found that this was true in relation to quality of work performance, but not in relation to total productivity. If the results are generalizable, it would appear that initiating structure (or thrust for productivity) is sufficient for acquiring productivity but must be accompanied by consideration if quality also is desired. I presume that such results would be particularly important for education, since the quality of work is always of great importance.

Emotional maturity, cooperation, and tact.   Campbell et al. reported on research that indicated that peer judgments of emotional maturity, cooperation, and tact were unrelated to subsequent promotion (1970:114). However, at the same time, such traits as independence of thought, leadership qualities, and ability to think analytically were strongly related to promotion. Perhaps the reason for the lack of correlation is that the variables are difficult to differentiate or discriminate among subjects. For example, Peres and Garcia (1962:285) reported that in letters of recommendation the variables of "urbanity" and "cooperation-consideration" were least discriminating among those studies, whereas those dealing with "mental agility" were most discriminating. If, therefore, a variable like cooperation is rated virtually the same for all individuals, it is unlikely that it would be found to be related to any dependent variables such as productivity or quality of output.

However, if they are valuable in themselves, one should be wary of eliminating these variables from consideration in the evaluation process. If among twenty-five administrators only one of them is uncooperative or tactless, the correlation with some measure of productivity would be approximately zero. Yet, it may be important that all be evaluated on the variables in order to correct undesirable behavior in only the one person. This is a matter of validity as well as differentiation. One might desire to include variables that are considered to be high validity and low differentiation because of the utility with the exceptional case (Bolton, *Selection and Evaluation of Teachers,* 1973:157−158).

Perceptual accuracy and interest.   Along with the nature of the administrators' interests, their ability to assess others and situations may be of concern when considering the broad category of personality. Campbell et al. (1970:129) indicate that both of these are predictive of proficiency in executive and managerial jobs.

Persuasion, verbal interest, interpersonal contact. These qualities are common to effective managers, but they are not very well defined at present. They should be discussed and agreement should be reached among local leaders before they are included in evaluation systems (Campbell et al. 1970:133). It may be that persuasion is really an evidence of power need, that verbal interest is inherent in communication skills, and interpersonal contact is a part of consideration; if so, they may be better measured under different headings.

Conflict Resolution and Bargaining. This function or task of administrators has increased in significance as organizations have become more complex and as teachers and administrators have viewed professionalism as more important. Griffiths (1977:15) believes that in the future, "The key administrative process in organizations is very likely to be *bargaining* and not necessarily collective bargaining." If such is the case, many more administrators are likely to be involved in bargaining activities.

Although there are many strategies that can be used for the purpose of resolving conflicts, Sayan and Charters (1970:43) indicate that many people overlook one of the most important strategies used by school administrators when faced by conflict situations, viz., acting to alter the expectations or demands of the parties involved. Only when the people holding the competing expectations are seen as intractable does the administrator search for other means of resolution. If this strategy is successful, it resolves the conflict by eliminating it. It may be that this type of conflict resolution is very similar to the bargaining discussed by Griffiths. At any rate, it is evident that this variable should be considered by most school districts for inclusion in an evaluation system; the exact behavior in terms of strategies to be used may be expected to vary from district to district.

Using Judgment. Some of the literature makes very little distinction between *using judgment* and making decisions; however, judgment is somewhat less systematic than decision making. Odiorne describes it in this way:

> Judgment is that untheoretical and apparently intuitive (at least often described as such) reaction to questions which are presented without much warning and to which almost immediate responses are demanded. The quality of this reaction to an inescapable demand for decision forms the quality of judgment which we attribute to the manager (1969:124–125).

Although a decision is involved in the situation described by Odiorne, there is no opportunity to collect data, devise alternatives, predict consequences, or examine value systems in relation to the consequences predicted as an administrator would ordinarily do in making more substantive decisions. It may be that judgment is simply a special case of decision making in which time is short and yet a creative selection of alternatives is needed. If such is the case, "good" judgment may be directly related to prior experience with similar circumstances, intelligence and ability to assimilate quickly all of the relevant cues involved in the situation, and the creative ability to devise several alternatives in a short period of time. It may also involve the ability to determine whether a short delay, which would allow more systematic and comprehensive procedures to be used for making the decision, would prove detrimental to the organization.

The extent to which the local school district expects administrators to use their own judgment in relation to their jobs should be specified in the job description. The nature of the behavior to be exhibited could be specified in a summary report device applicable to a set of administrators, or in an individualized MBO statement.

Boundary Spanning. The function of an administrator identified by Gaynor (1975:2−3) as *boundary spanning* is probably recognized intuitively by most school personnel. Its significance is probably incorporated in the outcome area for which many administrators have some responsibility, viz., school-community relations and the process of communication that is often emphasized in relation to this outcome area. But Gaynor discusses it as a role rather than either an outcome area or process and indicates that the principal and the superintendent are in particularly critical positions in relation to the interface between the school system and the community. This role allows them to be sensitive to evolutionary changes in the school environment. Gaynor says:

> It can be hypothesized that in those school systems still operating in placid-clustered environments, the role of the principal remains internal and primarily bureaucratically oriented; however, as school systems find themselves in increasingly turbulent environments, the role of the principal should become more externally and politically oriented. . . . it seems critical for us to understand precisely what the relationship is between the role expectations held for the school principal and the nature of the changing environments of schools (Gaynor 1977:2-3).

It would appear, then, that this variable would be most important to consider under circumstances where the community is dynamic rather than stable, since the information provided by the interface would aid the school district in adapting and responding.

Being an Entrepreneur. One does not ordinarily think of an educational administrator as an *entrepreneur*. However, as one thinks of adapting and responding to the environment, the words of Drucker concerning the business administrator are pertinent. He indicates that the manager has to be an entrepreneur as well as an administrator, in the following sense:

> He has to redirect resources from areas of low or diminishing results to areas of high or

increasing results. He has to slough off yesterday and to render obsolete what already exists and is already known. He has to create tomorrow (Drucker, 1968:45).

If the entrepreneur's significant activities include (a) redirecting resources to improve results, (b) eliminating the obsolete in order that the more pertinent may prevail, and (c) creating changes that make the future more significant than the past, then certainly many school districts should consider this function as they design administrator evaluation systems. It may be considered as a separate function, or it may be included in more traditional tasks such as coordination, leadership, and planning.

Developing Means for Measuring

Determining the means for collecting data and for measuring the procedures and results of procedures for administrators is more difficult than for the evaluation of teachers. Basically, this is true because of the difficulty of observing many of the actions of administrators. Developing means for measuring includes determining what information will be collected, understanding the limits involved in collecting data, and agreeing on the data-collection procedures to be used. An important consideration is that the development of measurement should occur *before* action is taken (that is, before the administrator implements any procedures) and before information is collected. This prevents the outcomes from influencing the criteria for judging.

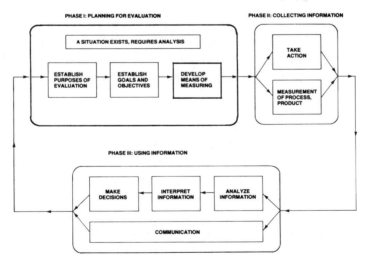

BASIC WAYS OF COLLECTING INFORMATION

Information can be collected in one of three ways: observating behavior, asking questions, and examining written documents. Each of these ways may be used in the evaluation of administrators, but agreement on the type of data collection to be used with each objective should be made during the planning period. Certain processes used by teachers are difficult to observe (e.g., the handling of emergencies), but many people consider *most* of the processes used by administrators unobservable or difficult to observe without severely altering the situation by the presence of the observer. For this reason, more emphasis is likely to be placed on information from records and from questions asked of the evaluatee and clients of the evaluatee such as students, teachers, and parents. Simply because questions and written records may be easier to obtain does not mean that creative means should not be used to observe administrators, since observation can be a very beneficial source of information. For example, faculty meetings, parental conferences, public meetings, and teacher conferences can all be observed for the purpose of evaluating performance, but this is seldom done systematically.

DIMENSIONS TO CONSIDER

As one considers the collection of data, there should be an attempt to reach agreement regarding what data will be collected, how it will be collected, who will collect it, and when and where it will be collected.

What.   The basic question most people have regarding their work is "What works for me, in my situation?" The question itself furnishes clues to what information should be collected. The "what" refers to the processes to be used; therefore, one should collect information regarding those processes. The "works" has to do with the results or outcomes of the processes; therefore, one should collect information regarding the products. It is this interest in process-product relationship which is at the heart of the evaluation process. Information about the product is needed in order to determine whether desired results were obtained; information regarding the process is needed in order to know how to replicate or to modify so that desired results can be obtained.

How.   There are many ways of classifying how one collects data, but one should at least consider whether it is to be collected on an individualized or a uniform basis. If it is to be collected on a uniform basis, a common data collection form may be used for a group of administrators. If an individualized procedure is to be used, it will be beneficial for a school district to develop a group of data collection forms that may be useful in a variety of situations. This will assist an evaluator and an administrator to determine which data collection form might be most appropriate for use. Care should be taken to avoid choosing a recording form simply because it is available, however (Bolton, *Selection and Evaluation of Teachers,* 1973:34, 111–112). Instruments should *not* be chosen solely on the basis of the evaluator's familiarity with the document, its availability, or the fact that other districts are using it! Considerations should include:

- relevance to the goals and objectives established
- acceptability to those who are involved, including the administrator, the

evaluator, and anyone who may be responsible for responding to a self-report device
- accessibility of information to those who will complete the device
- time needed to acquire the information
- the cost of information

Who. Deciding who should be involved in the collection of information involves many of the same considerations as the question of *how* it should be collected. Certainly of major consideration should be the nature of the goals and objectives and the type of information to be collected. The possibilities of *who* should be involved include the administrator, the evaluator or some other person(s) external to the evaluatee, and a combination of the evaluator and external people. With a single objective one is likely to choose either self or external collectors; but with the total evaluation process, a combination is more likely.

When and Where. If one has decided on the what, how, and who regarding the collection, many times the *when* and *where* will be self-evident. For example, if a principal has an objective which relates to his or her effectiveness in conducting faculty meetings, the following may have been decided:

1. The *what* will include procedures used in the meeting, with particular interest in the amount of participation by all members of the faculty. In addition, the product will involve the faculty's feelings of inclusion in the decision process and their satisfaction with the process.
2. The *how* will be individualized. An observation guide will be developed and used to determine how many people participated, the frequency and time taken by each participant, the percentage of time taken by the principal, what decisions were made, and how long it took to make each decision. In addition, a self-report device will be developed to obtain the reactions of the faculty to the faculty meeting.
3. The *who* will include the evaluator as an external observer of the meeting, using the structured observation guide developed by the principal and the evaluator. In addition, the faculty will respond to the short self-report device designed by the principal and the evaluator. The principal will be responsible for duplication of the device and for designing procedures for collecting them after they have been completed anonymously.

Once all of this has been determined, it is evident that the observation will need to occur *during* the meeting and the self-report device will need to be completed *immediately following* the meeting. It would not be beneficial to have the faculty complete the device a month after the meeting because their views may be altered by other circumstances; in addition, they may forget certain information about the meeting. However, a decision will need to be made regarding whether the faculty is to complete the device at the location of the meeting or whether they will be given the option to complete it elsewhere (e.g., at home or in their own classrooms) and turn it in the following day. Note that usually the information collection procedures, as well as goals and objectives, should be determined mutually. The only exceptions would be in cases where an administrator is unwilling to face behaviors that are detrimental to organizational goals.

A final idea should be emphasized in relation to these dimensions to be considered in the collection of information. In evaluating administrators, the emphasis should be on making judgments in relation to established objectives, *not* on judging the personal worth of individuals. Judging the personal worth of an administrator is in another realm (perhaps in the legal or even the spiritual) not in the realm of the evaluator. If the evaluator is concerned with the administrator being an appropriate model for teachers or students, then the appropriate behavior should be put in the form of an objective and evaluated accordingly; but this does not involve the question of personal worth of the individual.

SOME PROBLEMS OF MEASUREMENT

Regardless of whether the measurement planned will be based on direct observation, asking questions of others, or examination of written records, certain problems can occur. Most of these problems are inherent in the capability and training of the person gathering the information. This person must translate raw data into a usable format, and she or he can affect the translation in ways that cause problems.

Prejudice, Bias, or Poor Judgment.   For example, a person's prejudices or biases regarding behavior may affect the translation of raw data. If a person who is observing an administrator (in a faculty meeting, or in a face-to-face conference) has an aversion to certain personal characteristics of the administrator, it may affect the measurement of how a discussion is conducted or how the administrator reacts to questions. Or, because the observer thinks that nonverbal behavior is extremely important in communication, he or she may improperly measure the substantive element of a conversation.

Inconsistency of Reaction to Behavior.   A person who reacts positively to a given behavior or fact on one day and negatively on another day is reacting inconsistently. Likewise, a person who indicates that an administrator "seldom" behaves in a particular way and the next day indicates that the administrator "occasionally" behaves that way is being inconsistent. The reasons back of such inconsistency may be diverse, but regardless of the reason(s) the inconsistency poses a problem of measurement.

Ratings and Classifications Requiring High Inferences.   Rating devices that require an individual to come to a conclusion about several bits of information and to respond to a single scale can sometimes cause problems. For example, to ask one individual to rate another on the function of "communication" by marking a point on the scale below requires him or her to make an inference from many observations of the individual.

poor_____fair_____satisfactory_____good_____excellent_____

In addition, the scale forces the observer to attach a value to the sum total of the observations. The combined task of summarizing the information collected and attaching a value to it by coming to a conclusion about which classification is appropriate can cause inconsistency—both within and among measurers.

Outside and Inside Influences. Each person who is responsible for measuring any process or product of an administrator is influenced by his own physical and mental health (internal feelings) as well as by surroundings. When a person is frustrated or engaged in a conflict immediately prior to collecting data, these external influences can have dramatic effects on results.

Attempts to Measure Too Much. Undoubtedly all school administrators can re-member their first attempts to observe a classroom full of students and a teacher. It probably was during the time they were training to become teachers, and there was the attempt to observe everything that happened in the classroom. After some ex-perience of teaching, and perhaps some training in observational techniques, the administrator learned which cues were important for the particular objective being sought by the teacher. Consequently, this cue reduction process enabled the adminis-trator to focus on a limited number of things to observe. When one attempts to measure too much, only some type of global impression is obtained—which may not be very helpful in terms of measurement.

Continuation of a Prior Viewpoint. Sometimes impressions of an individual gained from a particular situation tend to carry over into other situations even though the behavior of the individual changes. For example, in a superintendent's cabinet meeting an evaluator may form an impression of an administrator based on a discus-sion of teacher evaluation procedures. Because of what is said, the impression may be created that the administrator does considerable classroom observation followed by individual conferences with teachers. If this impression persists when the evaluator is examining the teacher-observation reports completed by the adminis-trator, it may affect the reaction of the evaluator to the number of observations and conferences completed. The prior viewpoint should continue only if the new infor-mation warrants it; in essence, the two measures should be independent.

Consistent Over- or Under-valuation. Some people have a tendency to be consis-tently lenient while others tend to be harsh. These tendencies naturally affect the measurements they make and may be directly related to optimism-pessimism ten-dencies. Stories of such people exist in profusion. One of my favorites consists of three characters: a dean of a college of education and two professors. It happened that at the end of one quarter the dean was examining the grade distributions of each professor's classes. As he examined these grades, he noticed that the professors had rather unusual distributions of their grades. Professor "A" had given a large number of As, a few Bs, two or three Cs, and no Ds or Fs. Professor "B" had a distribution that was the reverse of Professor "A": no As, no Bs, two or three Cs, a few Ds, and a large number of Fs. Since these two professors had such different grade distributions, the dean decided to discuss it with them. To Professor "A" he said, "I notice that you have a rather skewed distribution of grades, with many As, a few Bs, two or three Cs, and no Ds or Fs. I wonder if you could explain this to me." "Why, of course," said Professor "A" "That is merely due to my superior teaching." The dean then encountered Professor "B" and posed a similar question: "I notice your grade distribution is rather skewed, with no As, no Bs, two or three Cs, a few Ds, and a large number of Fs. I wonder if you can explain this to me." With a slight pause, Professor "B" declared, "Well—you can't flunk 'em all." Over- and under-valuation can be a real problem of measurement.

TYPES OF SCALES

It may be recalled that measurement is described as "the quantification or quasiquantification of events, behaviors, or results of behaviors; as such, it does not incorporate any judgment making or require any value system to be applied" (see p. 29). The only value required for measurement to occur is for someone to desire that something be measured. Classical scaling theory discusses nominal, ordinal, equal interval, and ratio scales. However, for our purposes another classification of scales may be more beneficial. In examining documents in use by school systems, one finds rank ordering, forced distribution, absolute categories, verbal descriptors, degree of existence, and extent of agreement scales (Bolton, "Collecting Evaluation Data," 1973:80−82).

Rank Ordering. Rank ordering uses a scale for ranking individuals in a group according to some item or characteristic. For example consider the item and the scale below:

Ability to communicate with groups of people in structured situations.
Superior_____ Above Aver._____ Aver._____ Below Aver._____ Inferior_____

Note that this ranking is against a reference group, but rank ordering may also be against an absolute standard or criterion. For example, the scale may be:

Excellent_____ Good_____ Satisfactory_____ Poor_____ Inadequate_____

This latter scale requires only that one define each point on the scale in terms of behavior that would represent the point; whereas, the first scale requires that *some* reference group be known well enough to determine each point. On the first scale, one could not have 90 percent of a group in the "Superior" category, since that would violate the meaning of average.[4] However, one might well have 90 percent of the administrators of a group in the "Excellent" category, since they could conceivably satisfy that criterion or standard.

If one desires to use a rank ordering scale, care should be taken *not* to mix criterion referenced scales and norm referenced scales. For example, the following scale is mixed:

Poor——— Average——— Good——— Very good——— Superior———

Since poor, good, and very good are absolute standards and average and superior require a norm group, the scale is confusing to anyone trying to use it; error of measurement is "built into" the scale itself.

The rank ordering scale may be used with specific items (as illustrated with the communication item above) or with general and overall type items, which may be illustrated as follows:

General item: Professional responsibility

Overall item: Indicate your estimate of the service rendered by this administrator by placing a check in front of the most appropriate term.

Forced Distribution.   A forced distribution requires that a certain percentage of the people being considered be placed in each descriptive category. For example, consider the specific item which we combined with the norm referenced scale:

Ability to communicate with groups of people in structured situations.
Superior——— Above Aver.——— Aver.——— Below Aver.——— Inferior———

If we required that the categories include ratios of 10 percent, 20 percent, 40 percent, 20 percent, 10 percent, we would in fact be changing the item to:

Ability to communicate with groups of people in structured situations.
Upper 10%——— Next 20%——— Mid 40%——— Next 20%——— Lowest 10%———

As with the norm-referenced rank ordering scale, it would be necessary to define the norm group.

The forced distribution scale may also be used with general areas or overall items; the items could be similar to those used to illustrate the rank ordering scale.

Absolute Categories.   Absolute category systems describe individual behaviors or total behavior of an administrator by placing incidents into discrete descriptive categories. For example, a *specific* item combined with this scale might be:

The administrator provides background information from official school district policies or procedures.

---

[4]If the reference group is all of the administrators in a state, one might well have 90 percent of the administrators in a given district in the "Superior" category, but not if the reference group is the given district.

_____(count the number of times this occurs during the meeting observed)

It appears that this type of scale does not readily combine with a *general* type of item, but it may combine with an *overall* item; for example:

My recommendation for this administrator for the coming year is:

_____ should remain in the present position
_____ should have a parallel change of assignment
_____ should receive a promotion
_____ should request leave of absence
_____ services should be terminated

Verbal Descriptors.   Verbal descriptors are used to express what has been perceived and may be used in sentence, phrase, single word form, or scaled with bipolar adjectives. The example below uses a *specific* item combined with bipolar adjectives.

The manner in which the principal evaluates teachers can best be described as (put a check in the space you consider to be appropriate):
continuous ____ : ____ : ____ : ____ : ____ : ____ : ____ erratic
rational ____ : ____ : ____ : ____ : ____ : ____ : ____ irrational
systematic ____ : ____ : ____ : ____ : ____ : ____ : ____ disorganized

For a more *general* item, the following might be required:

Write a brief paragraph describing characteristics that are most pertinent
to the administrator's potential for promotion to the next higher level.

An *overall* item may simply ask for comments regarding areas needing improvement. The examples used in this category indicate that the specific items merely supply the descriptors and the behavior or characteristic to be described, but the more general item or the overall item leaves the responsibility for devising these descriptors to the person doing the measuring.

Degree of Existence.   The degree of existence scale is concerned with how often an event or type of behavior occurs. An example of a *specific* item would be:

Exhibits confidence in teachers' doing a professional job.
always_____ often_____ occasionally_____ seldom_____ never_____

The same type of scaling could be used with a more *general* type of item such as "uses good judgment," but it does not appear to be appropriate for the *overall* type of item.

Extent of Agreement.   This type of scale usually makes a statement with which a person may express an amount of agreement or disagreement. For example, teachers may be asked to respond to the following *specific* item:

The evaluation procedure used by my principal has encouraged me to initiate and maintain a systematic procedure for self-evaluation.

SA_____A_____U_____D_____SD_____

in this case, SA = Strongly Agree, A = Agree, U = Undecided, D = Disagree, and SD = Strongly Disagree.

A more *general* item might be:

The principal of this school is well organized.

Strongly Agree _____ : _____ : _____ : _____ : _____ Strongly Disagree

An *overall* item might be:

This administrator should be retained in the present position next year.

Yes_____No_____

It is probable that this type of scale will be more useful for the specific item, but some may find it beneficial for either the general or the overall type of item.

The scales and types of items that have been described are not intended as a prescription for use in specific school districts. However, under conditions where administrators in a school district desire to construct their own measurement or information recording devices (rather than borrowing them from another district or having them designed by a consultant), the classification scheme may be of benefit. Care should be taken to choose the types of scales and items that contribute most to the purposes for evaluation. For example, the use of a forced distribution scale on an overall item may be quite beneficial for making administrative decisions about reduction in force; however, under conditions where such decisions are not being made, the scale may induce anxiety, apprehension, and even hostility.

SOURCES OF INFORMATION

It has been mentioned that the behavioral sciences obtain information from three sources: observation, asking questions, and written records. And all of these can be used for obtaining information for the evaluation of administrators.

Observation. Observation of administrators by external evaluators can occur in both a systematic and an incidental way. Systematic observation of administrators may occur in certain structured situations such as faculty meetings, departmental or level meetings, or meetings with groups of parents. In addition, one might systematically observe the office routines used by an administrator or an observer could keep an accurate log of the way an administrator manages his time. Less systematic observation is likely to occur in meetings of administrators, superintendent's cabinet meetings, individual conferences with a supervisor or another person, committee meetings, or task force meetings. In these situations all individuals are likely to be concentrating on the substance of the encounter and only incidentally observing the behavior of the participants.

Because an evaluator may have many more contacts of an incidental nature with an evaluatee than contacts where systematic observation is designed and carried out, there should be a conscious effort to review criteria, circumstances where information might be collected, and critical incidents occurring in these circumstances. Where the review occurs between the evaluator and the administrator, not only is communication likely to be improved between the two of them, but also both are likely to become better observers of events contributing to the evaluation.

Asking Questions.   Asking questions of others can occur via interviews or structured self-report devices. Questions may be asked of subordinates, peers, or clients. For example, subordinates of principals would be teachers and vice principals; peers would be other principals who may interact with each other on projects or in coordination of programs; and clients would include students, parents, and voters. An assistant superintendent in charge of personnel would have a different set of subordinates, peers, and clients, however.

Suppose, for example, that an assistant superintendent has responsibility for a series of meetings in homes where the purpose is to provide information about a school levy for operations during the coming school year. He may desire to acquire information from those who attend the meetings (clients) in order to evaluate his own effectiveness in conducting the meetings. The self-report device might include such items as the following:

A. Please respond to the following items by placing a checkmark (✔) in the space you judge to represent your views.

1. The ideas presented and discussed, in relation to my own concerns regarding the school levy, were

   pertinent ____ : ____ : ____ : ____ : ____ : ____ : ____ missed the point

2. The presentation was

   valuable ____ : ____ : ____ : ____ : ____ : ____ : ____ worthless

3. The question and answer period was

   interesting ____ : ____ : ____ : ____ : ____ : ____ : ____ dull

   worthwhile ____ : ____ : ____ : ____ : ____ : ____ : ____ worthless

   clear ____ : ____ : ____ : ____ : ____ : ____ : ____ hazy

4. There were opportunities today for me to clarify my thinking

   considerably ____ : ____ : ____ : ____ : ____ : ____ : ____ not at all

5. The combination of the presentation and the question-and-answer period allowed me to feel

   free to
   participate ____ : ____ : ____ : ____ : ____ : ____ : ____ stifled

B. Complete the following sentences:

6. I would like _____

    7. The main problem _____

    8. I found out _____

C. Please respond to the following:

    9. What questions or topics were not discussed as fully as you would have liked? _____

    10. Please indicate how you think meetings of this type would be of more benefit to voters _____

Such information may be used to (a) facilitate communication between the administrator and his supervisor (probably the superintendent) regarding the exact nature of the meetings and how they are perceived by those who attend; (b) suggest changes in format or content of meetings during the levy campaign; (c) assess information regarding differences in reactions in different parts of the community; and (d) compile summary information for use in planning future information dissemination.

An additional advantage of this type of information is that it can be acquired and analyzed quickly; ten items such as those suggested above can be completed in five to seven minutes by those who attend; a clerk can summarize a set of twenty-five in approximately fifteen minutes; and the administrator and supervisor can analyze and interpret the results in fifteen minutes or less. The major time factor would be in devising the precise questions. However, one could soon accumulate sets of items that could be used in a variety of situations, and then a questionnaire could be devised in a fairly short time.

Written Records.   An administrator's written records fall into two categories: those which result from the normal activities of the administrator and those made by the administrator in order to answer some question of an evaluative nature. An example of the first category is the records a principal may keep of all observations of classrooms during a school year. An example of the second category is the record a principal may decide to keep of the number of telephone calls received from parents—classifying them by nature of the inquiry, duration of call, and when they occur, in order to determine how this places a constraint on use of time. In each case, the written records would be subject to analysis and interpretation by both the administrator and the evaluator in relation to certain objectives established prior to the data collection (or at least prior to the analysis).

USE OF FORMS

Forms are used to collect information and to summarize that information for reporting purposes. The collection of information is basically a measuring process, and general conclusions may not be needed. However, summary report forms usually require conclusions to be stated.

One of the major problems with forms currently in use by many school districts is that these two functions (i.e., collecting and summarizing/reporting) are combined in the same form. When this happens, it is often the case that the summarizing/

reporting overshadows the collecting function rendering the form inadequate for use in collecting information. A solution to this problem is to design a summary report form and use it for that purpose only. It may then be necessary to design individual information collection devices in terms of the needs of specific administrators. A "bank" of devices is helpful for designing these forms.

Summary

Planning for the evaluation of administrators is considered to be the first phase of a three-phase, cyclical process that also includes collecting information and using information. The information used during the third phase becomes the basis for planning as the cycle repeats itself. The *planning for evaluation* phase includes analysis of a specific situation, establishing purposes for evaluation, setting goals and specific objectives, and deciding on means for measuring the processes used and the eventual outcomes.

The planning phase may involve primarily one-to-one relationships between and evaluator and evaluatee, but it is more likely that some parts of the planning phase will occur with groups of administrators. For example, as the situation within which administrators function is analyzed fully, both the external and the internal variables are likely to be examined by groups of administrators. They may be *reviewed* by individual evaluators and evaluatees, but the initial examination may be by groups. The same may be true of other parts of planning.

There is some evidence that the level of an administrator's position and the nature of subordinates supervised have an impact on the type of cognitive skills needed in a position. In addition, at least the following variables should be considered by administrators analyzing local situations: (a) the number of individuals and groups that have an impact on the commitment and support of schools, (b) the size of the organization, and (c) the value system and expectations of those with whom the administrator works.

Job descriptions for administrators vary from organization to organization—in substance as well as extent of use. The three areas of responsibility often included in job descriptions are (a) performance of regular and/or routine duties, (b) achieving satisfactory solutions to problems, and (c) completing new and innovative projects. The job description is generally considered a beneficial tool in managing an organization when used as a basis for discussion about priorities, significant elements of the job, and elements that have changed since prior discussions.

Studies of the expectations others have of administrators in local situations appear to offer clues to what type of behavior causes people to be satisfied with the functioning of schools. Since others' expectations regarding such things as thrust for productivity and attention to the concerns of people vary among situations, it appears important for school districts to identify locally what characteristics and behaviors are valued by subordinates, administrators, and clients. Such empirical evidence may be quite beneficial in planning for evaluation of administrators.

The identification, discussion, and agreement on the purposes of evaluating administrators is extremely important because the purposes provide the direction and reason for existence of additional activities in the evaluation process. Without purpose, activities tend to be generated or omitted on the whim of those involved. Problems encountered in the process of reaching consensus on purposes of evaluation include (a) stating all purposes that are important to the individuals and to the organization without becoming embroiled in meaningless arguments over whether one is primary or more important than another and (b) stating underlying assumptions and the value system of the evaluation process so they are meaningful to everyone.

Although a list of purposes cannot be recommended to fit all situations, consideration should be given at least to changing goals or objectives, modifying procedures, determining new ways of implementing procedures, improving performance of individuals, supplying information for modification of assignments, protecting individuals or the school system, rewarding superior performance, providing a basis for career planning and individual growth and development, validating the selection process, and facilitating self-evaluation.

Establishing goals and specific objectives is basically a process of determining a standard against which comparisons can be made. Many differences exist in relation to this task, including differences over perceptions of role expectations, how goal statements should be written, and the significance of performance standards generally.

The following points relative to establishing goals and objectives should be observed when attempting to individualize the evaluation process in terms of the uniqueness of the situation: each administrator has a responsibility for establishing objectives compatible with and contributing to the goals of the school district; the objectives of the administrator are not synonymous with the goals of the district or the objectives of the teacher; the evaluator has the responsibility for approval of the objectives; and establishment of objectives means commitment of time and effort as well as support via school district resources.

In contemplating what should be evaluated, the following are pertinent variables that are often omitted from consideration: cognitive complexity, awareness, decisiveness, personality, consideration, emotional maturity (including cooperation and tact), perceptual accuracy and interest, persuasion, verbal interest, interpersonal contact, conflict resolution and bargaining, using judgment, boundary spanning, and being an entrepreneur.

Administrators may be involved in the triple roles of managers, judges, and helpers. Reduction of potential conflict between these roles may occur if precise expectations in each of these roles is put in writing in the form of general goals or specific objectives and if the communication is open and authentic between an administrator and the evaluator.

A well-written objective should be clearly written, focus on an identifiable outcome or result as a target, specify the action to be taken and the activities to be engaged in, specify who should accomplish the objective, be time limited, specify cost in terms of all resources needed, and be stated so that it is verifiable. After objectives are stated, they should be given priorities in order to indicate which objectives are to be met first in case some cannot be accomplished.

Means of measuring the procedures and results of procedures for administrators should be developed *before* action is taken by the administrator to implement any procedures and before information is collected. Developing means for measuring includes determining what information will be collected, understanding the limits involved in collecting data, and agreeing on the data-collection procedures to be used. Measurement itself is considered to be the quantification or quasiquantification of events, behaviors, or results of behaviors; as such it does not involve judgment making or application of values.

Information can be collected by observation of behavior, by asking questions, and by examining written documents. As one prepares to use one of the means of collecting information, an attempt should be made to reach agreement regarding what data will be collected, how it will be collected, who will collect it, and when and where it will be collected. Throughout the evaluation process, and especially as measurement is being considered, the emphasis should be on making judgments in relation to established objectives, *not* on judging the personal worth of individuals.

In designing measurement procedures, one should be aware of certain problems that often occur in measurement: prejudice, bias, or poor judgment; inconsistency of reaction to behavior; ratings and classifications requiring high inferences; outside and inside influences on the measurer; attempts to measure too much; continuation of a prior viewpoint; and consistent over- or under-valuation.

Scales used in measurement procedures by school districts may include rank ordering, forced distribution, absolute categories, verbal descriptors, degree of existence, and extent of agreement scales. Most of these scales may be used with specific, general, or overall type items. One should be careful in designing forms for use in the evaluation process not to attempt to design a single form for the purpose of collecting information and also for summarizing that information for reporting purposes. If individualization is to occur in the evaluation process, conclusions and summary statements may need to be based on information collected via several different devices.

3 PHASE II: COLLECTING INFORMATION

Evaluation must be based on information that has been collected according to a specific plan. The *collecting information phase* has two parts: (a) the administrator being evaluated takes some action based on the plans made during Phase I and (b) measurements are made of what happens during and as a result of the action taken. Although the administrator being evaluated is taking the action during this phase, one should not assume that all of the measurement is being done by the external evaluator. The evaluatee is also often engaged in measuring either the process or the product related to the objectives established.

Take Action

In most organizations, administrators are concerned with taking actions that bring about both productivity and satisfaction with the work being done. Their actions, as such, are not *directly* productive, in the sense of seeing that major

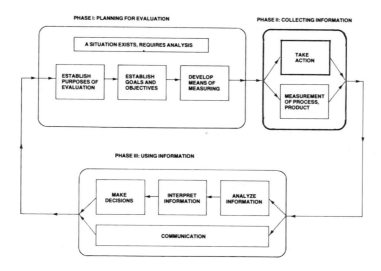

products or services of an organization result. But their actions are productive in the sense of providing support designed to improve the processes of teachers and providing a desirable environment for students and teachers.

The idea that administrators are playing a supportive role is not new, but it is one which is easily ignored in the pressure-laden environment of the administrator. Providing service to others does not mean that one does not have outcomes as goals or that one should be unaccountable to others for processes used; however, it does mean that the processes and products identified for a given administrator are unique to the types of services provided.

To illustrate the viewpoint that different administrators have different products, consider figure 3.1. Note that the functions and responsibilities of the principal are

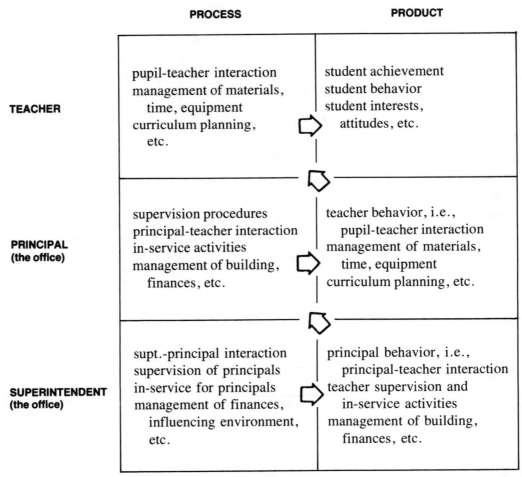

Figure 3.1: *The relationship among teacher, principal, and superintendent processes and products*

not focused directly on student behavior and achievement.[1] Likewise, the focus of the superintendent is not directly on teacher behavior and processes used in and out of the classroom. As one examines the figure (or school district operations which it represents), it is evident that there are many outcomes or products and not all personnel are working to affect all of these products directly; in effect, some people's products are others' processes.

Although figure 3.1 shows processes of the principal concerned with improving teaching techniques, and the activities of the superintendent related to their impact on principal behavior, these do not encompass all of the responsibilities of administrators. Administrators are expected to produce outcomes in a variety of areas; therefore, they may be expected to use a variety of processes. Figure 3.2 illustrates

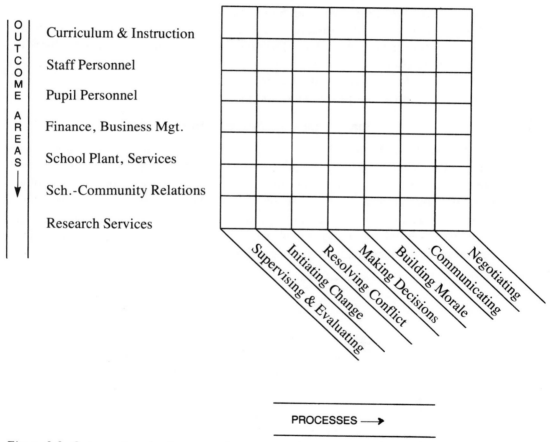

Figure 3.2: Outcome (product) areas and processes related to responsibilities of educational administrators

---

[1]Figure 3.1 and the discussion related to it are based largely on a prior discussion of evaluation of processes and products as a responsibility of school principals (Bolton, 1974:181-183).

several outcome areas and processes that are beneficial for attainment of objectives in these outcome areas.

Each cell of the figure represents an outcome area and a process that may or may not be related to it (depending on the specific outcome identified). Actions of administrators may be classified in one of the cells of the figure. For example, if an administrator conducts a conference with a teacher for the purpose of evaluating a lesson that was observed, the action would be classified in the cell represented by the staff personnel outcome area and the supervising and evaluating process. One can classify administrator objectives by such a classification scheme and determine whether a group of administrators are ignoring certain outcomes or processes in their planning. For example, in a study conducted in a single school district, it was found that 19 percent of the objectives were communication processes, 12 percent were decision-making processes, and none were concerned with resolving conflict; also, 63 percent were concerned with outcomes in curriculum and instruction, 11 percent with personnel, none with research services, and 9 percent with pupil personnel services (Bolton & Sullivan, 1978). The point is not that the percentage of objectives in a given classification is correct or incorrect for that school district but that such a classification allows a given school district to examine whether emphases are being placed on outcomes and processes in the manner desired.

Measurement of Process and Product

Measurement during this phase includes collection of all information necessary to make decisions regarding whether goals and objectives are being accomplished. Even though the establishment of purposes of evaluation, setting of goals and objectives, and development of measurement in Phase I were done sequentially, the two activities of Phase II are done concommitantly. This means that the action is not taken by the administrator and then measured at some later time. For certain actions, measurement *must* be made while the action is being taken or the measurement is

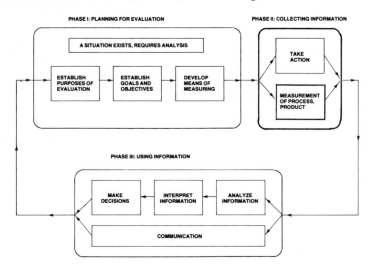

unreliable. As previously noted, to try to observe and remember all of what happens in a faculty meeting and to make a record of it two weeks later would certainly introduce considerable error of measurement.

Of course, the purpose of examining the outcomes of an administrator is to determine if the goals have been met. The purpose of examining processes used is to determine whether a specified plan is being followed. And the purpose of comparing outcomes with procedures is to determine whether the procedures should be modified (if outcomes were not accomplished) or replicated (if outcomes were accomplished).

WHO COLLECTS INFORMATION?

To evaluate administrators, information should be acquired regarding processes used with groups of people, processes used alone, and the impact of these processes on the organization and on subordinates and clients. For example, a principal will be engaged in activities with faculty and parent groups, in individual planning and organizing, and the impact of these activities should make a difference in how teachers behave in the classroom. *Who* collects information about these activities and behaviors depends on what plan is agreed upon by the principal and his evaluator. In this instance, at least the following people may be involved: the principal's supervisor, the principal, vice principal(s), teachers, students, department heads, subject-matter specialists (consultants, supervisors), personnel specialists, peers (other principals), and parents.

It seems reasonable that any person involved in the collection of data would not be expected to collect *all* of the information needed in relation to a specific objective. Likewise, not all people who will be involved will be *collectors* of information. For example, the principal may collect information on his product (e.g., the behavior of teachers) by observing the classroom behavior of teachers and keeping a record of the behavior and the conferences with the teachers regarding the observations. On the other hand, the teacher's views may also be recorded as an analysis and interpretation of the data collected. Likewise, the teacher may collect information from students about achievement and attitudinal changes. The evaluator of this principal may not collect any information related to the principal's *product* but may be involved in observing some of the principal's procedures in working with teachers. Even though several people may be involved, they are involved in various roles in terms of the processes and products being examined—in relation to specific objectives.

A clear specification of the role and responsibilities of the people collecting information should do two things. First, it should alleviate any anxiety on the part of the evaluatee as to whether information is being collected secretly. Second, it should fix responsibilities so that there is no ambiguity and so that collection of information is not left to chance. The evaluator has the responsibility to see that these roles and duties are specified; however, the evaluatee should be involved in making these decisions.

ACQUIRING INFORMATION ON SELF

An administrator can obtain information about processes used and products resulting from his processes. Where the administrator is solely involved in the analysis and interpretation of this information, i.e., where the process is one of self-evaluation, there are certain advantages. For one thing, there is the opportunity for improvement without external threat, which may potentially increase motivation and creativity where risk taking is associated with change. However, there is also the possibility that the information collected may not relate readily to criteria considered important to the needs of the school district.

Another problem area in relation to acquiring information on self is in the area of personal perception. Zimmerer (1970) reviews prior research in this area and indicates that: (a) knowing oneself makes it easier to see others accurately (i.e., when one is aware of what one's own personal characteristics are, one makes fewer errors in perceiving others), (b) one's own characteristics affect the characteristics he or she is likely to see in others (e.g., more secure people tend to see others as warm rather than cold), and (c) persons who accept themselves are more likely to be able to see favorable aspects of other people. Where a principal, for example, is collecting information about the behavior of teachers (as his or her product), the principal's own self-knowledge, characteristics, and security may have considerable impact on the type of information collected and the analysis and interpretation of that information. Zimmerer indicates that since accuracy in perceiving others is not a single skill, one question to be asked is, Am I looking at him and forming my impression of his behavior in the situation, or am I just comparing him with myself?

Evidently, there are considerable differences in perception of information. For example, one study found that individuals identified as "least promotable" (LP) were not able to identify criteria for promotion, but the "most promotables" (MP) were more able to do so. Likewise, the MP seemed to be more able to determine what their superiors thought of them than were the LP (Zimmerer, 1970). If these results generalize, it would tend to indicate that any group of administrators who are engaged in collecting information about themselves (and analyzing and interpreting it) should be given training to help them identify information which is pertinent to organizational goals and a framework to help them analyze and interpret the information once it is collected.

When administrators want to get information directly from subordinates regarding their own behavior or characteristics, several procedures may be used. For example, they might use one-to-one conversations, small group meetings, or written feedback. In some of these instances, the subordinate may feel there is a risk involved in being perfectly candid. Dyer (1974) provides some suggestions that administrators can use to reduce risk in such circumstances:

1. The evaluator may describe a specific instance to break the ice.
2. A small group may meet and report in summary fashion in order to assure anonymity.

3. In a regular staff meeting they can stimulate open and direct interchange.
4. With a large staff, over a period of time, they can use standard instruments and questionnaires.
5. They can share a performance assessment and ask for comments.
6. They can use an outside consultant to add perspective and confidentiality to a high-risk, tense feedback setting.

In addition, if one desires to encourage feedback from employees, Dyer suggests that one: (a) listen before defending, (b) ask for further elaboration, (c) react honestly, and (d) express appreciation and indicate plans for the future.

It is doubtful that one could function as Dyer suggests unless there is an inner attitude that sincerely desires honest feedback. Therefore, it is suggested that one examine attitudes about feedback before asking for it. One of the major questions in acquiring information about self is how secure one is psychologically and how much self-control one has. Levinson (1968:253–254) indicates that the basic problem the executive has to contend with is himself; the primary source of the dilemmas leaders face is their own inner conflict. In effect, one must have his own psychological house in order and be keenly aware of self and others to be able to acquire, analyze, and interpret information about oneself. An attitude of willingness to be critical of one's own performance rather than the performance of others is needed.

RATING SCALES AND CHECKLISTS

Information on either the processes or the products of administrators may be recorded by using highly systematic or less systematic observation procedures. The more systematic observation procedures would be used most often with the products of the administrators, especially where those products include the teacher's classroom behavior. There are many reviews of these systematic classroom observation procedures (e.g., Bolton, *Selection and Evaluation of Teachers,* 1973:113–115; Simon & Boyer 1970, a and b), so it is not necessary to review them here. Not much has been done to adapt classroom observation procedures to the observation of administrator behavior, but this could be done rather easily with some of the interaction analysis processes.

The less systematic recording procedures include such devices as rating scales and checklists. The chief advantage of nonsystematic techniques is that the observer is able to consider clues from a variety of sources before making judgment. However, this can also be a disadvantage because the delay in recording information can cause errors. Also, when raters are too lenient, too harsh, or unwilling to be decisive and objective, ratings tend to cluster rather than differentiate. Generally, middle-range ratings are more difficult to justify, since it is easier to identify the extremes on a given scale.

Collecting and Displaying Data. Sometimes problems arise in the development of ways to handle data because people do not distinguish between ways of collecting, displaying, and treating data. For example, one might collect data by means of analysis of written records; the data may be in raw form or they may be transferred onto a form designed for recording the information. This information may then be displayed on a checklist, graph, or in a summary paragraph. However, the treatment of the data may include some sort of statistical analysis or review by several people. Problems of communication arise when people lump all of these processes (i.e., collecting, displaying, and treating data) into one category such as "techniques of evaluating." As one designs administrator evaluation and information collection procedures, it is important to distinguish between collecting and displaying information—since different forms and though processes are needed.

When one is interested in reducing the errors related to leniency and halo, Blanz and Ghiselli (1972:186) suggest the use of a set of three ordered statements on which the rater is asked to indicate whether she or he considers the ratee to be better than the description, to fit the description, or to be worse than the description. The rater must respond to each of the statements; therefore, the procedure is somewhat more time consuming than normal rating procedures. However, the authors did find that errors were reduced and that the procedure worked as effectively with managerial level people as with worker level.

It has been recognized for some time that certain person-oriented scales that cast supervisors as judges instead of observers cause problems. In spite of the fact that such scales tend to cause the observer to be less certain of ratings, and the rater to be less pleased with the ratings, Brumback (1972) found that some person-oriented scales yielded acceptable criterion validities. Therefore, it may not be necessary to discard all scales dealing with characteristics of administrators, especially if certain precautions are taken regarding defining the scales and training the observers.

In general, reviews of standardized personality measures indicate a rather poor record for measuring or predicting managerial effectiveness. A better plan is to develop a personality or interest measure for the specific situation because there is some evidence that the development of special scoring keys based on measures of effectiveness in particular organizational settings can be effective (Campbell et al., 1970:131−133). Brumback and Vincent (1970) recommend the use of both structured and unstructured personality measures, which may facilitate adaptation to local needs and constraints and reduce rating errors because of the precision of the structured scales.

Carvell (1972) reports on a practice of selecting four important areas of performance and devising a bank of instruments for collecting information on these behaviors and characteristics.[2] Once a set of characteristics and behaviors is decided upon

---

[2]Carvell's "bank of instruments" idea is basically that one would have a collection of instruments acquired over a period of time. As one plans with an evaluatee, instead of devising a completely new instrument, there would simply be a selection from among those collected.

as being important for a group of positions, then the development of a bank of measurement devices can be very useful. It would be particularly useful for routine expectancies, but it also might be used for recurring but special behaviors that are individualized.

In developing less systematic measuring devices, one should take care that each measure developed does indeed measure something different from other measures. For example, scales intended to measure "leadership" qualities may not be entirely independent of scales intended to measure "initiation of change" activities. Even though the face value of the two measures may appear different, they may cause the rater to think of the same behaviors on the part of the administrator being assessed. When this happens, the two measures may not be independent of each other and, therefore, may not be as beneficial as assumed. Forehand (1963) provides an example of this in his work concerned with measuring innovative behavior. He emphasizes that it is essential that this measure be independent of overall effectiveness, at least to the degree that it correlates with general effectiveness only when assessors report by an independent measure that they value innovative behavior highly.

In general, ratings and checklists can be used by the person being evaluated or by external evaluators. Heneman (1974:638) reports that "a number of studies have found that self-ratings tend to have higher means values (leniency error) and less variability (restriction of range error) than do superior ratings." However, Heneman found the reverse in his study, and speculates that his results may have been due to the fact that these scores were acquired for research purposes only—rather than for evaluation purposes. He did find that the self-ratings he collected contained less halo error than did superior ratings (which is a factor in favor of self-ratings), and these results are consistent with previous evidence. Heneman's results indicate that self-ratings can provide useful information, especially if a relationship of trust between the evaluator and the evaluatee has been developed.

Determining Criteria and Appropriate Techniques. For some time, there have been discussions regarding whether evaluation procedures, and especially information collection procedures, should be objective or subjective. In many cases the person who raises this question is either unwilling or unable to define the terms being used. Ingle (1977:243−244) does a good analysis of the argument, indicating that people tend to migrate to one of two poles. One side tends to say that subjective judgments allow for too much bias, which Ingle describes as a "my biases are as good as their biases" argument; the other side tends to say that those aspects of the job that can be objectified are not what make a good or bad administrator, which he describes as an "if you can measure it, it does not matter" argument. Ingle proposes that one is better off not attempting to answer the question at all during the initial stages. He says:

> Rather, determine mutually the criteria for the evaluation and then determine the most appropriate techniques for data gathering. Once the criteria have been established, the

techniques are usually obvious, and the objective-subjective question tends to disappear (1977:243−244).

If people were to follow Ingle's suggestions, many of the general and philosophical arguments would be reduced to examining the details in relation to specific situations. It would cause decisions to be made at the point where they need to be made—rather than stalling information collection by what appears on the surface to be irreconcilable differences.

Where one's general purpose is to allow administrators to exercise considerable self-control over their activities, insistence on highly quantified measures may be self-defeating. Ivancevich, Donnelly, and Lyon (1970:149) stress that it is generally more important for measurement to be clear, relevant, and feasible than to be highly quantified. They say, "It is far better to ask subordinates to participate in goal setting than to state specifically that quantitative goals are mandatory." This is particularly good advice when MBO procedures are being initiated because many people have reservations that can turn into resistances. With experience in devising their own measurement procedures, administrators' anxieties will normally drop and more precision can be initiated. As McConkey points out, the importance of the objective should take priority over the precision of measurement:

> In terms of being prudent, it is more worthwhile to the company to approve an objective of considerable importance even though the objective can be quantified to a lesser degree than it is to approve an objective of lesser worth which can be quantified to a greater degree (1972:15).

However, the choice may not be the one described by McConkey. The logical approach is to establish significant objectives and then attempt to find the best possible measures of these objectives. Problems occur when one starts with what can be measured and then attempts to write objectives that are compatible with the measures.

Reddin (1970:5−6) warns against measuring qualities that contribute to what is described as "apparent" effectiveness rather than measuring variables that measure output or what an administrator produces from a situation by managing it appropriately. For example, such qualities as being on time, answering communications promptly, making quick decisions, or writing well may give the appearance of effectiveness; yet, they may not contribute to outputs in a given situation unless combined with other behaviors. Wallace (1974:403−404) discusses a similar idea and indicates that we can predict what people will say about an individual's performance better than we can predict the performance itself. He suggests that we may exist in a system where we value a quality that we might call "the ability to make people say good things about oneself." If this is the case, we should be very careful to identify precisely what we want to measure rather than fall prey to being influenced by the ability of a person to cause others to think well of her or him.

The idea is, of course, that the work to be done and the outputs desired should influence what is to be measured more than the personal traits of the individuals doing the work. If one focuses on the results desired and the tasks needed to produce these results, there is less of a tendency to draw up measurement devices in isolation from the job. Brumback (1972:571) indicates that empirical evidence is preferable to subjective judgments in making decisions regarding measurements. "It is much easier to sit down and draw up a list of traits than it is to go out and analyze the work being done," he says.

In devising measurement devices and procedures, it may be desirable to obtain the assistance of a staff person or an outside consultant. In special circumstances, it may also be desirable to use a neutral person (i.e., neither the evaluator nor the evaluatee) for actual collection of the data. Gaslin (1974) describes a procedure where an outside person helped the faculty and the administrative team to devise the instrument, collected the data, and then interpreted the data to the administrator. Such a procedure may be beneficial in some special cases; but if the outside person were to assist the administrator and the evaluator to develop skills, they might benefit more from the analysis and interpretation by doing it themselves.

The following suggestions are made to improve the accuracy of measurement procedures and to reduce the discrepancies among evaluators:

1. Clearly define the focus of the evaluation, and in so doing be sure to specify results desired.
2. Develop specific, low-inference items.
3. Specify the circumstances under which information is to be collected.
4. Use a record form agreed upon by evaluatees and information collectors, making sure that the record is distinct from the summary report device.
5. Provide adequate training for those collecting information.

When items are specific, interrater reliability is increased to the point where rating scales are comparable to systematic categorical observation systems (Rosenshine, 1970). This indicates that homemade devices can be as useful as standardized procedures if they are carefully developed.

Summary

Collecting information, the second phase of evaluation, consists of the actions taken by the administrator and the measurement of these actions and their results. The measurement of actions and results of actions may be done by the evaluatee as well as by the external evaluator and others.

The actions of administrators are productive in the sense of providing supportive services to others and to the organization. Such services should make teachers and others more productive and more satisfied with their jobs, and should help the organization proceed in a purposeful direction. The processes and products identified as significant for a given administrator should, therefore, be unique to the types of services she or he is providing to others and to the organization. Since there are many outcomes or products in a school system, one should be aware that not all personnel are working to affect all of these products directly. In certain cases, some people's products are others' processes.

The measurement of the actions and results of actions of administrators involves collection of all the necessary information to make decisions about whether goals and objectives are being accomplished. This is done concurrently with the action that is occurring, rather than waiting for a period of time and trying to recall events and results. The purpose of measuring outcomes is to determine whether objectives have been met. The purpose of examining processes is to determine whether a specified plan is being followed. The purpose of comparing outcomes with procedures is to determine whether procedures should be modified or replicated.

Measurement during this phase of evaluation may be done by a variety of people, including the administrator's supervisor, the administrator being evaluated, other administrators, teachers, students, subject-matter specialists, department heads, personnel specialists, and parents. Who is to collect the information depends on the nature of the data to be collected; all who are involved in the collection may not be involved in collection of all the data.

Collecting information on one's self may reduce external threat and increase the possibility of creativity and motivation. However, care should be taken to ensure that information collected is related to school district criteria, and self-perceptions should be checked with others.

Systematic observation procedures, rating scales, and checklists may be useful in measuring processes and products of administrators. In using less systematic procedures such as rating scales, care should be taken to differentiate between ways of collecting, displaying, and treating data. The development of rating scales has certain advantages over using standardized scales, but care should be taken to develop scales that are independent of each other. Research studies have reported self-ratings to be valuable information, and they may prove helpful as an adjunct to external ratings.

The objective-subjective question, in relation to evaluation procedures, tends to disappear when adequate time is spent determining criteria and appropriate techniques for data gathering. Also, highly quantified measures may be less important than the involvement of the evaluatee in the goal-setting process and the determination of important goals. Measurement of "apparent effectiveness" may be avoided by focusing on results desired and the tasks needed to produce these results.

In general, the accuracy of measurement may be improved by clearly defining results desired, developing specific items, specifying circumstances under which information is to be collected, using appropriate recording procedures, and providing adequate training for information collectors.

4 PHASE III: USING INFORMATION

This phase consists of the sequential activities of analysis of information collected during Phase II, interpretating that information, and making decisions based on the analysis and interpretation. Throughout these activities, communication is occurring between the evaluator and the evaluatee; this communication not only should help in the analysis and interpretation, but it also should assure high-quality decisions that are satisfactory to those involved.

Planning Evaluation Conferences

Much of the communication during this phase occurs in a conference (or conferences) between the evaluator and the evaluatee. If this communication is to be precise and beneficial to both the evaluatee and the evaluator, it should be planned carefully. Planning should consider some of the research findings related to conducting evaluation conferences. One important conclusion reported in the research is that the evaluation may be designed to serve many functions; therefore, the purposes of

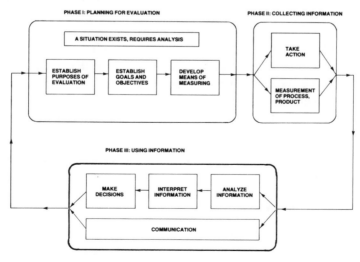

the conference should be identified and made clear to the people involved (Solem, 1960). For example, some organizations consider the conference to be an essential part of the supervision process, intending that it be designed to *develop* individuals as well as to provide feedback to them on their performance. With these purposes in mind, the conference may be designed to motivate, warn, praise, develop potential, treat individual problems, or recommend future courses of action regarding professional plans. Although motivation, warning, etc., may be natural outcomes of a conference in certain organizations, the outcomes should be planned in terms of what is desired.

NATURE OF FEEDBACK

As one considers the process of dealing with the information collected in Phase II, the question of how feedback can be provided is a reasonable one. Where an external person is involved in evaluating administrators, Ritchie (1976:34) suggests that at every formal evaluation session each supervisee be required to evaluate progress toward each goal. The self-evaluation is matched with that of the external evaluator for each goal, and then a performance rating is established. In this way the feedback process includes a reconciliation of independent assessments. Whether this increases reliability of the final measurement (or conclusion reached) is not known, but it probably does lead to higher satisfaction with the process.

Odiorne (1969:114–115) recommends that where feedback is interpreted as a report of failure or success, only those actions that are under the control of an individual should be included in periodic reviews. For example, illnesses on the part of faculty may reduce their responsiveness to supervisory treatment, and this should be taken into account during the feedback process. This suggests that during the feedback conference some review of circumstances and constraints during the review period should be made.

To be most useful, feedback should be prompt. The accumulation of information over a long period of time is not as beneficial as providing it soon after events occur. Odiorne (1969:114–115) says "the teaching effects are totally lost when they are deferred until some arbitrary periodic review is indicated."

Medley (1971:160) provided information showing that feedback is not being used very effectively by supervisors of student teachers. The experiment indicated that neither the supervisory process nor closed-circuit television had any effect on the outcomes. He concluded that educators are failing to make effective use of two very powerful agents.

> It is known that TV equipment displays mercilessly accurate information to the teacher about his teaching and that sage counsel of an experienced supervisor contains information of considerable value. The problem is to make this information available to the student in usable form (1971:160).

If supervisors of practice teachers are not making wise use of counsel and TV equipment, one might raise the question as to whether evaluators of administrators are making wise use of feedback and technical equipment in order to have an impact on the people they evaluate. To do so requires ingenious planning in order to get good results; not to do so assures unsatisfactory results.

The substance included in feedback sessions should be directly related to the goals established and the work task. The evaluator may provide instruction in relation to these goals, encouragement and motivation, and guidance so that the evaluatee may make better decisions (Ivancevich, Donnelly, and Lyon, 1970:149). In order to do all of these things, it will be necessary to allocate time to the feedback process; the amount of time allocated will vary from person to person.

Written Reports. Written reports are one form of feedback. Although no recent research has analyzed the written reports about administrators, Guthrie and Willower (1973) did analyze principals' written reports of classroom observations. They found that these reports are pervaded by ritualism that tends to be positive or laudatory in tone, not critical; they labeled such feedback "the ceremonial congratulation." Of the observation reports examined, 86 percent were ritualistic, and only 14 percent were goal oriented. Of the ritualistic reports 72 percent were positive and the remainder were either negative or neutral; approximately half of the goal-oriented reports were negative or neutral; hence, of the total reports 69 percent were positive and 31 percent were negative or neutral. The percentage of ritualistic to goal-oriented statements was unrelated to teacher experience or principal experience, being above 80 percent in all categories of experience. Guthrie and Willower (1973:289) are not totally critical of these results, however:

> The ceremonial congratulation plainly is functional for the principal-teacher relationship; it can be viewed as one form of adaptation on the part of the principals that guards the delicate balance in role relations between themselves and teachers. Its consequences for students are less clear. In any case, the observation report is unlikely to be a vehicle for the promotion of serious dialogue on instruction between principals and teachers.

If the conclusions from this study are pertinent also to the written reports for administrators in school systems, two implications seem clear: (a) the ceremonial congratulation may well have an impact on the morale of those being congratulated and the maintenance of harmonious relations between the evaluator and the evaluatee and (b) the ceremonial congratulation may have no impact whatsoever on the productivity of administrators or the serious consideration of that productivity by either the evaluator or the administrator. As with oral feedback, one should seriously consider the function one desires it to serve when considering its form and content.

Use of Conference Time. Campbell et al. (1970:144) warn against using the conference time for the purpose of making far-ranging inferences and suggest a strategy of keeping things simple while staying close to the data available. This suggests the idea that this phase is primarily concerned with conclusions based on the information collected; whereas, Phase I is concerned with devising hypotheses regarding what should be done next.

Carroll and Tosi (1973:93−97) offer the following general guidelines for conducting a conference to review performance:

1. Be prepared for the meeting.
2. State the purpose of the interview and put the subordinate at ease.
3. Facilitate discussion of the subject (listen actively, use reflective summary, reward insight and self-criticism).
4. List disagreements (resolve when possible—if not, list and seek facts).
5. Close the review with a summary and a plan.

EFFECTS OF FEEDBACK

Studies reporting effects of feedback on educational administrators are scarce indeed. Therefore, the best inferences we can make are from studies made with teachers and in noneducational settings. For example, Smithman and Lucio (1974) found that pupils whose teachers were evaluated by objectives outperformed those pupils whose teachers were evaluated on a rating scale. The sample was from Canadian schools; therefore, there may be a difference in teacher preference for nature of feedback due to type of school system. Even so, one should consider whether a standard rating scale will accomplish what an individualized MBO process will.

Where students provide feedback to instructors, Pambookian (1974) found that instructors who were initially rated moderately by students showed more change in several areas (as measured by a second rating by students) than did the lower rated or the more favorably rated instructors. The results, of course, do not indicate why this occurred. However, one hypothesis might be that the instructors rated high had very little modification to make (in their perception of the initial ratings), but the instructors rated low may have rationalized the results in some manner. This may mean that feedback from subordinates has very little effect on some people unless they are assisted in using the information for diagnostic purposes. If this is true, it speaks to the role of the outside evaluator in relation to feedback from subordinates.

Feedback provided in group meetings may not be too beneficial, especially where individuals have been provided adequate information regarding their tasks and responsibilities. Niedermeyer (1977) found that information provided teachers about pupils and strategies for working with pupils had an impact on the teachers and on student achievement. However, follow-up group meetings regarding the instructional improvement strategies did not appear to assist teachers in cases where they had strategies available ahead of time. The group meetings did tend to help teachers who had information on students only. It may be that only individualized follow-up meetings will have any impact on individuals who are relatively well prepared for their responsibilities.

Feedback Regarding Results. Some information shows that individuals appreciate feedback that indicates accomplishment of objectives. For example, Moffett (1966) conducted an experiment with student teachers who had preinstructional contracts based on instructional objectives. Not only were these student teachers able to produce more achievement gains in students (as compared with normally graded student teachers), they also expressed more confidence in the supervisory procedure used and were more satisfied with their midterm grades. But in addition, 94 percent of all subjects participating in the experiment (i.e., both the experimental and the control groups) expressed a preference for having their teaching performance based on pupil achievement as a result of instruction rather than rating scale measures.

McNeil found similar results (1967:71), in that where teachers emphasized results (rather than procedures), their students achieved more in an identified area of deficiency. Not only that, but their students achieved more in other types of related but not predetermined skills indicating that "the focus of instruction upon overcoming a specific deficiency did not preclude desirable outcomes in other related areas." Although this was done with student teachers rather than with experienced administrators, people in general may value feedback regarding accomplishment in relation to objectives more than they value feedback on their traits or characteristics.

One might wonder whether feedback regarding results (and setting expectations in terms of results) places undue pressure on individuals. In another study with practice teachers, McNeil (1967:71) found that the practice of supervision by objectives with its emphasis on attaining results with pupils does not appear to produce undue pressures. If these results occur with practice teachers, one might expect similar results with mature teachers or administrators, *provided* they have such experiences early in their careers. However, this may not be true with experienced personnel who are used to considerable independence and little examination of the results of their efforts. A period of anxiety may occur; however, once individuals are accustomed to a practice and the feedback has proved to be useful, the anxiety should be reduced.

Manner of Providing Feedback. Reduction of anxiety is, of course, related to the type of communication occurring during the feedback session or the evaluation conference. A study conducted by Indik (1961) in an industrial setting suggested that a high level of productivity tends to be positively associated with (a) openness of communication, (b) satisfaction with superior's supportive behavior, (c) mutual understanding, and (d) local influence and autonomy on work-related matters. The first three of these factors is related to the manner in which feedback is provided, while the last is concerned with the substance that may be communicated.

In an experimental setting where some subjects received feedback that was definitely negative and others received feedback that was definitely positive, Skolnick (1971) found that people reacted more favorably to the positive feedback than to the negative, regardless of how well they had been told they had performed on a total score. The implication seems to be that individuals will react more positively in the affective domain to people who say good things about them and that they will perceive their performance more positively than with a negative note. This experiment is provocative in that it raises the question regarding whether the affective screens out the cognitive. Does negative information cause the person not to like the sender of information to the extent that the reality of the information is missed? Is the interpretation of positive/negative feedback related to the personal security of the individual receiving the message and the relationship already established with the sender? No information on these questions is provided by Skolnick's study, but the questions point out the need of a psychological support system based on a trust relationship between the evaluator and the evaluatee so that both can deal with the reality of feedback.

Administrators do appear to respond to feedback regarding their behavior (Daw & Gage, 1967). Principals were provided information about teachers' perceptions of their actual and their ideal principal behavior. After a period of time another measure was taken of teachers' perceptions of principal behavior. A change had occurred in the principals who received feedback, and these changes did not seem to vary with age, experience, or form used for measurement. The implication is that the principals responded to the information provided; the type used could have been a self-evaluation or it could have been done in cooperation with an outside evaluator.

Meyer, Kay, and French (1961, 1965) came to four conclusions about the evaluation conference, based on research in business and industry:

1. Criticism has a negative effect on the achievement of goals because it builds defensiveness.
2. Praise has little effect on the achievement of goals.
3. Mutual goal-setting improves performance.
4. Coaching should be day-to-day, not a once-a-year activity.

One might tend to conclude that these findings are contrary to personal experience, where people have appeared to respond positively to praise. However, the results of this research do not recommend that praise should be abandoned but that one should not expect too much from it. Praising most individuals is likely to cause them to persevere in the activity that has been praised—assuming that praise is regarded highly by the person being praised, which would be true of sincere praise coming from a significant other—but it may not cause them to produce more. Mutual goal setting does cause an individual to set higher goals, which in turn does improve performance. The combination, then, of praise and mutual goal-setting is more likely to accomplish what one desires than either activity alone. The praise will probably foster attitudes that will produce harmony during mutual goal setting and encourage desired behavior to continue, while goal setting will cause striving for higher levels of performance.

These conclusions are compatible with Rose's (1963) study of teachers, where he concluded that the manner in which feedback is provided to teachers can halt or enhance their growth and improvement. Since the conference allows the evaluator to treat each administrator in an individual way, the evaluator should know enough about each person to understand what is important to him and how he will respond to communication and feedback. Both businesses and schools have found that individuals more readily accept communications about themselves if the major focus is on improving rather than finding fault.

The idea of coaching on a day-to-day (or at least a frequent) basis can be justified for several reasons. For one thing, individuals respond more to feedback occurring soon after an event. Also, the frequency and quantity of feedback increase the possibility of having an impact. Since a limited number of improvements can be accomplished, frequent feedback reduces the possibility that individuals will experience an overwhelming feeling of failure accompanying a long list of "needed improvements" (Noland & Moylan, 1967). Where conferences are infrequent (or annual only), the evaluator may tend to overwhelm the administrator with a long list of needed improvements, or to be overgenerous in such a way that the evaluatee benefits little and there is little basis for decision making (Lopez, 1965; French, Kay & Meyer, 1966).

In the first of two studies reported on appraisal interviews, Greller (1975) investigated the question, What relates to a subordinate's perception that the appraisal helped? He found the following significant correlations: who talks most (where the evaluatee talks a lot) was .42; the opportunity of the evaluatee to state his own side of the issues was .44; and the composite score representing psychological participation was .38. In the same study, Greller also found that when the evaluator asked for the opinion of the evaluatee, the subordinate was more satisfied with the supervision provided (r = .42).

In a second study Greller found that both the "invitation to participate" and "goal setting" related significantly to the evaluatee's satisfaction with the appraisal process (r = .65, and r = .52, respectively). In addition, he found that "goal setting" was significant at the .05 level of significance with the evaluatee's overall satisfaction with the job (r = .22).

Evidently, participation in an evaluation can have a facilitative impact on the evaluatee. The act of setting goals has a substantial effect, even though the nature of the control over these goals may have little effect. Greller (1975:546) put it this way:

> Talking a great deal and having the opportunity to state one's side of the issues are associated with feelings of being helped by the interview, while having one's opinion solicited by the boss is associated with satisfaction with supervision.

Analysis and Interpretation of Information

The evaluation model being discussed indicates that the use of information culminates in making decisions. But preceding the decision process, there must be analysis and interpretation of information. Basically, analysis of information includes clustering or grouping of data of a similar nature, arrangement of data into a

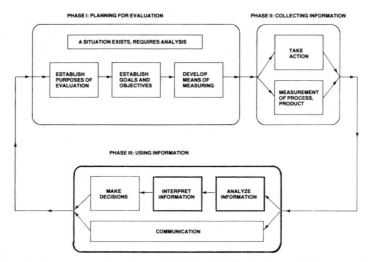

format or visual display so that it can be seen easily, and statistical manipulation in order to represent the behavior, events, or results of events being examined. Interpretation allows one to attach meaning to the analysis that has been made. This is a matter of answering the question, What does this all mean? or What conclusions can I come to as a result of examining the data in this way? Since much has been written about the analysis and interpretation processes, this section will focus on some rather rudimentary aspects and conclude with a few comments on how feedback should occur and the effects of feedback.

EXAMINING THE INFORMATION

Let us examine some rather simplified information regarding the outcomes of an administrator's actions. Suppose a principal decides that he or she would like for all teachers of advanced level academic subjects to be asking at least 50 percent of their questions at the "analysis" level of Benjamin Bloom's *Taxonomy of Educational Objectives* by the end of the third quarter of the school year. In addition, the principal wants each teacher to establish an objective related to how the use of this questioning level affects student achievement in the area of problem analysis in the course. The level of achievement will be established in terms of the academic ability of the students and the objective will be mutually agreed upon with the teacher.

The principal now has two outcomes to check, each having to do with the processes used by teachers. But in addition, another outcome must be set. Since the principal would like to be perceived as a leader, the teachers' perceptions may be checked by asking them to respond to the following items:

1. Concerning new methods and techniques of teaching, my principal:
   encourages and
   supports me ____: ____: ____: ____: ____: ____: ____ discourages me
2. Discussion and conferences with my principal regarding my teaching are:
   very helpful ____: ____: ____: ____: ____: ____: ____ not helpful

It will be considered that the objective is attained only if no teachers respond on the negative side of either item.

Once the outcomes have been specified, the principal must establish a process for accomplishing these objectives. He decides to do the following:

1. Set a deadline for each teacher to establish the objective regarding the results of questioning level on the classes involved. In relation to this, establish a series of two individual conferences with each teacher to discuss, clarify, and reach agreement on the objective(s) set by each teacher.
2. Conduct a group study with all teachers involved. The group would meet every two weeks during the first semester of the school year and would study Bloom's *taxonomy,* research data on learning styles of bright students, and experimental data regarding the impact of higher level questions on achievement and creativity. The principal would be responsible for the sessions but would make use of resource people and the members of the group for presentations and discussions. Reading material would be provided on the various topics.

Data on the first two outcomes, regarding teacher behavior, should be relatively easy to analyze and interpret. For example, each teacher can classify all questions asked during certain randomly chosen time periods by listening to a tape recording of the sessions. The number of tapes to be analyzed can be predetermined and agreed upon, and the ability of each teacher to classify questions can be checked during the training sessions. The objective regarding establishment of objectives by teachers can be checked by simply keeping records of teacher/principal conferences and the copies of the objectives written by teachers. If one is interested in analyzing the information in terms of the dates objectives are written, a visual display of a time line with frequencies along the time line can be drawn. If an analysis of when certain groups wrote their objectives is desired, the total group can be broken into smaller groups (e.g., according to subjects taught, age, recency of training, etc.) and each small group can be plotted along the time line.

Data on the teachers' perceptions of the principal can illustrate the difference between analysis and interpretation. After teachers respond to the questions, the principal (or a clerk) can tally the data and express the total information by putting a number representing the frequency of response in each of the spaces as shown with the following hypothetical data:

1. Concerning new methods and techniques of teaching, my principal:
   encourages and
   supports me _4_ : _10_ : _4_ : _2_ : ___ : ___ : ___ discourages me
2. Discussion and conference with my principal regarding my teaching are:
   very helpful _1_ : _5_ : _8_ : _4_ : _2_ : ___ : ___ not helpful

Analysis of the data is partially complete at this point; however, an even better picture can be obtained if a visual display is made. This may be done via a graph, as follows:

1. Concerning new methods and techniques of teaching, my principal:

encourages and
supports me ⊏━━:━━━━:━━━:━━━: ____: ____: ____discourages me

2. Discussion and conference with my principal regarding my teaching are:

very helpful ⊏━━:━━━━:━━━:━━━: ____: ____not helpful

The key to a graph of this type is illustrated below, where the lower horizontal bar represents the range (a measure of variability), the upper bar represents the middle 50 percent of the responses (another measure of variability), and the vertical line represents the midpoint, or median, of the responses (a measure of the central tendency of the distribution).

Now the analysis is complete, since the data have been clustered or grouped and a visual display has been made. What, then, can be done by means of interpretation? What do the data mean, and what conclusions can be reached? It appears that the objective has not been met as far as the second item is concerned because two responses are to the right of the middle of the scale. Another conclusion can be reached by comparing the responses to the two items, namely, the teachers perceived that the principal encouraged and supported them better than he conducted discussions and conferences. This can be concluded on the basis of the comparisons of the total frequency distributions and by examining the midpoint and the middle 50 percent of the graphs. Still another conclusion can be that there was more diversity of view related to the discussions and conferences with teachers than regarding the encouragement and support provided. This can be concluded by examining the variance, as indicated by the range and the middle 50 percent displayed on the graph. With these conclusions based on the data, the principal and his supervisor are in a position to proceed with the remainder of Phase III.

Making Decisions

The decisions to be made during Phase III are basically concerned with a single question, What works for me, in my situation? This is the question administrators are asking about their performance. They are not concerned with what works for some administrator in another state, or another city, or even in another position within the same district. They are concerned with what produces results for them. In

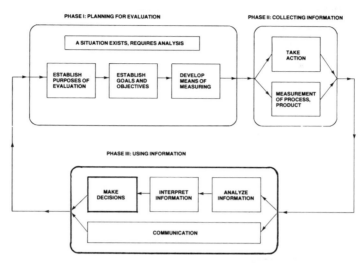

effect, the "what" is the procedure used by the administrator, and the "works" is the product or the outcome. So, the primary concern in decision making is the relationship between the process and product in a specified situation. There is no need to compare with other administrators or to establish some complex research design; what one is interested in is situation-specific results on the basis of the procedures used.

Planning during Phase I allowed the administrator to make decisions regarding what *should* happen. The decisions during Phase III focus first on what *did* happen. Once these decisions are made, attention can be given to the next steps to be taken. Focusing on what *did* happen may be facilitated by examining the following questions:

1. What were the results? Were they satisfactory? Did we accomplish what we wanted to accomplish? This involves comparison of the outcomes with the original goals. If a clear standard has been set during Phase I, and if information pertinent to the standard has been collected during Phase II, this comparison should be straightforward. The extent of discrepancy can be noted, whether it is more or less than the target, and this information can be used in reacting to other questions.
2. Were the goals set reasonable for the situation, or should they be lowered or raised? The response to this question involves judgment, based on the perspective of hindsight and all of the information analyzed regarding how things functioned after the goals were set. It also should consider the discrepancy between the outcomes and the goals.
3. Were the procedures fully implemented as planned? When it was decided that certain outcomes were desired, a process was identified to accomplish these outcomes; was this process implemented as designed? To answer this question

involves making a comparison of actual procedures with those planned during the first phase of the evaluation process. To make this comparison, the process must be described in operational terms and then adequate information must be collected, analyzed, and interpreted.

4. Were the initially designed procedures effective? Did the planned processes produce the desired results? Since these questions involve an examination of both procedures and products, they cannot be answered unless the procedures were implemented. In effect, a nonimplemented process should not be considered ineffective—merely not implemented.

Once decisions have been made regarding what *did* happen, one can concentrate on the next steps. Additional general questions should be considered in this regard: What should be the next steps? Should control mechanisms be established to assure that the process is implemented? Should the procedures be changed? The answers to questions regarding what *should* happen next are based on the total information regarding what *did* happen to both the process and the product during the time interval being examined. This decisional analysis may be illustrated by means of the flowchart in figure 4.1. It will be noted that following the examination of process and product (step 6), a series of questions are asked. Two things are significant about the sequence: (a) even if the results are satisfactory, one still asks questions about the goals for the next cycle (step 8) and whether the procedures should be continued (step 9); and (b) if the results are not satisfactory, one then raises questions about the goals and their implementation simultaneously rather than sequentially. The last point is important because one may need to change both the goals and the controls on the implementation before going back through the cycle; if the questions were sequential, one might change the goals and go through the cycle again before making a definite decision on implementation. Also, it should be noted that one *concludes* that the process should be changed *only* after it has been determined that the following conditions exist: the results were not satisfactory, the goals should remain unchanged, and the implementation was satisfactory.

DECISIONS REGARDING AN EXAMPLE

At this point, we want to reexamine the information discussed in the last section. It will be recalled that information was collected on teachers' views of their principal, following a time period when he had worked with them on question-asking techniques designed to increase the analytical skills of students. The principal's processes included conferences with teachers to assist them in setting goals for their students and a series of group meetings with teachers where they studied levels of questions, learning styles of students, and information about the impact of higher level questions on achievement and creativity. The teachers had deadlines for setting goals, and group meetings were held every two weeks. Resource people and reading material were provided for the meetings.

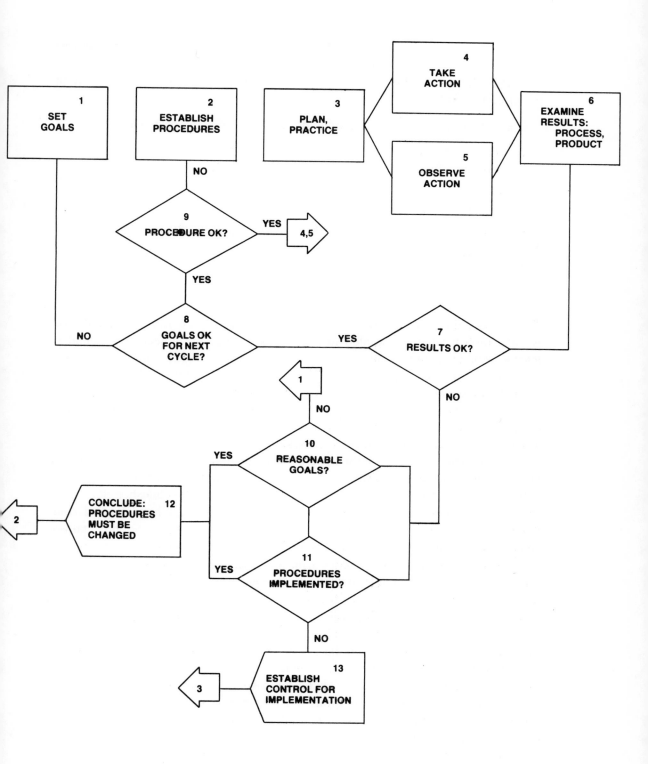

Figure 4.1: Decisional analysis of processes and products

The information obtained by having each teacher respond to questions about the principal was as follows:

1. Concerning new methods and techniques of teaching, my principal:

encourages and
supports me __4__ : __10__ : __4__ : __2__ : ____ : ____ : ____ discourages me

2. Discussion and conferences with my principal regarding my teaching are:

very helpful __1__ : __5__ : __8__ : __4__ : __2__ : ____ : ____ not helpful

The first question to be asked is, What were the results? Were they satisfactory? Did we accomplish what we wanted to accomplish? Since the objective was that no teacher would respond on the negative side of either item, the response has to be that the objective was not accomplished in relation to the second item. The extent of the discrepancy is two of the twenty teachers responding, or 10 percent.

The second question is, Were the goals reasonable? Considering the nature of the group of teachers, should the goals have been set at a higher or a lower level? The response to this is a judgment to be made with more information about the group than we are able to provide in the hypothetical situation we are considering, but the principal may reason in this way: "I do think that it would be unreasonable for me to expect to have none of the teachers on the negative side of this question during this first year of conducting individual conferences with them. I have learned some things about these conferences this year which I won't repeat again. So, the goal was somewhat high for this year, but I think it is very reasonable for me to keep for next year. After I have had more practice with the procedure, I may even want to set a higher goal." Other reasoning may be equally logical, depending on the reasons that might be generated as to *why* the results were what they were. Regarding question number one, the principal may conclude that the goal was about right.

The third question to be asked is, Were the procedures fully implemented as planned? Here, the principal and the evaluator would need to examine the information collected and recorded by the principal as to the number and dates of the individual conferences with the teachers, the dates of completion of objectives, the number and dates of the study sessions, the resource people used, and the materials provided. The records may indicate that all of the study sessions were held on the dates planned, that six resource people were used, and that six books and twenty-three journal articles were made available to the teachers. On the other hand, the records may indicate that six teachers were not scheduled to have their second conference with the principal prior to December 1 and that four of these conferences were interrupted by telephone calls or by the secretary. This would indicate that some decisions need to be made about the implementation of the conference procedures. It may be that the principal would decide to attend a workshop on time management and that some retraining of the secretary would be necessary. With such changes, it may be hypothesized that responses to question number two would be changed.

A fourth question to be asked is, Were the procedures effective as they were designed? The answer to this question cannot be ascertained except in cases where the procedures are fully implemented as designed. In our example, it appears that the answer to the question is clear in relation to item number one. The procedures were implemented as designed and the results were satisfactory; therefore, we can conclude that the procedures were effective. However, in relation to item number two, the results were not acceptable for the goal set; but the procedures were not implemented fully. Therefore, we cannot conclude that the procedures were ineffective in relation to the way they were *designed;* we can only conclude that they were not effective in relation to the way they were *implemented.*

The fifth question is, What should be the next steps? Considering all of the information collected regarding the processes and the products, what action is justified? This involves basically determining whether to change goals, initiating controls over the implementation of procedures used, or changing the procedures in some way. In the case we have been discussing, there would probably be a change in the goals of the principal in regard to helping teachers in question-asking procedures, but the principal may decide to continue with similar goals in relation to perceptions of teachers regarding leadership of the principal. The principal would probably initiate some type of control mechanism over how and when conferences are held with teachers in the early part of the school year but would not change the general style of providing encouragement and assistance to the teachers.

With these decisions made, the principal is ready to go back to Phase I and go through the cycle again. It should be noted that the cycle for this set of goals and objectives took an academic year to complete. However, one should not conclude that all cycles are annual; the duration of the cycle should be determined on the basis of the type of objective and the need for feedback in relation to that objective. The important consideration is that the function of the evaluation is to provide feedback in order to keep the operation moving in the direction of goals and to correct any errors that creep into the system. The duration of cycles can be too long for this function to be performed adequately.

DECISIONS REGARDING PAY

Evaluative decisions regarding differential pay are made in a similar manner to other evaluative decisions in that they involve establishing objectives, collecting data in relation to those objectives, and comparing the data with the statement of objectives. However, decisions about pay are usually considered to be a special case of evaluative decisions in that they are more sensitive and emotion-laden. This is because they are often interpreted as symbolizing personal worth. In many cases, it is not that the person is worried about financial security; rather, there is a concern with social status or a need for a tangible statement of worth. As with other decisions, care should be taken to identify the criteria that will be used, how the decision will be made, and who will make it and communicate it.

Hunaday and Varney (1974:27) indicate that MBO processes should be tied to pay. They point out:

> It is our belief that MBO can be a powerful tool to help an organization improve productivity by tying part of the salary administration program to individual performance relative to mutually established goals.

They indicate that this belief is based on the view that tying pay to MBO is better than tying it to age or seniority because it (a) stresses productivity and performance, (b) assures differential treatment based on performance, (c) is easily explainable to employees, contains no surprises, and the boss and subordinates can be open with each other, and (d) lends itself easily to using percentage of goals achieved. One unresolved problem related to the last point is how to ensure the setting of realistic and significant goals (not merely easily achieved goals) where the stakes are considered to be high by the evaluatee. Unless this problem is solved, the use of percentage of goals achieved as a basis for pay becomes a trivial criterion.

In making evaluative decisions regarding differential pay, some authors (Beer & Ruh, 1976) suggest that three different functions should be done at different times so that they will not become confused in the minds of evaluator and evaluatee. For example, they suggest that MBO be used in determining goal accomplishment and providing neutral feedback in relation to the goals. The MBO procedures should be done at a different time from performance development review (which appears to be a supervisory treatment rather than evaluative feedback). However, both of these should be done at a different time from performance results evaluation for salary and placement decisions. These recommendations were made on the basis of experience in a business and industrial setting.

In educational settings, one is more liekly to find recommendations for pay to be based on duties and scope of responsibility than on performance. For consideration of pay for principals, Todd and Manning (1974) suggested the use of such factors as special classes, cafeteria responsibility, school size, and student turnover rate; these factors were used in the Cupertino, California school system.

On the other hand, an article in the *American School Board Journal* (1974) entitled, "How to Make Staff Accountable for What It Does—Not What It Is," reported that the Kalamazoo, Michigan school district incorporated feedback from peers, assistants, teachers, students, self, and supervisor in a multifaceted evaluation system that tied into salaries. This emphasis on performance of administrators as a basis of pay allowed for as much as 10 percent (plus or minus) modification of salary on some administrators. In this case, the reactions of the administrators involved were mixed.

Madison, Wisconsin, has also used performance as a basis for administrator pay (Ritchie, 1976:36). Because the system is based on performance rather than experience or training, degree status is not a consideration for salary improvement. No monetary credit is given for advanced degrees, even though the administrative staff is encouraged to pursue training and degrees. In effect "the program acknowledges that degrees do not automatically cause a person to be a better administrator."

Another school system, the Pennridge School District in Bucks County, Pennsylvania, provides an example of the use of MBO in conjunction with merit pay for administrators. The superintendent and his assistants evaluate the administrator's goal achievement and can award up to 5 percent of the base salary as merit pay for high achievement. This system is founded on a strong team-management concept.

In general, the use of evaluation for purposes of determining pay of administrators is not done extensively in education. Where it is being done, the reactions are mixed to exuberant. Those who combine MBO with determination of pay report that the practice is functional for them.

Communication

There is not much doubt that the process of communication is extremely important during Phase I. However, it becomes even more important during Phase III. For one thing, there is a tendency for both the evaluator and the evaluatee to avoid contact during this time. The choice of each is to analyze, interpret, and make decisions (a) before a conference with the other person, (b) during the conference with the other person, or (c) following the conference with the other person. The tendency is to choose the first option, doing an analysis and interpretation and

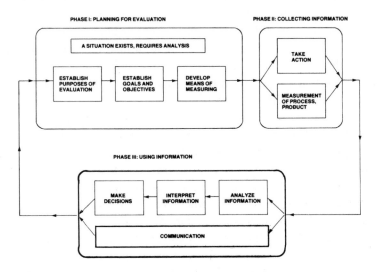

making decisions prior to communicating with the other person. However, when this is done, one should be cautioned to make only tentative conclusions regarding the data and tentative decisions about what should be done next. Otherwise, the benefit of the other person's insight is lost and poor decisions may be made.

Some evaluators favor one of these times for all decisions. When the first option is always used, it may indicate a rather authoritarian posture in relation to subordinates. When option number two is always used, it may show high consideration for other's views. When the third option is always chosen, it may indicate an unwillingness to share this responsibility with others. A reasonable guideline may be to choose one of the options in terms of the purpose to be accomplished by a particular conference or decision. For example, if the purpose of the conference is to assist the administrator in improving performance and providing assistance with regard to changes in procedures that might be used, the second option may be most appropriate. However, if the decision to be made by the evaluator has to do with whether the administrator should be placed on probation for ineffectiveness, the evaluator may delay the decision until after the conference in order to use information obtained in the conference (or perhaps from other sources suggested during the conference) to make the final decision.

GOALS AND ACTIONS RELATED TO ADMINISTRATOR STATUSES

One important aspect of the substance of communication is the status of the evaluatee. Unless this is clear, the evaluatee may misinterpret the purpose of ideas expressed or data analyzed. Basically, an individual is either in a status of "retain" or "consider for release." Most of the discussion about decision making in the last section had to do with administrators who are in the "retain" status, which is the initial status of all administrators. However, after several evaluations of performance, this status may change. When it does, it is important that this information be communicated to the administrator; otherwise, the administrator cannot be expected to take the appropriate action to change status, and it appears unethical not to allow this opportunity. The goals and actions of the administrator are different in the two categories, and the actions of the evaluator are also different. For example, consider table 4.1. It will be noted that the evaluatee goal in the "retain" category or status is to improve performance in relation to individual and organizational goals. The actions of the evaluatee are basically to plan and implement those activities that are likely to improve performance. The evaluator actions are mainly to provide assistance and feedback. The assistance is with all three phases of the evaluation process and with suggesting any in-service training or supervisory treatment that may be beneficial in improving the performance of the administrator. The feedback is to allow the administrator to know when objectives are being met and to correct errors that come into the administrator's management system.

However, one will note that the goals and actions are somewhat different on the "consider for release" side of the table. The evaluatee still has a goal of improving performance. However, in addition there is the goal of changing status in order that

Table 4.1
GOALS AND ACTIONS RELATED TO TWO DIFFERENT ADMINISTRATOR STATUSES

	STATUS	
	RETAIN	CONSIDER FOR RELEASE
Evaluatee goals	To improve performance in relation to organizational and individual goals.	To improve performance in relation to organizational and individual goals.
		To change status from "Consider for release" to "Retain."
Evaluatee actions	To plan and implement activities.	To modify behavior to such an extent that it is acceptable.
Evaluator actions	To provide assistance.	To provide assistance.
	To provide feedback.	To provide feedback.
		To provide direction.

release will *not* occur. This goal, of course, causes the evaluatee to have a somewhat different approach to actions. The actions to be emphasized first are those that will modify behavior to such an extent that the behavior is acceptable—and thereby precipitate a change of status. Likewise, the evaluator's actions are somewhat different, in that specific directions must be given regarding behavior that is to be changed in order to become acceptable. This must be communicated to the evaluatee. Note, however, that the evaluator does not discontinue providing assistance or feedback. This is done because *it is the obligation of the evaluator to help the administrator, at all times, to change status.* It is not the function of the evaluator to cause the administrator to be released; if the evaluator does not do everything possible to assist the administrator to change status, the evaluator is negligent.

It should be noted that placing a person in a "consider for release" category is a judgment decision. But the decision should be made on a similar basis to other evaluative decisions, viz., by comparing outcomes with predetermined criteria. This means that there should be some standards for behavior and productivity that are known to all administrators and that data collected will be compared with these standards in order to make a judgment about whether behavior is acceptable. Without such standards, capriciousness can enter into the judgment. When such standards are known and communicated, administrators can be expected to fulfill them.

PLANNING MODE OF COMMUNICATION

Before any Phase III conference is conducted, the evaluator should plan the mode of communication use during the conference. Once the purposes for the conference are clearly established in the mind of the evaluator, a tentative agenda should be prepared for sharing with the evaluatee. In addition, the evaluator should think about how the evaluatee is likely to respond and react to different types of communication. Most people react differently to telling than they do to asking or exchanging, to a demanding tone of voice than to an encouraging tone. The evaluator should keep in mind at all times what type of relationship is desired with the evaluatee and how the communication can contribute to this relationship.

Even the choice of words is extremely important. Sometimes a simple conjunction in a sentence can change the entire meaning. For example, a sentence beginning with "I agree with you, *but* . . . " may be interpreted differently from a sentence beginning with "I agree with you, *and* . . . ". As an evaluator chooses words, he might be reminded of the story of two young women who were examining a new engagement ring being worn by one of them. The one young lady was overheard to say, "I didn't say I thought your ring looked cheap. I said it looked like it was all paid for."

PREVENTING CONFLICT

One of the major problems that can arise in relation to Phase III communication is a conflict between the evaluator and the evaluatee. Conflict can create a gap between the two which affects morale of both, and sometimes this can affect productivity. One of the major causes for conflict is inadequate communication in Phase I. Unless adequate time was spent discussing the context of the evaluation, the reasons for the evaluation, the goals and objectives, and the means whereby the objectives are to be measured, conflict is likely. Likewise, during the Phase I conference(s) is the time to discuss what communication will occur during Phase III. For example, there should be open communication about what will be written in a summary report form for the personnel files, and written copies of these should be provided for the administrator being evaluated. Open personnel files are essential to maintaining authentic communication.*

RECORD KEEPING

Much that has been said and written concerning record keeping in relation to evaluation implicitly assumes that the responsibility for keeping records and writing conclusions and decisions is the evaluator's. Further, it is assumed that the evaluatee has no responsibility in this regard. But when this assumption is examined, it seems to imply that evaluation is something that is done *to* the evaluatee, not *by* or *with* the evaluatee. If one thinks about this, certain questions arise. For example, what happens to the relationship between the evaluator and the evaluatee when the evaluatee has the responsibility for writing down conclusions reached in the Phase

---

* For a discussion of authentic and phony communication as related to open files see Bolton, *Selection and Evaluation of Teachers,* 1973:153 – 155.

III conference? What happens to the ownership of the decisions when they are written by the evaluatee and a copy is provided to the evaluator? Would concepts of "team management" and "sharing of authority" be more meaningful if the evaluatee had a major responsibility for writing summary statements about a given evaluation period? The research literature is silent on such questions, perhaps because the responsibility for writing and record keeping has been solely the evaluator's. It seems that the idea of the evaluator's sharing responsibility with the evaluatee for record keeping and written communication is compatible with modern concepts of leadership and management and would be worth trying in a school system.

Summary

The third phase of the evaluation process consists of the analysis and interpretation of information collected during Phase II and making decisions based on this information analysis and interpretation. Communication between evaluator and evaluatee facilitates the analysis and interpretation and helps to assure high-quality decisions that are satisfactory to those involved.

Phase III conferences should be purposeful and carefully planned. The feedback should be assessed by both the evaluatee and the evaluator, as soon after data collection as possible. The substance of the feedback should be directly related to goals and the work task. Ritualistic written reports in the form of "the ceremonial congratulation" have little impact on productivity but may affect the relationship between evaluator and evaluatee. General guidelines for conferences for reviewing performance include preparing for the meeting; sharing the purpose and the agenda; facilitating discussion by using good listening techniques; exhibiting a responsive attitude; resolving disagreements when possible or noting facts that are needed to resolve them when not possible; listing next steps; and summarizing the conference.

Studies of feedback to principals appear to have similar results to those of feedback to teachers and workers in industrial settings. Feedback does have an impact on behavior and results, and the responsiveness of principals to others' perceptions of them does not appear to be related to age, experience, or form used for measurement. Although criticism tends to have a negative effect on achievement of goals by inducing defensiveness, praise tends to cause the person to persevere at a given level (rather than to improve or to retrogress). Communication regarding mutual goal setting improves the performance of individuals by allowing them to become committed to goals at a higher level.

In appraisal interviews, both "invitation to participate" and "goal setting" relate significantly to the evaluatee's satisfaction with the evaluation process, and "goal setting" relates significantly to overall satisfaction with the job. Evidently, participation in the evaluation process can have a facilitative impact on the evaluatee.

Analysis of information involves grouping or clustering of data, visual display of that data, and statistical manipulation of data representing behavior, events, or results. Interpretation is a deduction of the meaning of the analysis that has been made.

Analysis and interpretation are for the purpose of making decisions basically concerned with the question, What works for me, in my situation? This question is a matter of determining the relationship of the procedures used to the products that resulted. By focusing on what *did* happen, decisions can be made on the following sequence of questions: What were the results? Were the goals reasonable? Were the procedures fully implemented as planned? Were the initially designed procedures effective? Once these questions have been answered, one can then concentrate on decisions regarding what steps should be taken next; this involves determining whether the same goals should be pursued, whether control mechanisms should be established to assure process implementation, and whether the procedures should be changed.

Evaluative decisions about pay are made in a similar way to any other evaluative decisions, but they are more sensitive and are more emotion-laden. There is some evidence that evaluation of performance is being used in educational systems for determination of pay, but the number of cases reported is not large. Those who combine MBO with determination of pay report that the practice is functional.

Communication during Phase III is extremely important and usually should occur throughout the time that the information is being analyzed and interpreted as well as during the decision process. Evaluatee goals and actions are different in a "retain" status from in a "consider for release" status; likewise, the evaluator's actions are different in these two cases. The evaluator should take care to provide assistance, feedback, and direction when the evaluatee is in the "consider for release" category, since the function of the evaluator is to do everything possible to help the administrator to change status.

The evaluator should carefully plan the type of communication to be used during and following the evaluation conference, since people respond and react differently to different types of communication. Conflicts at Phase III will be reduced if communication at Phase I included a plan for what would be discussed at Phase III and what type of written reports would be made. Both the evaluator and the evaluatee should make written statements at the conclusion of Phase III so that the evaluatee will more willingly accept responsibility for taking action on the decisions made.

5 ASSESSMENT OF THE EVALUATION PROCESS

As one considers the assessment of an evaluation process, certain questions may arise. For example, why should there be any need for assessment of the evaluation process? What are some of the problems that one might expect to encounter? How should one collect information regarding an evaluation process? How should evaluators be trained? How can information on the evaluation process be analyzed? How can activities be initiated to modify processes or install new ones? These questions will be discussed in this chapter.

Need for Assessment of the Evaluation Process

It is implied throughout this book that evaluation should be an integral part of the total management stategy used in an organization. This means that any time a system has been developed for use in an organization, whether it is an instructional system, an in-service training system, a managerial development system, an evaluation system, or any other system, it should be assessed to determine whether it is functioning in the way it was intended to function. Too often a system is simply *deduced* to be effective at the time it is installed; or the information collected to determine whether it really is effective is gathered in a haphazard and/or biased fashion and analyzed and interpreted in a similar way.

Periodic assessment of the evaluation system is needed to determine (a) whether any errors have crept into the system due to implementation or changes of circumstances, constraints, or environment and (b) whether the evaluation system is producing the results desired.

RELATED FINDINGS ON MBO

One's expectations regarding an evaluation system may be conditioned by prior research findings, especially those in the area of management by objectives. In a review of the MBO literature prior to 1970, Ivancevich, Donnelly, and Lyon (1970:142−143) reported the following conclusions:

1. Changes in performance in the positive direction appear to be associated with MBO programs.
2. Active participation of employees appears to be well received by managers.
3. Anxiety and tensions of not knowing how well one is performing are partially reduced because of increased communication between participants.
4. Lower level managers are participating the least in the MBO programs.
5. There are some major problems in presenting MBO programs, e.g., excessive formal requirements and paperwork.

The same authors reported (1970:148−149) findings of their own study in a business setting:

1. *The need satisfaction of participants is influenced by the program.* The most effective way to implement MBO is for the top level executives to explain, coordinate, and guide the program. When top level managers were actively involved, the philosophy and mechanics of the program filtered through and penetrated the entire organization. Thus, a possible motivation strategy to improve perceived need satisfaction at lower levels of management would be to involve the top level management in the MBO program.

2. *More attention must be given to the method of implementation than is suggested in the current literature.* This is related, of course, to the first conclusion, which implies that the strategy of implementation is to involve the top administrators of the organization. Without their support and modeling of the process, behavior of lower level administrators will either remain as it was prior to initiation of MBO procedures; or, if initially changed, it will soon regress to the prior behavior.

3. *The exact number of feedback sessions to employ in order to optimize the need satisfaction of participants is not known and must be determined on an individual organization basis.* Although the number of sessions must be determined on a local basis because of the nature of the personnel involved, it is generally assumed that individuals who receive frequent reports on performance tend to have better attitudes toward the entire process.

4. *Prospective users of MBO should recognize some of the problem areas.* These problem areas include the potential for excessive time spent on counseling, overemphasis on quantitative goals, and some people being independent of or out of the mainstream of the MBO program.

Raia (1965:51) cites these four main advantages that resulted from using an MBO process in the Purex Corporation: (a) planning and use of resources were improved; (b) problem areas were pinpointed; (c) performance was more objectively measured; and (d) communications and mutual understanding were improved. Carrol and Tosi (1973:14) identify three similar positive effects of MBO: (a) changes in performance and behavior; (b) aid to managers in performing their jobs, including greater satisfaction with the basis for performance measurement and more task-oriented communication with their supervisor; and (c) more positive attitudes toward the work situation.

On the other hand, Raia (1965:51) also specifies these disadvantages of using an MBO process at Purex: (a) the managerial philosophy was distorted, particularly at the lower levels; (b) there was a lack of full participation, again at the lower levels; (c) there was increased paperwork; (d) some people tended to decrease their goal levels for the fiscal year; and (e) there were problems of setting measurable goals in certain areas of work. Carroll and Tosi (1973:15) also indicated that excessive paperwork and the difficulty of measurement of performance of certain objectives were negative effects of MBO. Also, they found that the inaccurate data collected and the instability of the organization were related to negative effects of MBO. The latter is particularly important when there are rapid reorganizations, rapid changes in technology, or an inordinate number of crises in the organization.

Tosi and Carroll (1968:425) indicate that enthusiasm and support may wane for MBO programs, and they suggest that assessment of implementation and results are particularly important:

> The novelty wears thin and the need to cope with the difficulties of an objectives approach may force managers toward the path of least resistance, compliance with the minimum formal requirements, use of unimaginative goals, and only surface support.

Where the potential for both positive and negative effects is great, systematic assessment of the system is imperative.

Problems and Issues to Be Resolved

In assessing the administrator evaluation system in a school organization, certain problems and issues need to be faced, mostly concerned with the manner in which the system has been designed and the way it has been implemented. The major problems and issues will be phrased in the form of questions, followed by a brief discussion.*

DESIGN OF THE EVALUATION SYSTEM

Reality of the Design.   One of the first problems one may encounter, yet one which is often overlooked, is concerned with the reality of the design. *Is the system based on the reality of the situation that exists, and is everyone involved in the evaluation process well informed regarding this reality?* For example, has the evaluation system taken into consideration two real and disparate forces: (a) external clients who expect educational administrators to be productive and to be accountable to them for this productivity and (b) members of the administrative corps who seem to ignore this expectation of clients and/or to establish means of resisting any kind of interference by nonprofessionals. Is there any evidence of accurate measurement of these

---

*This discussion of problems and issues leans heavily on a chapter of a *Phi Delta Kappan* of a *Phi Delta Kappan* publication (Bolton, 1977).

two forces, the impact they have on each other, and how they change from time to time?

Also, is there evidence that communication regarding the activities of administrators takes into consideration the preferences of the different administrators for precision? In describing identical events, some administrators use very precise language while others are much more vague and ambiguous. Each may have real or imagined reasons for thinking that his or her means of communication is advantageous, yet others with whom he or she communicates may wish that events were described differently.

Additionally, does the evaluation system take into account the varying degrees of commitment to using evaluation as an integral part of the managerial style? Some administrators are unwilling to learn to use evaluation as a part of their managerial style, maintaining that it is an impediment to creative activities and their relationships to their subordinates. They may even rationalize their position by suggesting that evaluation is just another passing fad and their present style of managing is adequate. Related to this question is another one: Is there evidence that the evaluation system takes into consideration the different levels of enthusiasm for task accomplishment? Some people obtain their highest levels of satisfaction from their work while others appear to endure work in order to participate in outside hobbies and activities. The person who is highly preoccupied with outside interests or problems may be minimally competent but considerably lacking in enthusiasm for work productivity.

The overall issue, then, is whether or not the evaluation system is designed to take into account such elements of reality. If one assumes that no such reality (with its attendant problems) exists, the design is likely to exhibit a very limited view of how the designer thinks people and the world *ought to be*. Further at issue in relation to these realities is how they should be considered. Should one try to improve productivity by attempting to change the people involved or by trying to change the environment and the tasks? Etzioni (1972) believes that changing the environment and tasks may be more successful (and even more ethical) than trying to change the people; further, it may be that too much money is being spent in an effort to change people in view of the difficulty of the task.

Reasons for Evaluation.   Another major issue related to the design of evaluation systems is the matter of purposes, or reasons for evaluating administrators. *Is there evidence that all purposes for evaluating administrators have been stated clearly and that the evaluation system is designed to accomplish the stated purposes?* Sometimes there is a tendency to get embroiled in meaningless arguments over whether one purpose is primary or more basic than another. The major consideration is that *all* purposes have been stated in such a way that they are acceptable to all parties and yet are precise enough to assist in the design process. Since the purposes must be translated into actions, they must be specific enough to imply actions. For example, if the evaluation process is going to be used for modification of assignment or release of personnel, this should be stated in clear, concise terms. In addition, the data collection and use of data should be designed to carry out this purpose as well as other stated purposes.

A question related to the one on purposes has to do with a more general statement regarding the philosophical bases for the evaluation system. *Is there evidence that the evaluation system has been designed with a consistent view of the nature of the administrators, the organization, and the roles to be performed by the administrators in the organization?* Is it clear to anyone examining a statement explaining the evaluation system that the school system is assumed to be purposeful rather than simply an organization that responds to external and internal pressures to act in a particular way? Are there any statements that indicate how conflicts between individuals or groups will be resolved? Are any assumptions stated as to the need to restrict administrators' behaviors? What is assumed regarding whether each administrator desires to improve his or her own performance? What is the organization's view about being fair to all individuals in the organization, i.e., will all be treated alike, or will consideration be shown for unique circumstances, interests, and talents? Are expectations clearly stated so that administrators are not evaluated on activities or results if the external forces prevent their doing those activities or, conversely, is the administrator given credit for supportive forces that he did not influence? In effect, this issue is concerned with whether there is a general statement that clarifies the total philosophical basis for the evaluation system, stating beliefs and assumptions that provide guidelines for the design of the system.

Criteria for Evaluation. The next issue has to do with the area that is central to most discussions about evaluation—the criteria for evaluation. *Is there evidence that the criteria for evaluation of administrators are sufficiently specific, written to clarify the relationships of processes and outcomes, flexible enough to be pertinent for various situations, and real enough to evoke commitment?* The meaning of the term "criteria for evaluation" should be specified clearly enough to assist in development of measurement devices. For example, when the term is used it may mean any or all of the following:

> . . . some people are referring to characteristics or personal qualities of administrators (such as emotional stability, appearance, and sociability), others are referring to certain functions performed (such as implementation or maintenance), others are referring to procedures used by administrators (such as conducting inservice programs for teachers, planning with PTSA groups, or initiating a change in some aspect of the curriculum), while still others are referring to results of behavior (such as changes in teacher behavior, or changes in school climate or parental satisfaction) (Bolton, 1977:74).

Since there is an almost unlimited number of behaviors and results of behaviors that might be specified, how much detail and what level of generality should be used in specifying standards of performance for administrators? Should this level of generality be different for different administrators? Too much detail may cause a lack of attention to the important tasks, tend to drive out creative and assertive people, and attract only the passive and conforming; yet, the standards of performance should be specific enough to give direction and allow judgments to be made about excellence and progress.

Evaluative criteria (in the form of job descriptions or job "targets") should be written so there is a clear relationship between the processes to be used and the outcomes expected. Since research does not clearly specify what administative behaviors or characteristics produce particular results, local organizations must specify both the results desired and the first estimates of what behaviors are likely to produce those results.

Since most administrative jobs are dynamic rather than static, criteria need to be specified so that they are pertinent despite fluctuations of expectations due to situations and changes. They should be flexible enough to be up to date and yet stable enough to give direction to the organization. If the criteria themselves are not flexible, the procedures for adapting the criteria to situations and time should be flexible. In addition, they must be real enough to administrators so that they will become committed to act on the basis of the criteria. Role expectations and job descriptions must be translated into objectives that are measurable and meaningful to the individual administrator; commitment of time and energy are made to specifics, not to generalities.

Collection of Data. Another issue involves collection of data. *Is there evidence that the system for evaluation clearly indicates who will collect information, when the information will be collected, and under what circumstances the information will be collected?* How will telephone calls and complaints to the central office from teachers and parents be handled? What responsibility will the administrator have for documenting certain processes and outcomes? Under what circumstances will it be appropriate to observe the administrator? What "incidentally collected" information will be used? How will the information be recorded and what forms will be used? Because the judgments regarding whether objectives have been accomplished must be made on the basis of information, it is extremely important that the design of the evaluation system include specifications as to how this information will be collected. Even with written statements about information collection provided in the design, misunderstanding will occur; therefore, periodic review of the means of collecting information by the administrators involved will likely reduce the conflict possibilities as well as facilitate the beneficial use of data.

Is System Functional? A final problem area has to do with whether the evaluation system is designed to be functional. *Is there evidence that the evaluation system for administrators is designed to be cyclical and continuous, to be a functional subsystem of the overall strategy of management, and to attend to the organizational and individual needs?* The evaluation system should not be designed merely to satisfy legal requirements or board of education demands for an annual review of activities.

Neither should it declare to all concerned that one can merely "walk through" the process without either thought or effort. School systems should be purposeful institutions; therefore, administrators of school systems should be purposeful, and the systems designed by educational administrators should be purposeful and functional.

One of the functional aspects of an evaluation system is that it is cyclical and continuous rather than linear and spasmodic. In most people there is a desire to reach closure and seek permanency. Perhaps this is because much of society and many work situations are changing, and there is a desire to have parts of life remain stable so that one can cope with the changing segments. At any rate, there is the tendency to categorize a person as a "good" administrator because of some activities observed or some results at a given point in time—and to discontinue evaluating that person, leaving him in the category of a "good" administrator. But this misses the major point of evaluation, which is to make judgments about the value of events, behaviors, and outcomes in light of predetermined objectives. The point is that evaluation is designed to assist in making decisions about what to do in specific situations, *not* merely to categorize a person and leave him in that category. The cyclical and continuous aspect of an evaluation system allows decisions to be made often enough so that errors can be corrected before they become serious and plans can be made quickly to adjust to changing situations.

The linear style of management might be shown in a flow chart, such as figure 5.1. Note that the first step is to specify general goals. This is quite common and may include a statement such as "improve staff development." The second step would include an emphasis on the positive and a repetition often of the general goals established. This is all designed to encourage people to exert effort toward the goals set. The third step, maintaining the organization, takes into account the fact that certain activities deteriorate during the course of the year. Therefore, there is a need to replace materials and equipment, listen to complaints, and see that repetitive functions are performed. But then administrators wait for problems to occur, because they know that this is the pattern with all organizations. When they do occur, administrators solve them. As they solve problems, they become better at problem solving and more people bring them their problems. This establishes a relationship of dependency that exists throughout the year. Eventually the year ends!

You may not know an administrator who functions on a linear strategy, but those who do have as their major intent to finish the year. Their real aim appears to be to get the year finished, the reports completed, the children out of the building,

Figure 5.1: A linear strategy for management

and the teachers' last paychecks delivered before some major catastrophe occurs. Their actions imply that they have no more purpose than to solve the problems that arise and to finish the year.

Contrast this with the cyclical model of figure 5.2. This strategy may also have some general goals, but the focus at the beginning emphasizes four facets of planning that need to be identified: (a) specific objectives, (b) activities needed to accomplish the objectives, (c) people who will be engaged in each of the activities, and (d) the time sequence of events. Implementation includes putting the total plan into operation by taking the initiative of seeing that the activities are begun and kept on schedule. Maintenance is the same as the one identified in the linear strategy, except that the focus is on the plan specified earlier rather than on repetition of prior activities. Finally, evaluation provides feedback necessary to aid in correction by replanning, modifying implementation procedures, or changing maintenance activities. The duration of the cycle depends considerably on the plans that are made and implemented, but it may be short enough that the cycle is completed several times in an academic year. When this style of management is incorporated in a total school system, evaluation is seen as an integral part of the total operation. Teachers then see a relation between this administrative strategy and the teaching strategy they have been encouraged to use, viz., diagnosis, prescription, implementation, and evaluation. Also, they see the benefit of making long-range plans and of correcting those plans on the basis of short-term evaluation.

People model others whom they view to be significant. Teachers often model administrators, and administrators model those who provide their direction and supervision—regardless of the administrative style used. The design of the evaluation system should be such that it encourages all personnel in the organization to incorporate evaluation into their style of operation. Unless they see how evaluation helps them to do their jobs better, they resist incorporating it into their managerial style.

In addition, the evaluation system should be designed in such a way that it facilitates the harmonizing of individual aspirations and organizational goals. The normal method of accomplishing this in the evaluation system is to incorporate a self-evaluation component as well as an external evaluation component. The function of self-evaluation is to provide continuous and instant feedback on the elements

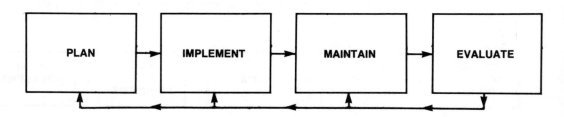

Figure 5.2: A cyclical strategy for management

of the job that are of most concern to the individual administrator. The function of the external evaluator is to assure that individual objectives are compatible with organizational goals and that organizational goals are being met. In effect, the external evaluator is needed to assure that criteria are compatible with the goals of the organization. This prevents the well-known centrifugal force, which causes people to be spun off in all directions (their own specific interests), from becoming too great for the organization to be functional.

IMPLEMENTATION OF THE EVALUATION SYSTEM

Commitment to Evaluation. Once an evaluation system has been designed, the temptation is to assume that it will be implemented immediately—and in the way designed. If there is no commitment to either the purposes or the procedures of the system, there will be resistances that lead to poor implementation and ineffectiveness of the system. Therefore, it is important to ask: *Is there evidence that those involved in implementing the evaluation system are committed to it as it has been designed?* Sometimes a lack of commitment occurs when an individual is not involved (at least to the extent that views and opinions are asked for) in the design phase or in planning for implementation. When this occurs, difficulties of implementation may be overlooked; plans and goals may need to be changed to take into consideration the reality of these difficulties.

It can be concluded, on the basis of this reasoning, that a sufficient number of those people involved in implementing the evaluation system should also be included in the design of the system. This is reasonable because they have a stake in the outcome, and they should be able to contribute to the decisions being made by predicting the outcome of procedures designed. In addition, where the total group involved in the implementation is very large, the planning group can function as a communication link with the total group.

If a group is used for planning the design and implementation procedures, there still may be an issue with regard to the nature of the group. For example, should it be a committee or a task force? The distinction between the two is often in terms of the time blocks provided for meeting and working and the duration over which the groups function. The committee usually meets for short periods over a long duration, but a task force meets in larger time blocks and finishes the work more quickly. Recent experiences of some school districts with the task force is good, provided that adequate time is allotted for communicating with those who have a stake in the outcome. The use of committees over a long period of time tends to cause people to lose interest in the project.

Morale Factors. Another problem of implementation has to do with putting the evaluation system into operation in such a way that adversarial relationships and surprises are minimized. The question should be asked: *Is there evidence that the implementation of the evaluation system has adequately considered such morale* *factors as potential adversarial relationships and surprises?* To accomplish the dual goals of high productivity and high morale, it is generally considered desirable to have open, authentic communication, to adopt a futuristic and goal-oriented posture (rather than looking backward at problems) in order to evade adversarial relationships, to limit the responsibility of individuals to the extent that they do not feel harassed by the multiplicity of tasks, and to realistically face the resistances to evaluation procedures. This means that implementation should be done in such a way that data and events are viewed realistically and problems are not evaded. The focus should not be on finding fault with others but on examining the existing situation to see what could be done during the next cycle to accomplish the desired outcomes.

Morale tends to be lowered under conditions where the expectations for individuals are set too high or where they are unclear. People are motivated by challenging tasks they believe they can accomplish but hesitate to spend valuable time on hazy goals or unclear procedures. Those who are involved in implementing an evaluation system deserve to know how they will be able to perform any new tasks and still accomplish prior expectations. In addition, adequate information should be provided regarding the criteria to be used; the conference and report schedules should be explained; and the meanings of measuring devices and summary report forms should be clarified so that no surprises will occur during the early stages of implementation.

Training of Evaluators.   The concern for reasonable expectations and minimization of surprises leads to another problem of implementation. *Is there evidence that adequate training of evaluators has been provided so the evaluation system can be implemented as designed?* Have evaluators received training in management of time so that they are capable of establishing priorities in terms of maximum contribution to the organization? Are they aware of how their supervisors view the importance of various tasks they perform? Are their listening and communication skills such that they will feel comfortable in the role of an evaluator and be able to develop a trust relationship with those they evaluate? Do they understand procedures thoroughly and follow through with them? For example, where MBO procedures are required, have they developed skills in writing and critiquing objectives, in conducting conferences, and in providing feedback?

In order for the procedures to be implemented as designed, the evaluators need (a) knowledge about evaluation processes in general and the procedures of this system in particular, (b) skills in planning, collecting information, and using the information to make decisions about the next steps, and (c) an attitude that is compatible with the basic assumptions underlying the evaluation system and which views the total process positively so the evaluator is willing to act on the knowledge and skills he has. The training procedure established for evaluators should take into consideration all three of these requisites; to focus on the knowledge aspect only will produce evaluators who evade certain elements of the evaluation design with which they are uncomfortable.

Can Evaluation System Sustain Itself?   The next problem of implementation has to do with the following question: *Is there evidence that the evaluation system has been implemented in such a way that it will sustain itself over a period of time?* All systems have a tendency to die, whether they are physical organisms or organizational structures (Smith, 1956). The support that is necessary for an evaluation system to continue to exist is usually provided in the form of reinforcement by people who have an impact on the school system. The strength of the support is often determined by the status and power of the people providing the reinforcement. Therefore, implementation should be planned so that top level administrators and the board of education will provide support and reinforcement of the intent and procedures of the evaluation system. This reinforcement and support, which comes from the top management of the school district, should have two characteristics: (a) it should be reviewed frequently rather than annually, in fact almost continuously, and (b) it should be a natural consequence of the successful use of evaluation as a part of day-to-day operation. These characteristics will be exhibited only if evaluation is implemented as a truly integral part of the total management strategy and style.

Sources of Information

What are the sources of information that will help one to know whether the evaluation system for administrators in a school system is working effectively and efficiently? Since sources of information are direcly related to the types of questions being asked about the system, a listing of some of these questions should be helpful.

1. *Is the evaluation system helping administrators do their job better?* It is the administrator's task to provide services to others so that they can perform better and be more satisfied with their job and also to provide service to the organization so that it can proceed toward its goals. Therefore, information is needed concerning (a) performance of those being supervised by the administrators; (b) satisfaction of teachers and administrators with their jobs (morale and esprit indices); (c) accomplishment of specific goals of the organization (e.g., indications of satisfaction by parents, completion of new building programs, follow up of graduates indicating success in activities immediately following completion of school); (d) quick solution to problems (as indicated by perceptions of parents and teachers of the responsiveness of the organization to problems identified). The sources of this information would be observation of the administrators and self-report devices completed by teachers, principals, parents, and central office administrators.

2. *Is evaluation functioning in all aspects of the management system?* Are central office administrators setting goals for management development programs that help principals to develop skills of evaluating teachers? What reactions do princi-

pals and teachers have to how they are evaluated? Are central office administrators discussing with principals the objectives set by principals—and then helping the principals to collect, analyze, and interpret the necessary data to make decisions about these objectives? Are central office administrators who encourage principals to obtain feedback from teachers regarding the principals' functioning also asking principals for feedback on their own functioning? The sources of information for such questions will be primarily the records kept by each administrator as well as the self-report devices completed by teachers, principals, and central office administrators.

3. *Is sufficient time being spent to implement the evaluation procedures?* One evidence of the priority of any task is the amount of time spent on that task. If an administrator spends only fifteen minutes a week on a task, one would have to conclude that it is relatively unimportant in comparison to other responsibilities. Likewise, one can conclude that *no system of evaluation* is likely to accomplish very much unless there is opportunity to implement the designed activities. Evidence on this aspect of the evaluation process can be collected from the records of each administrator. For example, a periodic sampling of how each administrator spends time during a given two-week period can be obtained by allowing secretaries to keep records of the amount of time the administrator spends in observing teachers and in conferences or by recording on planning forms the amount of time spent on conferences and data collection.

4. *Is the system of evaluation purposeful?* Are the statements of purposes clear, and do they explain concisely why the administrator evaluation system exists? Is it clear to all that evaluatees will set goals, and that the goals will include specifications of who will do what? Are the purposes clarified further by sufficient details of how the system of evaluation will be implemented? These questions imply, as a source of information, a written document that describes not only the reasons for the evaluation system, but also the evaluatee goal-setting process and the remainder of the implementation procedures. Such a document serves as a source of information to all administrators. In addition, information can be collected from administrators. In addition, information can be collected from administrators to determine whether they perceive the purposes as reasonable and real (or whether the real purposes are masked). Feedback from those involved should indicate whether evaluation is realistic and compatible with the procedures implemented or only occurring as a "game" to be played.

5. *Is the evaluation of administrators cyclical and self-correcting?* When evaluation is cyclical it has a sequence of activities that repeat themselves; when it is self-correcting, this repetition is sufficiently often to minimize the damage done by errors. A linear sequence of activities does not allow for repetition or self-correction; therefore, any deviation from established goals is amplified as time progresses and eventually leads to catastrophe and major correction in the form of drastic modification of the organization. The information needed to check this aspect of the evaluation system comes from records and summary report forms of

administrators, as well as from the description of the process itself. Other information may be obtained to determine whether evaluation procedures are incorporated in other activities of administrators. For example, when administrators intitate new activities or programs, is a plan made to evaluate them to determine their effectiveness and to make adjustments if needed?

6. *What results can be attributed directly to the administrator evaluation system?* Is there any evidence that feedback provided from administrators to teachers is affecting the learning of students? Are teachers improving their skills? Are problems of administrators being solved in such a way that fewer errors are being made? What is happening to the morale of both the evaluators and the evaluatees? What is happening to the satisfaction of parents with the functioning of schools? These questions suggest collecting information from the records of evaluation conferences, examination of achievement records, observation of the behavior of teachers and administrators, and self-report devices from administrators and parents.

Data collection in any of the behavioral sciences can be done through observation, examining written documents or records, and asking questions via tests, questionnaires or other self-report devices, or interviews. Most of the information needed to assess the administrator evaluation system can best be collected by examining written records and by asking questions via questionnaires or other self-report devices. It also is possible to gather information by interviews, but the sample for interviewing must be limited due to the cost.

Information about the administrator evaluation system should be collected regularly (probably annually) in order to make sure that it is operating smoothly and effectively. Just as teachers should be encouraged to collect information from each of their classes on a regular basis, so administrators should collect information about their procedures on a regular basis. Reasonable self-report devices can be assembled in a short period of time by an administrator who collects items that can be used for acquiring information from selected groups.

It is not essential that all administrators respond to all items, or that all parents be sampled, in order to acquire reliable information about certain aspects of the evaluation system. If one desires responses from 100 administrators on forty items, it is much easier (and still quite reliable) to allow 25 randomly selected administrators to respond to ten items, another 25 administrators to respond to the next ten items, etc. This procedure reduces the time needed for the administrators to respond as well as the time needed to analyze the information.

Analysis of Information

Analysis and interpretation of the information collected regarding the administrator evaluation system is similar to the analysis and interpretation of information used for evaluation of administrators themselves. The actual analysis procedures used still depend on the nature of the data collected. The type of question being asked determines whether one pays more attention to the mean or the variance of a variable being measured, whether one displays the data in some visual form (e.g., in a scattergram, where one is interested in examining relationships of two variables, or in some type of graph form), or whether one computes correlation coefficients or determines the significant differences between certain means. In most cases, examining frequency distributions of individual items or determining the median of the frequency will be helpful.

The time invested in analysis and interpretation should be compatible with the risk involved in the decisions to be made. Since the risk is likely to be low, extremely sophisticated analytical techniques are not likely to be necessary.

Suggestions for Training Evaluators

Is is assumed that individuals who are responsible for evaluating administrators are not automatically prepared for it by the activities in which they have engaged prior to becoming evaluators of administrators. Therefore, specific activities should be designed to teach them how to perform their job.

The content of prior chapters of this book indicates some of what is needed to perform the role of an evaluator of administrators but does not suggest any strategy for learning the role. Since there is a difference between learning *about* the process of administrator evaluation and developing the capability of *doing* evaluation, goals must be established for training evaluators, providing them with information (ideas, constructs, concepts, theories) and motivation. Then they must be given opportunities to develop and practice the necessary skills. It is common practice to dwell on the information base and to ignore the motivation (attitude development) and the skill development. If the major motivation is merely exhortation to "do better" (sometimes accompanied by "or else") without the evaluators being given the opportunity to understand how their own effectiveness and satisfaction will be affected, and if there is no emphasis on skill development and practice, there will be a strong tendency to consider the ideas as mere rhetoric or meaningless theory.

TOPICS TO CONSIDER

Topics which may have an impact on the information, attitude, or skill development of evaluators include the following:

1. *Conceptual base.* Information should be provided regarding the current significance of evaluation, definitions and assumptions, model of evaluation, roles and responsibilities of people involved in evaluation, a perspective of recent trends, the effect of evaluation on the managerial style, measurement techniques, and resistances to evaluation.
2. *Planning for evaluation.* This topic includes information and skills in the analysis of the administrative situation (including variables and constraints to consider), the purposes of evaluation, the setting of goals and objectives, the establishment

of means for measuring both processes and products, and agreements and reconciliation to be reached.

3. *Collecting information.* This includes methods of observation, keeping of records, measurement of procedures and results, and collection from sources other than the administrator and the evaluator.

4. *Using information.* Skills should be developed in the analysis and interpretation of information about both processes and products, making decisions based on the information interpreted, communicating accurately regarding the information, making agreements as to the next steps to be taken, and making a smooth transition to new planning to be done.

5. *Management of time.* One of the deterrents to implementation of the evaluation process is poor management of time; and information and skills need to be transmitted regarding setting priorities, time study and analysis, and time planning and control.

6. *Getting started in evaluation.* Information needs to be provided and plans initiated relative to change strategies which might be used and the initial steps which can be taken.

PRACTICE IN SKILL DEVELOPMENT

The six topics identified above suggest information which should be provided and areas in which skills should be developed. In any training of evaluators of administrators, care should be taken to provide actual practice in the development of skills in the following tasks:

1. Analyzing specific situations in which administrators perform
2. Explaining purposes for evaluating administrators
3. Analyzing an evaluatee's objectives
4. Reaching agreement on objectives written by the evaluatee
5. Reaching agreement on resources needed by an evaluatee in relation to the objectives established
6. Identifying means for measuring objectives
7. Planning for a conference with an evaluatee
8. Conducting a conference with an evaluatee
9. Writing objectives for the evaluator which relate to the evaluation of administrators
10. Analyzing and interpreting information with an administrator regarding his performance
11. Making decisions with an administrator about his performance
12. Collecting information and keeping records on the performance of administrators
13. Analyzing the evaluator's use of time
14. Planning and controlling the evaluator's use of time

ACTIVITIES TO BE USED FOR TRAINING EVALUATORS

Since there is a desire to develop attitudes as well as skills, the activities used in the training of evaluators should include more than simply giving information. Consideration should be given to the following activities:

1. Presentations
2. Large group discussion, where questions can be raised and answers provided
3. Small group discussions, where issues can be clarified, problems analyzed and defined, effective practices shared, guidelines and strategies devised
4. Observing, in one of the following situations: (a) televised or filmed episodes of conferences or administrative action and (b) live conferences or actions in either a "fishbowl" type situation or in small group (3-4 people) situations
5. Role playing of planning sessions, conferences with evaluatees before and after information has been collected
6. Feedback, regarding observations of others and action taken in role playing situations
7. Analysis, based on observations of televised, filmed, or live (role played) episodes.

Activities 4 to 7 offer the opportunity to use concepts presented and discussed in activities 1 to 3 and furnish a check on whether the evaluators can apply the concepts presented. Since the proof of the value of the training is in the eventual application, practice in doing the activities is critical to the total training process.

PERSPECTIVE ON TRAINING EVALUATORS

Evaluation of administrators is a complex process; therefore, evaluators cannot be trained in a short period of time. When a new administrator evaluation system is initiated, there is a tendency to spend much time discussing it during the design phase and then to expect that everyone involved will not only understand it but also be able to perform the necessary tasks. Consequently, a very short period of time is spent in training evaluators, perhaps even as little as one or two hours. Then, when problems arise in the evaluation process, there is a tendency to fault the process—but the problem really lies in the implementation. And the implementation problem often can be traced directly to inadequate initial training of evaluators.

Therefore, the first guideline for training evaluators should be: *Spend enough time in the initial training to develop the skills and attitudes necessary for adequate implementation of the evaluation system.* Depending on the background of the evaluators, this initial training period should be two to five days.

After the evaluators have initiated the activities for Phase I of the evaluation process, they should receive additional training. This follow-up training should include discussion and analysis of problems encountered. In addition, any hazy concepts should be clarified and skill development should be continued. Therefore, the second guideline is: *After evaluators have had time to implement the initial phase of the evaluation cycle, additional opportunity for training should be provided.* Normally a one-day session is sufficient for this purpose.

By the middle of the first year that an evaluator has been using an evaluation procedure, the total cycle should have been completed for all evaluatees at least once, and many will have gone through the cycle multiple times. Therefore, this is a good time to have a half-day or a full day of training to check on any problems that may be arising and to continue development of skills. After this additional training, there is a strong tendency to consider an evaluator "complete" and, therefore, needing no further training. However, the concepts learned tend to be forgotten, the skills developed may deteriorate if not used properly or if feedback is not provided regarding their use, and attitudes may change due to pressures and constraints of a situation. Because of this, there is another guideline that needs to be remembered: *Periodic opportunities should be provided for evaluators to renew ideas, skills, and attitudes via training sessions; these opportunities should be provided throughout the time a person has evaluation responsibilities rather than merely during the first year.* This suggests that there should be at least an annual opportunity for evaluators to renew requisites for the evaluation process.

The activities and topics suggested for training of evaluators of administrators include the use of video or filmed episodes, role playing, and planning sessions in a simulated situation. The intent is that all three of these activities occur in a simulated situation described in a set of materials. There are several potential advantages of simulation over the more usual conference format of "present and discuss"; they are:

1. Simulation provides sufficient realism to develop interest and ego-involvement on the part of the learner. The increased commitment to the task is related to the reliability and validity of performance of the evaluator.
2. Simulation allows experience with the evaluation process under conditions that are relatively nonthreatening to the learner and where the consequences of decisions are not damaging to the evaluatees or to the school system.
3. Simulation furnishes an opportunity for learners to acquire feedback regarding their performance and to perform a similar act following this feedback; in addition, it permits an instructor to determine whether additional practice is needed before modifying certain elements of the activities.
4. Simulation provides opportunities in a variety of settings and at any time of the year regardless of the availability of live evaluatees.

The availability of simulated materials, then, makes it possible for instructors to provide a precise experience in evaluation for evaluators with responsibility for evaluating administrators. Such experiences allow activities to be repeated under virtually the same conditions, so participants can have practice under relatively controlled conditions. The advantage of practice is that it develops skills in *how to* evaluate rather than simply teaching *about* the process of evaluation. The advantage of practicing in a simulated setting is that it allows considerable flexibility and at the same time provides a means for systematizing the procedures used.

Organizational Use of Assessment Information

Probably the most important aspect to be assessed in the evaluation system for educational administrators is whether it is being used by the top leaders in the school system. If assessment of the evaluation system overlooks the importance of this concept, diagnosis of the problems in the system may be incorrect. Considerable research information indicates the importance of not only support by high-level leaders but also the use and modeling of the process by them.

For example, Beer and Ruh (1976) found that some people will not use a procedure until they are told to do so or until the top person in the organization uses it with his or her immediate subordinates. Other people seem willing to use a procedure but wait for follow up in the form of pressure from someone in authority. Because of this and because few people communicate their positive views to others, they found that highly accepted systems do not automatically permeate an organization, and "the availability of a good system is not enough to spread its use; a vigorously active program is necessary" (Beer & Ruh, 1976:66).

In discussing MBO, Carroll and Tosi (1973:67) point out that the most important key to its implementation is its use by top management, since participation is the best indicator of top-management support. In fact, they found that satisfaction with MBO is positively related to the way the subordinate feels MBO is supported and used by the boss. This means that support for an evaluation system must be more than training in how to use the process; the total environment must be supportive of the process. The strength of their position is stated in this way:

> . . . the ideas developed in the learning phase must be consistent with existing norms that underlie the superior-subordinate relationship and the managerial philosophy that generally permeates the organization. These, and the decisions and policies resulting from them, will have the most substantial effect on whether managers use MBO effectively and their attitudes toward it. If managers find that the reward system pays off for behavior other than that recommended in the objectives process, MBO will achieve only secondary status. If it is not part of the ongoing system of the organization, it will be shoved aside and viewed as a useless appendage to the manager's job. He will view it as excessive paper work to be completed only because the personnel department requires it. If this is his perception, MBO will be relatively valueless to him (Carroll & Tosi, 1973:54−55).

These conclusions were based on assessment of an evaluation system where the most common suggestions for improving the program were that (a) more review of performance should be provided in relation to goals established, (b) goals should be updated when conditions change, and (c) higher levels should participate more so that higher-level goals would be made known to lower-level personnel.

In discussing a collaborative form of MBO, French and Hollman (1975) stress that CMBO is not likely to be an easy process to implement for many organizations; therefore, one should not expect immediate results to be exceptionally high. Whatever iniitial successes appear are likely to result from a strong desire on the part of the top-management team to cooperate with each other in implementing the process. Since the total process requires some degree of skill in interpersonal relations and group dynamics, it is necessary to provide training in these skills. In addition, it should be recognized that it takes time to shift to a collaborative mode and that there is a need to attend to timing—making sure that the organization is ready for the process.

Research in school systems on the Executive Professional Leadership (EPL) of principals indicates that a principal's own professional leadership will be directly affected by experiences of a comparable kind with his superiors.

> These findings strongly suggest that higher administrators would be well advised to examine carefully how their own performance may be influencing the EPL of their principals and to consider the possibility that any efforts to upgrade principals' EPL may call for changes in their own performance (Gross & Herriott, 1966:70).

Ivancevich (1974:564) found that a plant that applied positive reinforcement on a systematic basis to an MBO process being used showed improved performance when compared with other support conditions. He concluded that the strategy of having managers attend a training program and then return to their organization with expectations to conduct themselves according to MBO training was unlikely to produce reasonable results, since this strategy fails to consider the significance of having an environment and managerial unit that support and reinforce the training program.

Neidermeyer (1977:48) found that approximately one-third of a group of principals failed to implement experimental procedures in a supervision program. He suggested that this most probably occurred because they did not see how the implementation of procedures that get results can give credit to both them and the teachers involved. Without such motivation, one can expect that any busy administrator who is pressed for time will drop such projects. This may be compatible with Levinson's (1968:64) view that top management rarely understands that the way supervisors handle people is a reflection of how top managers behave. If evaluators do not understand how the evaluation of administrators affects their own productivity, and if the behavior of the top administrators does not model the behavior desired in the evaluators, then training programs will not only be ineffective but may even be dysfunctional. As Levinson (1968:64) puts it, "no amount of training will undo the influences and examples set by higher management."

So, one of the important aspects in the assessment of an evaluation procedure is to determine whether it is being implemented at the top levels of the organization and fully supported by the chief administrators. Olds (1977:21) reinforces this view by stating that it is very easy to assume that the failure of a plan has been due to the plan and not to the people involved in its implementation. Under such conditions, he indicates:

> Chances are very good that the evaluation plan is not viewed to be essential to the success of the organization or even to have any decisive influence upon the quality of ongoing work being conducted by the organization (Olds, 1977:47).

This is compatible with the view that, at the end of a period of evaluation, the first thing one should check after confirming the satisfactoriness of the goals is whether the plan has been implemented as designed. It is *then* that one can come to conclusions about how good the method is.

Tosi and Carroll (1968:424) found that satisfaction with a form of MBO was positively related to the subordinate's perception of boss and company interest in the program and how much time the boss spent on it. They considered that this was

> strong evidence of the link between managerial support and the degree to which the program is accepted by an individual. It is only when all levels of management reinforce the use of the program by subordinates by *using the system themselves* that benefits can obtain.

Further, they indicate that unless the evaluation program is perceived as filling a legitimate need in the organization, it will be driven from any manager's list of priorities. Tosi and Carroll (1968:425−426) state that "the objectives approach cannot be sold in books, meetings, or theory. It can only be sold in practice." Simply because a new or modified program of evaluation is put into practice does not mean that problems of evaluation and motivation will diminish. In fact, when individuals' expectations about feedback and appraisal are raised and not met, problems may be magnified. Therefore, there is an extreme need to appraise the evaluation system effectively and to determine how it is being implemented at the higher levels.

Finally, in assessing the evaluation process, one should be fully aware of the time lag issue. Because evaluation is a complex process and has an impact on various parts of the management process, it takes time to permeate the total management system. Ivancevich emphasizes this point in relation to MBO:

> Each managerial level and the total environment of an organization implementing MBO must usually be modified before MBO becomes embedded into the system. These modifications require time to reach the first-line managerial level (Ivancevich, 1974:564).

Since the time lag phenomenon is present, there is an increased emphasis on the need to examine how the process is being implemented at the top levels of the organization. When malfunctions are occurring at lower levels of the evaluation process, one must examine even more carefully how the process is functioning at the higher levels.

Summary

The need for assessment of the evalution system for administrators is the same as for any other system, viz., to determine whether any errors have crept into the system due to implementation or changes of circumstances, constraints, or environment and to determine whether the evaluation system produces the results desired. One would expect evaluation systems to have an impact on the type and level of communication between evaluator and evaluatee, the satisfaction with work, the performance level of evaluatees, and the planning and use of resources. However, with some evaluation systems (e.g., those using MBO) there has been difficulty with attaining full participation at all levels of the organization, with increasing levels of paperwork, and with problems of setting goals. When enthusiasm and support wane, it may be particularly important to assess what is happening in the evaluation system.

The following are areas where major problems with the *design* of the evaluation system may occur: (a) acceptance of the reality of the situation by those who design the system; (b) clear evidence that the system is purposeful and that those purposes are clearly stated and well known; (c) evidence that the roles of administrators are consistent with the organization and its nature; (d) specific criteria that clarify processes and outcomes expected of the administrators being evaluated; (e) clear specification of how and by whom information will be collected on which evaluations will be made; and (f) description of the evaluation system in such a way that it is cyclical and continuous, a functional subsystem of the overall strategy of management, attending to organizational and individual needs.

Major problems involved with the *implementation* of the evaluation system include: (a) commitment to the design by those who are responsible for implementing the evaluation system; (b) consideration of morale factors such as potential adversarial relationships and surprises; and (c) providing support and reinforcement for the evaluation system so it will sustain itself over a period of time.

Certain questions should de considered when one is deciding on the sources of information that may be appropriate in assessing a system for evaluating administrators:

1. Is the evaluation system helping administrators do their job better?
2. Is evaluation functioning in all aspects of the management system?
3. Is sufficient time being spent to implement the evaluation procedures?
4. Is the system of evaluation purposeful?
5. Is the evaluation of administrators cyclical and self-correcting?

6. What results can be attributed directly to the administrator evaluation system?

Most of the information needed to assess the administrator evaluation system would most successfully be collected by examining written records and by asking questions via questionnaires or other self-report devices. This collection of information should be done regularly (probably annually) in order to make sure that the system is operating smoothly and effectively.

The analysis and interpretation of information depends on the nature of the data collected. In most cases, extremely sophisticated analytical techniques are not likely to be necessary; frequency distributions, some measure of variance and central tendency along with some visual display will usually suffice.

In many cases it will be profitable for evaluators of administrators to engage in reasonably comprehensive training in evaluation procedures so that they can develop skills in actually doing evaluation rather than simply being competent in knowing about evaluation. Evaluators need to have good information about what is to be done, skills in doing the tasks, and an attitude that causes them to perform the tasks well. Therefore, the training of evaluators needs to include much opportunity to practice the skills needed in the actual act of evaluating. These include skills in analysis and conceptualization, planning and communication with others, decision making, collecting information, and use of time.

The activities needed to develop such skills include presentations, large group and small group discussions, observing of televised or filmed episodes and live conferences, role playing feedback sessions, and analysis of conferences and episodes.

Because evaluation of administrators is a complex process, time is needed to develop skills of evaluation. The initial training of an evaluator should allow enough time for the evaluator to be able to implement the system as designed, but periodic additional opportunity for training should be provided. The renewal of ideas, skills, and attitudes is needed throughout the time a person has evaluation responsibilities. To provide this training in a simulation setting has the advantages of furnishing sufficient realism to develop interest and ego-involvement on the part of the learner, allowing experience with the evaluation process under conditions that are relatively nonthreatening to the learner, furnishing feedback regarding performance, and providing opportunities in a variety of settings at any time of the year. Practicing in a simulated setting allows considerable flexibility and at the same time provides a precise experience for systematizing the procedures used for evaluating administrators.

Probably the most important aspect of the evaluation system for educational administrators is whether it is being used by the top leaders in the school system. Research information indicates that high-level leaders who support and model the processes desired obtain better implementation results than those who do not. Because highly accepted systems do not automatically permeate an organization, and because training alone will not communicate to administrators that certain processes are desired, it is essential for the total environment of the organization to support the function of evaluation. Even with adequate support, one should not expect a new or highly modified system of evaluation to be implemented immediately; a time lag is likely to exist until the organization is completely ready for the process. Without readiness and use of evaluation at the highest levels of the school system, the time lag will extend into complete abandonment.

6 APPLICATIONS AND EXAMPLES

As one discusses concepts and theories of evaluation with practitioners, the statement is often made, "Well, that certainly sounds promising and logical, but could you tell me a location where all of this is occurring?" The implication is that if all of it is not in practice in a given location (or preferably, in a large number of locations) it will not work. And this may be correct. However, almost everything that has been discussed thus far in this book has been in practice in some school district, even though the total system described may not be in effect in any one district.

The purpose of this chapter is to provide examples of applications of the ideas presented. The examples will be of school districts* of a variety of sizes and locations, with different clientele and organizational goals. It is assumed that the differences exhibited in their approaches to the total system of evaluation are due to differences in the situations being faced and the constraints that obtain in these locations.

As one thinks about using the ideas presented and the examples and applications discussed, two strategies for change can be envisioned. First, one can adopt a *problem-reduction* approach. This approach identifies problems in the present system, finds ways of reducing or eliminating these problems, and adopts the mechanisms necessary to reduce the problems. This approach is considerably different from the second, which is basically an *ideal-approximation* approach. To use

---

*The use of examples in this chapter does not make any claim to describing normative practice, nor does it claim to describe the best practices in use at the present time. The districts described were obtained in the following way: First, a group of districts surveyed in 1970 were approached again for information and materials. (The initial study was concerned with teacher evaluation and selection. See Bolton, *Selection and Evaluation of Teachers*, 1973, Appendix 8, for list of school districts.) In addition, the school districts used as cases in the Phi Delta Kappa *NSPER:75* - National Symposium for Professors of Educational Research - (Gephart, Ingle, & Potter, 1977) plus the fifteen districts suggested as resources were asked for materials. Also, AASA was asked for a listing of school districts that had been used as cases for National Academy for School Executives/American Association of School Administrators (NASE/AASA) seminars in administrator evaluation. The materials received were examined, and in several cases telephone interviews were conducted with the superintendents.

this approach, one first designs what is considered to be an ideal system of evaluation. Then, an examination is made of the situation in which the system must operate, considering especially the constraints that exist. Adjustments are made in the ideal design, and the closest approximation to the ideal is implemented. Note that in the first approach, one might eliminate all of the problems in a given system and still have a rather inefficient and ineffective system—simply because the basic elements of the system are inadequate. The effectiveness of the second approach depends on the approximation to the ideal of the design and the constraints (perceived or real) that cause modifications to the design.

The intent of providing the concepts of the first five chapters and the applications and examples of this chapter is to encourage school personnel to adopt the second strategy in implementing administrator evaluation systems. It appears more profitable to conceptualize the ideal system and then to approximate it as closely as possible than to simply attempt to reduce the problems of a current system.

The examples of applications include elements of the evaluation system, characteristics of procedural manuals provided, and effectiveness of MBO procedures used.

Elements of the Evaluation System

Fifteen different elements of an evaluation system will be examined, and examples from different school districts will be provided. The following school districts were sampled: Andrews, Texas; Beaverton, Oregon; Bloomfield Hills, Michigan; Bloomington, Indiana; Hyde Park, New York; Kent, Washington; Lake Washington, Washington; Madison, Wisconsin; Montgomery County, Maryland; Osceola, Indiana; Philadelphia, Pennsylvania; Salem, Oregon; Salt Lake City, Utah; San Diego, California; and Seattle, Washington.

1. *Are there districts using a process that is cyclical and/or continuous?* Almost all of the school districts examined provided an annual cycle with progress reports in the interim period. The number of progress reports varied, and some did not require any specified number. A very few simply required an annual completion of an evaluation report. In most cases, the cycle coincided with the academic year. However, Osceola used a cycle that ran from Arpil to April; and Hyde Park ran from March 1 to March 1.

   The advantages claimed for the April–April cycle (or March–March) were that: (a) it assures a continuity of planning and implementation of the system in that evaluation activities occur from April to June (some systems require a report by April 15, and then nothing happens from that time until mid August or even October), and (b) the plans for the following year are made at such a time that modifications can be made over the summer months, assuring that there will be no delay caused by not knowing the thrust of the total district until after school begins in the autumn.

2. *Does the school district approach the task of administrator evaluation from a*

systems analysis perspective, in that there is an emphasis on input, process, and output (product)? In general, there was more emphasis on the process used by administrators than on the other two aspects. In some cases, there was little distinction between the process and product specified. For example, the distinction between process and product made by the Andrews system was that the product was specified as measurable. Although operational in definition, the same type of distinction was not made by other school districts.

Several districts did place an emphasis on analysis of the uniqueness of the situation and *input* variables. Madison spent one to one-and-a-half days on establishing the initial contract for performance with each administrator; much of this time was spent analyzing priorities in terms of the situational needs. Philadelphia incorporated a self-evaluation as part of the job description of administrators. Lake Washington used a job description plus a description of unique factors to the job. Beaverton had a self-appraisal worksheet, although this was used more with the newer administrators than with more experienced administrators. Hyde Park examined role expectations in relation to performance standards prior to setting goals on an individualized basis. Likewise, Andrews incorporated a diagnosis by the evaluatee and the evaluator prior to setting goals.

Specification of *output* variables usually depended on MBO procedures. However, a few districts specified some common output variables in rather specific terms. These districts included Osceola, Hyde Park, Seattle, Beaverton, Bloomfield Hills, and Madison.

3. *Does the system of evaluation include a conscious attempt to interrelate the processes and products of various levels of the organization?* In no case was there evidence that the product of a higher level in the organization was considered to be the process of the next lower level. However, several districts did mention the necessity of harmonizing the objectives of the lower level with those of the higher level. Such districts included Philadelphia, Lake Washington, Salt Lake City, and Osceola.

4. *Does the school district design its evaluation system for administrators so that it is related to other subsystems within the district?* There was considerable evidence that a systems approach was being used, in terms of the design of various subsystems. For example, Osceola related the evaluation of administrators to its Planning, Programming, Budgeting System (PPBS) approach to fiscal matters. Also, Osceola and Montgomery County related evaluation to programs. Several school districts (Salt Lake City, San Diego, Hyde Park, Beaverton, Bloomfield Hills, Madison, and Montgomery County) interrelated evaluation and in-service training programs. Likewise, some districts used evaluation to validate the selection process; they were Kent, Bloomfield Hills, and Montgomery County. Kent related the evaluation process to the instructional system, and Bloomfield Hills related it to placement processes.

5. *Does the evaluation system provide direction to the individual and to the organization?* In general, the district orientations in regard to this question ranged from

direct statements relating to specific district goals or standards to statements indicating a need to set specific objectives. School district goals were identified by Bloomfield Hills, Seattle (also included specific objectives), Salt Lake City (included specific objectives), Andrews, and Montgomery County. Roles or standards for administrators were specified by Bloomfield Hills, Kent, Beaverton, Hyde Park, Osceola, Andrews, and Montgomery County (for principals only; central office administrators did not have role specifications). Madison, Bloomington, Philadelphia, and San Diego had a more open-ended approach to specifying direction.

6. *Does the evaluation system provide a planning phase that includes the acquisition of resources needed to accomplish objectives?* In many cases, this was provided but in different ways. For example, Osceola provided this via a joint consideration of evaluation and PPBS. Beaverton, Kent, and Philadelphia provided an item on the planning forms that required consideration of resources. Madison required that it be included in the written description of the contract negotiated between the administrator and the evaluator. Some districts specified that the assistance of the supervisor would be provided in the accomplishment of objectives; these districts were Hyde Park, Madison, and San Diego (which also required that a report be made of the results of the assistance). Montgomery County specified that the type of resources needed should be identified and provided when possible.

7. *Does the system of evaluation for administrators provide for the making of intermediate decisions?* In most cases this element was included but in various ways. A midyear conference was required by Philadelphia, Lake Washington, and Andrews. Multiple conferences were required by Madison (3 required, 4 more usual), Kent (2 required, plus others optional), Hyde Park (2 required), and Osceola (2 as minimum). Bloomfield Hills required a monthly report, Salt Lake City did not specify how often the intermediate reports or conferences were to be made but indicated that they were required. Beaverton built the intermediate decisions into the targets set, and Bloomington did not require intermediate decisions to be made via conferences or reports.

8. *Is there evidence that the organization provides support for the process of evaluation of administrators?* A variety of evidences was provided for the support of the evaluation system. Numerous school districts provided well-designed materials: Osceola, Andrews, Salem, Hyde Park, Madison, Beaverton, Kent, Lake Washington, Montgomery County, and Seattle. Osceola and Hyde Park indicated that the evaluation of administrators was a specific commitment of the board of education. Training programs for evaluators of administrators were provided by Philadelphia and Hyde Park. Osceola emphasized the need for a team approach to the success of the evaluation system. Both Osceola and Salt Lake City specified who was to monitor the evaluation system, and Hyde Park clearly indicated who was to evaluate whom. Allocation of time to the evaluation process was mentioned by Hyde Park and Montgomery County (where there

was a special mention of the need for the evaluator to visit schools). Bloomfield Hills provided monitoring via monthly written reports.

9. *Is the evaluation system for administrators designed to facilitate the making of terminal decisions?* Terminal decisions may be made on a variety of matters. The types of decisions and the districts that participated in them (as evidenced by the materials used) are listed below:

   a. overall assessment of performance: Madison, Bloomfield Hills, Kent, Hyde Park, Osceola, and Andrews

   b. decisions to terminate assignment or continue in the same assignment: Bloomington, Kent, Lake Washington, Beaverton, Salt Lake City, and Osceola

   c. decisions regarding appeal procedures: Kent, Lake Washington, Andrews, and Seattle

   d. decisions regarding compensation: Madison, Osceola, Salt Lake City, and Bloomington

   e. assessment of accomplishment of objectives: Salt Lake City, Madison, Bloomfield Hills, Philadelphia, Kent, Beaverton, Hyde Park, Osceola, and Andrews

   f. determination to proceed with a more intensive evaluation process: Beaverton

10. *Does the administrator evaluation system include a self-evaluation component?* In some cases, self-evaluation was done for the purpose of diagnosis prior to establishing objectives; districts that used this approach included Andrews, Hyde Park, Beaverton, Osceola, and Philadelphia. Completion of the final summary report form by the evaluatee was required by Andrews, Seattle, Lake Washington, Bloomington, and Bloomfield Hills (requiring a final written report). In some cases, acquisition of information from clients of the administrators was optional, while in other cases it was required: Andrews (optional), Beaverton (required), Bloomington (required, but not anonymous), Montgomery County (faculty in school buildings required, others encouraged). Mutual agreement on final summary statements was included by Osceola and Hyde Park. Periodic written reports by the evaluatee were required by Salt Lake City and Bloomfield Hills.

11. *Does the administrator evaluation system include external evaluators?* In all cases examined, external evaluators were involved in all phases of the evaluation process. In most cases, this person was simply referred to as the "evaluator" or the "supervisor," but in Montgomery County the specific evaluator was identified. In Andrews the system provided for a prime evaluator, contributing evaluators, reviewer, and multiple evaluators (in cases where an individual was responsible to more than one person, e.g., an athletic director who worked with several high schools).

12. *Does the administrator evaluation system incorporate a set of common criteria for the administrators being evaluated?* In many cases this was done, but the manner of inclusion varied somewhat. For example, the job description was

used to individualize the evaluation process; however, Madison used it to specify common criteria for positions that were the same or similar. Common standards or criteria (some specifying rather definite indicators to be used) were included by Kent, Lake Washington, Beaverton, Seattle, Hyde Park, Salt Lake City, Osceola, Andrews, and Montgomery County (for principals, but not for central office administrators and supervisors). General characteristics or areas of responsibility were specified by Bloomington, Philadelphia, and San Diego. In specifying common standards or criteria, Seattle used a hierarchy consisting of *major concerns, tasks, performance criteria, and indicators.* The *major concerns* were identified as planning, managing, evaluating, interacting (both internal and external). When the *major concern* of planning, for example, was broken into its components, it included such *tasks* as establishing goals, organizing and assigning, involving others, and developing programs. The section for *indicators* was left blank to be filled in by the administrator and evaluator during the initial stage of evaluation. Salem also used a similar hierarchical structure for specifying criteria.

13. *Does the administrator evaluation system include the opportunity for individualized goal setting and individualized criteria?* Virtually all of the school districts examined included some form of individualized goal setting with accompanying forms. Many of the forms were rather open ended, suggesting that the structure for the objectives was determined more by the training of the evaluators than by the forms to be used. Kent divided the objectives into three categories: regular objectives, problem-solving objectives, and innovative objectives. Most other districts appeared to expect regular and sometimes problem-solving objectives to be handled by "job expectations" or "standards" or "criteria" that were common to all or to a subset of the total group of administrators; this would leave innovative objectives as the domain for writing objectives. The Kent system also contributed to the individualization of the process by using criterion-referenced scaling rather than norm-referenced scaling. Many of the forms for individualized goal setting included elements similar to those of Seattle: *objective* (Where are you going?), *strategies* (How do you get there?), *evaluative criteria* (How do you know when you're there?), *estimated completion date,* and *report of outcomes* (What happened?).

14. *How often does the evaluation of administrators occur?* Virtually all of the districts required some sort of annual evaluation for all administrators, with some having variations for special cases. Bloomfield Hills required more evaluations for new administrators, and Beaverton required more evaluations for administrators who were placed on "intensive evaluation." Salt Lake City and Madison had an annual evaluation plus any additional evaluations as agreed upon during the establishment of objectives. Districts requiring at least one evaluation conference in addition to the annual evaluation were Andrews, Lake Washington, Philadelphia, and Montgomery County, which also required an evaluation once every three years for administrators who had been in a current

position more than two years. Osceola required at least two evaluation conferences in addition to the annual evaluation. Bloomfield Hills required monthly written assessments of all administrators. In most cases, the schedule for when evaluations occurred was specified in written or outline form. However, Kent provided a Gantt chart (see p. 171) of the tasks to be done and the date when each task was to be completed. Andrews provided a visual display of activities in the form of a flow chart, which also included a date when the activities were to be completed. This flow chart was related to an overall model for evaluation.

15. *Were the purposes for evaluating administrators clearly specified in the written documents regarding evaluation?* Districts provided either a rather general or an overall statement about the purpose(s) of evaluation, or a rather detailed and specific list. Those providing a general overall statement included Beaverton, Bloomington, Madison, Osceola, Salt Lake City, and Seattle. Those including a specific list of purposes included Andrews, Bloomfield Hills, Hyde Park, Kent, Lake Washington, San Diego, and Montgomery County. In four cases, the assumptions back of the evaluation system were also listed: Andrews, Hyde Park, Madison, and Montgomery County. One school district, Salt Lake City, provided an incentive for completing objectives by incorporating a 2 percent increase in annual salary if the objectives were completed as planned. This was not considered as a merit system but a payment for performance. All objectives had to be met, and only a very small number of administrators failed to meet this goal each year.

A summary of the elements of the evaluation system is provided in table 6.1.

Characteristics of Manuals of Procedures

Many school districts have developed manuals describing procedures used in the evaluation of administrators. The characteristics of these manuals are described below, and the districts that included good examples of these characteristics in their manuals are identified.

1. Provides definitions of terms used in the manual: Andrews, Hyde Park, Kent, and Osceola
2. Specifies who evaluates whom, responsibilities of the evaluators: Andrews, Beaverton, Hyde Park, and Montgomery County
3. Describes characteristics of the evaluation system, including assumptions: Bloomfield Hills, Hyde Park, and Montgomery County
4. Provides examples of objectives or targets: Hyde Park, Madison, Kent, and Osceola
5. Provides for monitoring or evaluation of the system of evaluation: Osceola and Salt Lake City
6. Emphasizes mutual goal setting: Osceola
7. Defines the roles of administrators: Andrews and Osceola

Table 6.1
SUMMARY OF ELEMENTS OF EVALUATION SYSTEM PROVIDED IN VARIOUS SCHOOL DISTRICTS

Elements of the Evaluation System	Andrews, Tex.	Beaverton, Oreg.	Bloomfield Hills, Mich.	Bloomington, Ind.	Hyde Park, N.Y.	Kent, Wash.	Lake Washington, Wash.	Madison, Wisc.	Montgomery Co., Md.	Osceola, Ind.	Philadelphia, Pa.	Salem, Oreg.	Salt Lake City, Utah	San Diego, Calif.	Seattle, Wash.
1. Cyclical process	x	x	x	x	x		x	x	x	x	x	x	x		x
• cycle from April–April										x					
• cycle from March–March					x										
2. Systems analysis															
• analysis of input	x	x			x		x	x			x				
• analysis of process	x	x	x	x	x		x	x	x	x	x	x	x	x	x
• analysis of output		x	x		x			x		x					x
3. Interrelate process/product of levels							x			x	x		x		
4. Relate to other subsystems															
• PPBS and budgeting										x					
• program									x	x					
• in-service training		x	x		x				x	x			x	x	
• selection			x			x			x						
• instruction						x									
• placement			x												
5. Provides direction															
• district goals identified	x		x						x				x		x
• roles or standards specified	x	x	x		x		x		x	x					
• rather open ended				x				x			x			x	
6. Provision for resources															
• via PPBS											x				
• on forms, specify		x				x						x			
• on contract, include								x							
• assistance of supervisor						x		x						x	
• identify, provide when possible										x					
7. Intermediate decisions															
• midyear conferences	x							x				x			
• multiple conferences						x	x		x	x					
• monthly written			x												
• unspecified, but required													x		
• built into target setting		x													
• none required					x										
8. Support for process of evaluation															
• well-designed materials	x	x			x	x	x	x	x	x			x		x
• commitment of board of education					x					x					

Table 6.1 *(Continued)*

Elements of the Evaluation System	Andrews, Tex.	Beaverton, Oreg.	Bloomfield Hills, Mich.	Bloomington, Ind.	Hyde Park, N.Y.	Kent, Wash.	Lake Washington, Wash.	Madison, Wisc.	Montgomery Co., Md.	Osceola, Ind.	Philadelphia, Pa.	Salem, Oreg.	Salt Lake City, Utah	San Diego, Calif.	Seattle, Wash.
• training program					x						x				
• emphasis on team approach										x					
• specifies who monitors program										x			x		
• specifies who evaluates whom					x										
• commitment to time needed					x				x						
• written report with response			x												
9. Terminal decisions															
• overall assessment	x		x		x	x		x		x				x	
• terminate or continue		x		x		x	x			x			x		
• provides appeal procedures	x					x	x								x
• regarding compensation				x				x		x			x		
• re: objectives accomplished	x	x	x			x	x	x		x	x		x		
• to determine intensive evaluation		x													
10. Self-evaluation component															
• as diagnosis at beginning	x	x			x						x	x			
• complete final form	x		x	x			x								x
• client information (req. or opt.)	o	r		r						r					
• mutual final form					x						x				
• periodic reports			x										x		
11. Outsider as evaluator															
• superordinate	x	x	x	x	x	x	x	x	x	x	x	x	x	x	x
• multiple evaluators + reviewer	x														
• specific person specified										x					
12. Common criteria provided															
• job description							x								
• standards or criteria	x	x			x	x	x			x	x		x		x
• general characteristics				x								x		x	
• uses hierarchy of standards													x		x
13. Individualized objectives															
• via MBO	x	x	x	x	x	x	x	x	x	x	x	x	x	x	x
• categorizes objectives, 3 types							x								
14. How often?															
• annual (min.)		x		x	x	x									
• annual plus one (min.)	x						x		x				x		
• annual plus two (min.)										x					

Table 6.1 *(Continued)*

Elements of the Evaluation System	Andrews, Tex.	Beaverton, Org.	Bloomfield Hills, Mich.	Bloomington, Ind.	Hyde Park, N.Y.	Kent, Wash.	Lake Washington, Wash.	Madison, Wisc.	Montgomery Co., Md.	Osceola, Ind.	Philadelphia, Pa.	Salem, Oreg.	Salt Lake City, Utah	San Diego, Calif.	Seattle, Wash.
• annual plus what is in objectives									x				x		
• monthly written assessments			x												
• more for new administrators		x	x												
• visual display of deadlines	x					x									
15. Purposes stated?															
• general overall statement		x		x					x	x			x		x
• specific list	x		x		x	x	x		x					x	
• assumptions also listed	x				x				x	x					
• includes payment for completed objectives													x		

8. Provides rules for dealing with ineffective or incompetent administrators: Kent
9. Requires that reasons be given for specifying objectives: Hyde Park and Philadelphia
10. Provides a hierarchy of goals: Salem and Seattle
11. Provides a time schedule in the form of: (a) a list of activities: Bloomfield Hills, Lake Washington, and Montgomery County; (b) a flow chart: Andrews, Beaverton, Philadelphia, and San Diego; and (c) a Gantt chart: Kent

MBO Procedures

ADVANTAGES

School districts that were engaged in MBO procedures were asked to identify the best features of their procedures, i.e., in what ways they were advantageous to the school district. Their responses were quite varied and included the following ideas:

1. The MBO procedures resulted in more productivity, with the administrative team moving in the same direction: Bloomington, Hyde Park, Kent, and Osceloa.
2. It provided self-correction, controls over the operation of schools, and better planning: Hyde Park, Kent, Osceola, and Salt Lake City.

3. It provided employee motivation and higher morale: Beaverton, Bloomington, Madison, and Salt Lake City.
4. It was not a system of evaluation "after the fact": Andrews and Beaverton.
5. It facilitated communication about the job; therefore, a person knew his boss' perceptions: Hyde Park and Osceola.
6. It provided each individual the opportunity of knowing where he stood and what to expect: Madison and Osceola.
7. It was nonthreatening, since it provided the opportunity for mutual goal setting: Beaverton and Bloomington.
8. It provided the stimulus for treatment of administrators as professionals: Andrews.
9. It promoted staff development: Osceola.
10. It recognized the freedom of action necessary to accomplish results: Osceola.
11. It was an individualized process: Beaverton.
12. It was a systematic approach characterized by accuracy, consistency, and thorough reporting: Bloomfield Hills and Montgomery.
13. The district knew what was happening in the classroom as a result of MBO: Bloomfield Hills.
14. It provided feedback on specific things rather than general information: Bloomfield Hills.
15. It provided support for other activities and systems, since it was the same basic structure as that used for teachers: Montgomery County.

DISADVANTAGES

Management by objectives was not found to be without problems, however. The major ones identified by the districts interviewed included the following:

1. There was too much paperwork: Andrews and Osceola.
2. At first, the objectives were insignificant, seemingly due to low commitment to the process: Andrews and Salt Lake City.
3. It was too complex for those involved: Osceola.
4. The performance criteria were too general: Osceola.
5. Termination of employment by means of the system was not easy—but it was better than without this system: Salt Lake City.
6. Certain unexpected events tended to crowd out monitoring and working with the process: Hyde Park.
7. There was too much variation in skill and commitment to the task: Beaverton.
8. There was not enough control over those who were somewhat removed from the top-level management: Kent.
9. Uncertainty reigned regarding how much to report on the progress review: Bloomfield Hills.
10. The process was too time consuming: Bloomington and Madison.

11. It was difficult to attach merit to MBO: Bloomington and Madison.
12. Collecting data was difficult: Montgomery County.
13. Too many administrators reported to one evaluator: Montgomery County.
14. Some evaluators and evaluatees had difficulty analyzing needs: Montgomery County.

It should be noted that the best features and problem areas encountered with MBO were identified in response to open-ended questions, i.e., *not* in response to a complete listing. Therefore, many of the districts might have checked additional items on either list if they had been provided a more complete listing. What the list represents is a set of items taken from those first mentioned by the person responding to the question, and they may or may not represent the most significant item on the list for the school district identified.

Examples of Procedures and Materials

The procedures and materials provided in this section are either relatively uncommon or are considered to be good examples of common practice. In no case are the total procedures or forms of a given school district presented but parts of several are presented to illustrate practices worthy of consideration by other school districts.

GENERAL PROCEDURES AND SPECIFICATIONS OF RESPONSIBILITY

Many school districts provide information in a set of written materials that describe the general procedures to be used. Selected from such descriptions are the following:

Definition of terms	Andrews
Assumptions	Montgomery County
Purposes and Objectives	Montgomery County
Characteristics of a School-Based Evaluation System	Montgomery County
Objectives of Appraisal	Hyde Park
Who Evaluates Whom	Andrews
Evaluation Process—Options	Andrews
Development of Routine Objectives	Salem
Purpose, Characteristics, Indicators, and Measurable Performance Objectives	Salem
High School Standards and Indicators	Bloomfield Hills
Management Contract Example—Primarily Evaluates Actions Rather Than Outcomes	Madison
Management Contract Example—Evaluation of Quantifiable Empirical Data	Madison
Client Evaluation	Osceola

1 - Andrews

DEFINITION OF TERMS

EBO
Evaluation by objectives - a process that relates the assessment of performance to specific objectives and action plans cooperatively determined by evaluatee and evaluator

EVALUATEE
The individual being evaluated

PRIME EVALUATOR
The person normally serving as the evaluatee's immediate supervisor and the one who makes assessments of his or her performance

CONTRIBUTING EVALUATOR
An individual having a staff relationship with the evaluatee and who serves in a supplemental evaluating capacity

CLIENTS
Those persons whom the evaluatee serves. Examples: clients of a principal - parents, teachers, and students; clients of a director - teachers, principals, and those who may report directly to the director

PERFORMANCE AREA
A major aspect of the evaluatee's duties and responsibilities

PERFORMANCE CATEGORY (INDICATOR)
A subelement of a performance area

DIAGNOSIS
The process by which the evaluatee and evaluator determine the status of current performance of the former

SPECIFIC OBJECTIVE
A job target that is responsive to a particular need that is identified as a result of the diagnosis process

ACTION PLANS
Strategies designed to achieve specific objectives

TASKS AND ACTIVITIES
Elements or specific steps in action plans that tell what will be done, when, and by whom

ANALYSIS
Clarifying the meaning and implications of the results achieved in the evaluation process

FOLLOW-UP
Making the necessary determinations and plans for the next evaluation cycle

MONITORING
Making observations and contacts with the evaluatee during the evaluation process to obtain information that will indicate how successfully the specific objectives are being achieved

2 - Montgomery County

Assumptions

A humane and effective system of personnel evaluation must have as its base certain assumptions about man's potential as a satisfied, productive worker. The Task Force on Professional Evaluation proposed a school-based administrator evaluation system built on the following assumptions:

1. When there is an environment that is conducive to respect for the worth and dignity of the individual, he will be better able to respect the worth and dignity of others.

2. Organizations achieve their objectives only in part from external direction. Individuals are motivated by participants in setting both personal and organizational objectives. Individuals committed by involvement to the achievement of objectives will also experience greater satisfaction.

3. When there is mutual participation in the total work situation and in the evaluation process, opportunities to exercise a relatively high degree of imagination, ingenuity, and creativity are made possible for all involved in the process.

4. The individual performs better and with greater satisfaction when there is opportunity for recognition of work well done.

5. An evaluation process which contains the elements of self-appraisal as well as appraisal by others according to agreed-upon objectives contributes to the improved performance of the individual.

3 - Montgomery County

Purposes

The assumptions given above are the bases of a belief that the primary purpose of a school-based administrator evaluation system is to help principals and assistant principals improve their effectiveness.

The evaluation system must also serve these purposes for the management of the school system:

> It must facilitate the achievement of the goals of the Montgomery County Public Schools and of individual schools.

> It must contribute to good morale by demonstrating just and equitable personnel practices.

> It must be a source of motivation for continuing improvement.

> It must facilitate communication and cooperation among school-based administrators and other members of the profession, students, and the community.

> It should provide feedback which can be used to identify in-service needs of principals and assistant principals; to appraise the effectiveness of recruitment, selection, and placement of school-based administration; and to appraise the effectiveness or adequacy of human and material supports for principals and assistant principals.

Objectives

A system of school-based administrator evaluation has short-range objectives which enable the individual and the school system to work toward the long-range purposes. All objectives of the evaluation system must be clearly stated and used as guides for determining the characteristics of the form and the process used and for appraising the effectiveness of the system of school-based administrator evaluation.

The objectives of principal and assistant principal evaluation are to:

1. Communicate with the principal or assistant principal about his performance on specific aspects of his work

2. Establish objectives for school-based administrator improvement or for emphasis in indicated areas

3. Provide information for use in identifying and counseling principals and assistant principals for promotion or other assignment

4. Provide the superintendent of schools with data which will enable him to classify professional certificates as prescribed by the Public School Laws of Maryland

4 - Montgomery County

<u>Characteristics of a School-Based Administrator Evaluation System</u>

The system for the evaluation of school-based administrators described in the following pages is built upon the preceding assumptions, goal, and objectives. This evaluation system has the following characteristics:

1. Principal and assistant principal performance will be evaluated on specific job objectives called criteria for school-based administrator effectiveness.

2. The evaluation process is divided into two parts. The major part consists of conferences between the assistant superintendent and principal and between the principal and assistant principal which will assist the school-based administrator in analyzing and improving his own effectiveness. His needs for support and assistance will be identified and provided to the extent possible. Throughout the year and in preparation for the conference, the principal or assistant principal will gather and use a variety of data for self-appraisal.

    The second part of the evaluation process is the completion of the evaluation form for permanent personnel records. At the evaluation conference, the evaluator and evaluatee review germane data gathered. The evaluator records his assessment of the evaluatee's performance on the evaluation form, which becomes part of the principal's or assistant principal's permanent personnel file.

    It should be stressed that the first step of the evaluation process focuses on data-gathering for the principal's or assistant principal's use in analyzing and improving his own effectiveness. The only time evaluative judgments are recorded about the school-based administrator's performance is that point at which the evaluation form is completed and becomes part of his personnel record.

5 - Hyde Park

OBJECTIVES OF APPRAISAL

The objectives which the Hyde Park Appraisal Program hopes to achieve are:

1. Clarify the performance expectations of the individual; i.e., make duties and responsiblitities of the appraisee and appraiser more clear.

2. Establish both short and long term targets.

3. Bring about a closer working relationship between the appraisee and appraiser.

4. Make appraisal relevant to on-going job performance.

5. Establish "ground rules" or plans for both the appraisee and appraiser to follow up on "target" achievement.

6. Maintain accurate records of all appraisal conferences and other appraisee-appraiser contacts.

7. Assess the effectiveness of job performance both by self-appraisal and appraisal by the appraiser; i.e., make it a cooperative process.

8. Conduct meaningful appraisal conferences directed toward improving performance.

9. Establish appropriate ways for follow-up of actions needed for further improvement.

10. Keep appraisal a dynamic process; assess its effectiveness periodically; revise it as necessary.

WHO EVALUATES WHOM

Evaluatee	Prime Evaluator	Contributing Evaluator(s)
Asst.Supt. of Instruction	Superintendent	
Director of Business Affairs	Superintendent	
Director of Operations/ Plant Services	Superintendent	
Tax Assessor/Collector	Superintendent	
Athletic Director	Superintendent	B.,C.,D.
Principal/Elementary Schools (4)	Superintendent	A.,B.,C.
Principal/Middle School (1)	Superintendent	A.,B.,C.
Principal/High School (1)	Superintendent	A.,B.,C.
Director of Accounting	Director of Business Affairs	
Director of Vocational Education	Director of Business Affairs	H. S. and M. S. Principals
Reading Coordinator	Asst. Supt. of Instruction	
Special Education Coordinator	Director of Business Affairs	A.,D.
Visiting Teacher	Director of Business Affairs	A.,D.
Assistant Principal	Principal, High School	A.

Key:

       A = Assistant Superintendent of Instruction
       B = Director of Business Affairs
       C = Director of Operations and Plant Service
       D = Principals

7 - Andrews

Evaluation Process - Options

The relationship between evaluatee and evaluator/s depends upon the level of position in the organization. In general, whenever administrators are available who can function in the role of consulting evaluator, it is the policy of the Andrews Independent School District that they be involved in the evaluation process.

The guiding principles governing evaluation relationships are as follows: (1) the person having the direct supervision over the evaluatee should serve as prime evaluator; (2) those persons who have staff relationships with the evaluatee and who can help set appropriate objectives, assist in the implementation of the action plans and participate in the assessment of results can serve as contributing evaluators.

OPTIONS

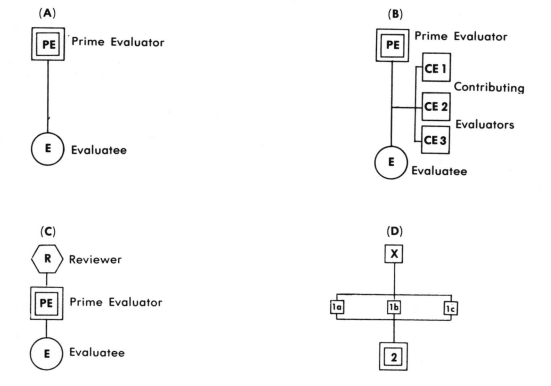

8 - Salem

DEVELOPMENT OF ROUTINE OBJECTIVES

STEP ONE

IDENTIFY PURPOSES OR REASONS FOR EVALUATING POSITION

STEP TWO

IDENTIFY THE CHARACTERISTICS OR FUNCTIONS THAT RELATE
TO THE POSITION BEING EVALUATED.

STEP THREE

IDENTIFY THE INDICATORS OR TASKS THAT WOULD INDICATE
THE FUNCTION IS BEING PERFORMED

STEP FOUR

STATE THE INDICATORS (TASKS) IN PERFORMANCE TERMS

1. MEASUREMENT SHOULD BE REDUCED TO QUANTIFIABLE TERMS
    WHENEVER POSSIBLE.

2. IF NOT POSSIBLE OR VERBAL DESCRIPTION OF OUTCOMES.

9 - Salem

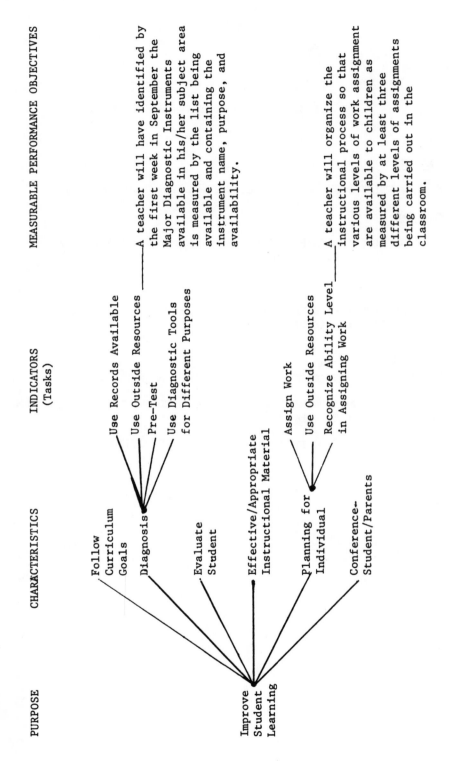

Figure 1

10 - Bloomfield Hills

BLOOMFIELD HILLS SCHOOLS

HIGH SCHOOL STANDARDS AND INDICATORS FOR 1977-78

INDICATOR	STANDARD
	BASIC SKILLS
1. Test of Academic Progress, Math and Reading	a. Seventy-five percent of the Bloomfield Hills' 11th grade students will achieve a score at or higher than the 50th percentile against national norms.
	b. Twenty-five percent of the Bloomfield Hills' 11th grade students will achieve a score at or higher than the 90th percentile against national norms.
2. Criterion-referenced Tests	At least 85% of the students will successfully meet the stated objectives of courses in which they are enrolled.

9/13/77
ss

11 - Madison

(Management Contract <u>EXAMPLE</u>--Primarily Evaluates Actions Rather Than Outcomes)

This would be <u>one</u> of four or five objectives

I. Mr. Principal will develop a program intended to increase and improve among his parent clientele relevant public information about the activities and curriculum of the school. In addition to information, Mr. Principal will provide the machinery through which parents can be involved in both a supportive and consultative role regarding the school program. To accomplish this he will do the following:

A. Organize a parent advisory council including three parents from each grade level. This council will meet monthly for briefings of the ongoing program, to express concerns or ask questions about the school program and to explore means of continuous parent information/involvement.

B. The principal will mail a newletter home every six weeks that provides descriptive general information about the program, describes any major or minor research or evaluation studies going on within the school, important dates of meetings to be held, and other professional/research information that might be helpful to parents. He may include a bibliography of books/materials that interested parents might want to read to further their understanding (e.g., <u>Schools Without Failure</u>). In the newsletter he will also answer questions posed by the Parent Advisory Group and questions sent in by parents on the "Parent Question Form" (a tear-off form in the back of each newsletter).

C. He will devise a parent volunteer program which provides a means for interested parents to volunteer their services (once a week, once a month, etc.) to the school. He will write materials describing the kinds of volunteer opportunities the school has open and how the parent can be most helpful in manning that position. He will hold an orientation session at the end of each volunteer day (or maybe monthly for regulars) indicating observations, suggestions, etc.

D. He will randomly select three children a month and write a personal letter to the parents of those children stating the progress the children are making.

E. He will personally invite (a number of) parents each month to visit school for the day and have a discussion with them at the end of their visitation.

II. In evaluation and support of this program the Area Director will:

A. (In reference to I-A) will attend at least one meeting a quarter of the Parent Advisory Group and two such meetings if requested by the principal.

He will evaluate the principal's role in terms of relevant content of information, prior preparation for the meeting and ability to answer questions. In those meetings not attended he will examine the minutes of the meeting in regard to information presented and questions answered.

B. (In reference to I-B) will receive a copy of the newsletter and subjectively evaluate content, relevance and recommendations.

C. (In reference to I-C) will attend the orientation and review sessions of volunteer parents, examine the materials developed for the volunteers and will examine the cumulative "end-of-the-day" forms. The orientation session/materials/forms will be evaluated as to evidence of preparation, logical placement of volunteers, and following through on observations.

D. (In reference to I-B) will receive copies of personal letters sent to parents and evaluate them in terms of thoroughness and comprehension to laymen.

E. (In reference to I-E) will sit in on at least one "end-of-the-day" discussion or two if requested by principal. Means of evaluating these discussions and the parent day in school will be defined and agreed to by the principal and Area Director.

III. A. Area Director will make arrangements with the Public Information Office (central office) to provide assistance to the principal in the development of the newsletter.

B. Area Director will make arrangements with the coordinator of science (?), math (?) and reading to provide the principal with appropriate bibliography/research material which the principal may want to include in his newsletter.

IV. Formal review sessions will be held on the week of November 15, January 12, March 25 and June 1.

V. No additional information needed.

12 - Madison

(Management Contract EXAMPLE--Evaluation of Quantifiable Empirical Data)

This would be one of four or five objectives

I. Mr. Principal will develop a procedure to show quantifiable improvement in the student's comprehension of mathematics as defined by acceptable standardized tests as well as logically developed criteria referenced evaluations. To do this he will:

12 - Madison (Cont.)

    A. Develop a document showing standardized scores over the past three years. These scores would be grade level and show standard deviations from norm. This would establish a base line.

    B. Develop with the faculty and Curriculum Department behaviorally stated criteria references.

    C. Develop instrument and test students against criteria reference identified in B above.

    D. Conduct at least one inservice meeting per month with staff which focuses on improvement of math teaching/learning. Cooperation with Curriculum Department will be arranged by Area Director.

    E. Hold one teacher conference with each teacher per month to discuss progress and review teaching techniques related to behaviorally stated goals.

    F. Administer standardized tests and tests against criteria references to show improvement in mathematics performance.

II. Area Director will:

    A. Review data collected by standardized tests no later than October 15.

    B. Receive for review behaviorally stated criteria references identified in I-B.

    C. Receive copy of test scores against criteria references as identified in I-C.

    D. Attend one inservice meeting per quarter as identified in I-D and one teacher conference per quarter as identified in I-E.

    E. Receive and review test results identified in I-F.

III.

    A. Area Director will make arrangements through the Curriculum Department to secure the assistance of the Coordinator of Mathematics for assistance in developing behaviorally stated criteria references and to develop the necessary inservice workshops to facilitate this program. The amount of time applied by the Coordinator of Mathematics will be cooperatively agreed to among the principal, the Coordinator and the Area Director.

    B. The Area Director will make arrangements to secure any agreed upon standardized tests within sufficient time for their use.

IV. Official review sessions will be held on November 2, January 3, March 15 and June 1.

V. A study of behaviorally stated criteria references for mathematics from the Santa Fe, New Mexico school system is underway. If they prove to be adaptable to the Madison Public Schools, the staff will not need to create a new set as cited in Part I of this agreement.

13 - Osceola

NAME_____

V - F

CLIENT EVALUATION OF

PENN-HARRIS-MADISON
PERFORMANCE-BASED APPRAISAL PLAN
(Appraisee)

Directions: Please complete and forward this questionnaire to the
Planning, Evaluation and Staff Development Office. We
would like to have the completed questionniare returned
by April 15 following the appraisal time period. Thank
you for your help.

A. Indicators of Administrative Performance

1. In your opinion, does Appendix A (Indicators of Administrative
Performance) direct the appraisee's attention to the important
key result areas of administrative performance which are related
to effective educational administration?

YES_____   NO_____   UNDECIDED_____

If your answer is no, to what additional behaviors within each
performance area of Administrator Performance should this plan
direct the appraisee's attention?

2. Is there a need to include additional performance area?

YES_____   NO_____

If so, what performance areas would you suggest be included?

13 - Osceola (Cont.)

3. It is possible to build an appropriate role description of your position by comparing the Indicators of Administrative Performance in the eight performance areas with your formal job description?

   YES _____   NO _____

   If no, what procedure would you suggest to correlate the Indicators of Administrative Performance with your particular job responsibilities?

B. Appraisal Procedures

   1. Is the appraisal time period from April 1st of one year to April 1st of the succeeding year of appropriate duration and placement within the calendar year to achieve the objectives stated for the appraisal plan?

      YES _____   NO _____

      If no, what time period would you suggest and for what reason?

   2. In your opinion, is everyone on the Penn-Harris-Madison Superintendency Team being appraised who should be appraised?

      YES _____   NO _____

      If no, who do you think should be appraised that isn't being appraised?

13 - Osceola (Cont.)

3. Do you think the Appraisal Team arrangement has contributed significantly to the performance-based appraisal plan?

   YES_____   NO_____

   If yes, in what specific ways have other Penn-Harris-Madison administrators served as a resource person in your self-appraisal plan?

   If no, what procedure do you think would be more helpful to you?

4. Do you think that annual appraisal program for administrators in Penn-Harris-Madison is appropriate and realistic?

   YES_____   NO_____

   If no, what frequency of appraisal would you suggest for the Penn-Harris-Madison Superintendency Team?

5. Please indicate to what extent each of the following types of conferences with your Appraisal Team contributed to your overall performance:

   a. Objective Setting Conference(s) Very Helpful Helpful No Help

   b. Progress Conference(s)   Very Helpful Helpful No Help

   c. Final Conference(s)   Very Helpful Helpful No Help

13 - Osceola (Cont.)

5. (Continued)

If any of the conferences with your Appraisal Team were of
<u>no</u> <u>help</u>, please state the reasons why as you perceive them.

6. In your opinion, did the various types of conferences with
your Appraisal Team help you to improve your administrative
and/or supervisory performance?

YES_____   NO_____

If your answer is yes, please state specifically how these conferences helped you to improve your administrative and/or
supervisory performance.

If your answer is no, in what ways could your conferences
have been improved?

7. What suggestions do you have for improving each type of conference with your Appraisal Team?

a. Objective Setting Conference(s)

13 - Osceola (Cont.)

    b.   Progress Conference(s)

    c.   Final Conference(s)

8. Did you feel free to discuss with your Appraisal Team their suggestions for improvement of your performance?

    YES_____   NO_____

    If your answer is yes, what made you feel free to discuss your performance?

    If your answer is no, why not?

9. Did you find that you were able to carry out the Appraisal Team's suggestions for improving your professional performance?

    YES_____   NO_____

    If so, why?

166

10. Did you find the appraisal steps and time schedule to be appropriate and realistic?

    YES_____   NO_____

    If your answer is no, please make suggestions for improving the sequence and time schedule.

11. Did you feel that your immediate superior fulfilled a helpful role in planning and implementing your self-appraisal program?

    YES_____   NO_____

    If your answer is yes, please indicate specifically how your immediate superior provided assistance to you.

    If your answer is no, please describe how your immediate superior could have been more helpful.

C. Self-Improvement Program

    1. Did you feel the development of a self-appraisal plan to be useful?

       YES_____   NO_____

13 - Osceola (Cont.)

2. Were you able to carry out your plan for self-improvement?

   YES_____   NO_____

   If not, describe as specifically as possible what prevented
   you from doing so.

3. Did you find that the strengths and weaknesses which you
   identified in developing a self-appraisal plan corresponded
   closely with the strengths and weaknesses identified by your
   immediate superior?

   YES_____   NO_____

   If your answer is no, in what ways did your judgment differ
   from your immediate superior's?

4. What suggestions do you have for improving the Objective
   Setting Conference procedure and forms?

5. Describe your feelings about the value of developing a self-
   appraisal plan.

13 - Osceola (Cont.)

6. Did you utlize client evaluation as a dimension of your self-improvement plan?

YES_____   NO_____

If yes, explain the nature and details of the client evaluation.

D. General

1. Did you receive all the assistance for improvement of your professional performance that you desired?

YES_____   NO_____

If your answer is no, what additional assistance did you desire that you did not receive?

2. Do you feel that your program of self-appraisal during the period made a direct contribution to the advancement of the teaching-learning process in the Penn-Harris-Madison School system?

YES_____   NO_____

If your answer is yes, please specify the contribution.

13 - Osceola (Cont.)

3. Do you feel that your program of self-appraisal during this appraisal period made a direct contribution to the advancement of the goals and objectives of the Penn-Harris-Madison School system?

   YES_____   NO_____

   If your answer is yes, please specify how:

4. Do you feel that your overall performance appraisal by your immediate superior was fair and accurately reflected your contribution to the education of youth in Penn-Harris-Madison?

   YES_____   NO_____

   If your answer is no, what suggestions do you have for improving this dimension of the appraisal program?

5. Did you receive effective supervisory assistance on a systematic basis from your immediate superior?

   YES_____   NO_____

   If your answer is no, what specific suggestions would you make to improve the quantity and quality of supervisory assistance from your immediate superior?

SCHEDULE OF ACTIVITIES

In many of the descriptive materials furnished by school districts, a schedule of expected activities is included. In some cases, this listing of activities is displayed in visual form. The two cases provided here show the schedule of events in a flowchart form according to stages (Andrews) and by means of a Gantt chart (Kent).

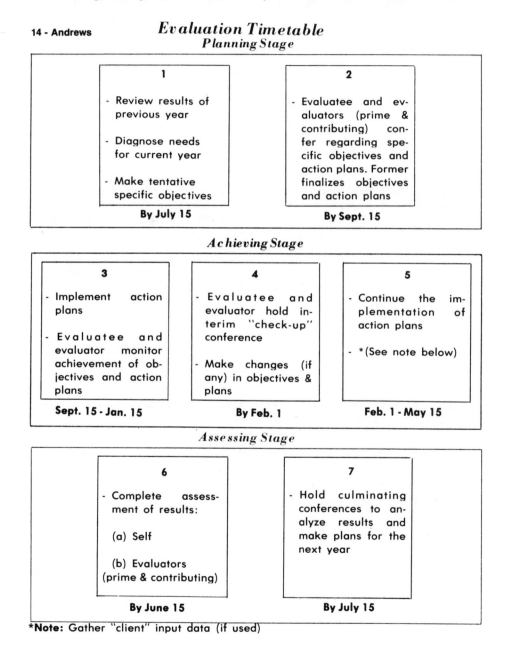

14 - Andrews   *Evaluation Timetable*
Planning Stage

1

- Review results of previous year

- Diagnose needs for current year

- Make tentative specific objectives

By July 15

2

- Evaluatee and evaluators (prime & contributing) confer regarding specific objectives and action plans. Former finalizes objectives and action plans

By Sept. 15

Achieving Stage

3

- Implement action plans

- Evaluatee and evaluator monitor achievement of objectives and action plans

Sept. 15 - Jan. 15

4

- Evaluatee and evaluator hold interim "check-up" conference

- Make changes (if any) in objectives & plans

By Feb. 1

5

- Continue the implementation of action plans

- *(See note below)

Feb. 1 - May 15

Assessing Stage

6

- Complete assessment of results:

  (a) Self

  (b) Evaluators (prime & contributing)

By June 15

7

- Hold culminating conferences to analyze results and make plans for the next year

By July 15

*****Note:** Gather "client" input data (if used)

PROJECT PLANNING & INFORMATION SYSTEM

15 - Kent

CERTIFICATED/CLASSIFIED EMPLOYEES
EVALUATION, PROBATION & NON-RENEWAL

◇ SCHEDULED
◆ COMPLETE

	Sep	Oct	Nov	Dec	Jan	Feb	Mar	Apr	May	Jun	Jul	Aug
Certificated Employees Evaluation												
New Employees:												
. observation compl.				◇*								
All Certificated Employees:												
.Preassessment conference			15 ◇									
.Est. MBO's												
.Performance Objs												
.Evaluation compl												
Admin Empl's					15 ◇					20 ◇		
Adm Empl's Copy to Area Mgr									15 ◇	23 ◇		
Other Empl's												
Other Empl's on Prob. Status						◇		◇	◇			
Other Empl's Copy to Supt										10 ◇		
.Notif'tn of employees not meeting minimum requirements												
Certificated Probation (Incl Act'n on Prov'nl emp's not being cons for re-emp)												
.Report poss probtn to Area Mgr in writing;cc employee				15 ◇	20 ◇							
.Evaluation Report						◇			◇			
.Area Mgr & Prin decide on probtn Recomm & report to Supt						◇	◇	◇				
.Supt notifies Employee									◇ ◇◇◇			
.Progress report to Area Mgrs									15 ◇			
.Probation ends												
.Area Mgr's reports to Supt.												
.Supt notifies employees												
Classified Employees Evaluation												
New Employees:(Evaluated 90 days after employment)									15 ◇			
Notification of Termination							15 ◇		◇			
Annual Evaluation												

*This date fits those employees who are hired by September 1; all other certificated employees are to be observed 90 days after they begin employment.

-69-

FORMS FOR SETTING GOALS AND OBJECTIVES

Many of the forms in this section have similar elements but different formats. In addition, several have relatively unique elements: Beaverton includes a preappraisal worksheet for analysis and determination of where efforts should be spent on objectives. Beaverton also includes a specific form for intensive evaluation of a person who is having difficulties of one sort or another. Philadelphia includes a job description on one form; Osceola and Bloomington have a relatively detailed explanation of how the objectives will be set. Seattle has a general goal-setting form plus aids for goal setting that break down major concerns into tasks, performance criteria, and indicators; and Osceola and Kent provide examples of completed forms.

10

16 - Beaverton   EVALUATION BY OBJECTIVES PROGRAM

SUPERVISOR APPRAISAL WORKSHEET

This evaluation instrument will be used in conjunction with the job description and priorities which apply to the administrator being evaluated.

The numbered statements below are the STANDARDS for which you are to gather data and indicate your suggestions for eventual use in the target setting conference. Each lettered indicator of the STANDARD must be considered and placed in a minimum of one of the spaces provided.

A standard must become a target if an indicator is placed in the Unacceptable space. An indicator placed in the Target space may or may not become a target based upon mutual selection by the supervisor and administrator in the target setting conference.

This appraisal form is to be completed by you to be used in the target setting conference.

INSTRUCTIONS: Enter the number of the Indicator in the appropriate space.

EXAMPLE:

AREA 1: MANAGERIAL SKILLS   Effective management necessitates the
                                   use of organizational skills and the use
                                   of alternative methods of decision making.

STANDARD 1: Decision Making

Target	Not a target at this time	Collecting data	Unacceptable
b	c	a	

INDICATORS
   a. using systematic methods of decision making.
   b. employing alternative methods of decision making.
   c. basing decisions on building/District/state policies
      and regulations.

ADMINISTRATOR EVALUATION PROGRAM
Self-Appraisal Worksheet

Administrator
Supervisor
Date

AREA 1: MANAGERIAL SKILLS

Effective management necessitates the use of organizational skills and the use of alternative methods of decision making.

STANDARD 1: Decision Making The competent administrator solves problems by:
INDICATORS:
a. using systematic procedures for decision making;
b. employing alternative methods of decision making by involving individuals or representative groups in the decision making process and making individual administrative decisions;
c. basing decisions on building/district/state policies and regulations.

STANDARD 2: Organizational Skills The competent administrator organizes for effective management by:
INDICATORS:
a. developing short and long range organizational goals;
b. demonstrating commitment to an organizational pattern whereby each member of the organization has an opportunity to participate in establishing goals;
c. assisting staff, students, and the community in reaching a common understanding regarding the goals of the organization;
d. conceptualizing, planning, implementing, and sustaining organizational changes;
e. utilizing the administrative team concept by delegating duties, responsibilities, and functions;
f. keeping records and completing reports on schedule.

AREA 2: COMMUNICATION

Effective management necessitates clear communication, facilitation of communication within the organization, and use of communication skills that demonstrate concern for people at all levels relating to the organization.

STANDARD 3: Clarity The competent administrator communicates effectively by:
INDICATORS:
a. selecting the method of communication which meets the needs of the audience;
b. organizing and expressing ideas in written and oral communication;
c. checking to see if others understand.

STANDARD 4: Human Relations The competent administrator demonstrates concern for people by:
INDICATORS:
a. being available to others;
b. receiving, listening, and reacting to all communication and suggestions;
c. encouraging others and self to examine, hold, or express differing opinions, ideas, or feelings;
d. showing respect and acceptance of others;
e. responding to people honestly, taking into consideration the sensitivity of individuals;
f. working to develop trust relationships;
g. having frequent shared communication with students, staff and community.

STANDARD 5: Facilitation The competent administrator facilitates communication at all levels relating to the organization by:
INDICATORS:
a. being able to define district and/or departmental goals.
b. providing for open communication between all subsystems and the total organization;
c. involving representative groups or individuals;
d. transmitting others' ideas;
e. managing school issues through established district channels;
f. discussing problems with the parties involved.

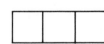

Not a target at this time | Collecting data | Requested target

INTENSIVE EVALUATION PROGRAM
TARGET SETTING SHEET

Beaverton School District
Beaverton, Oregon

Teacher/Administrator's Name _____

Date _____ Target No. _____

STANDARD NO. _____   INDICATORS (Indicate by letter _____

(1) What is to be changed? (List present situation):

(2) What desired change do you want to achieve? (Identify performance to be acquired):

(3) How will you know when you have achieved the desired change? (List level of achievement to be reached):

(4) What will you do to achieve the desired change? (Specify conditions under which change is to be made):

(5) What resources do you need to achieve the desired change? (Consider such resources as time, materials, training, supervision, etc.):

(6) When should the change be completed? (Specify date for target assessment conference):

Signatures:

Teacher/Administrator _____ Supervisor _____

PERS 37:7/31/76   Original - Personnel   Copy - Supervisor   Copy - Teacher/Administrator

19 - Philadelphia

THE SCHOOL DISTRICT OF PHILADELPHIA

EVALUATION OF ADMINISTRATORS AND SUPERVISORS

19   TO 19   PERFORMANCE OBJECTIVES STATEMENT

Note: All information must be typewritten to insure clarity of communication.	
Unit name:	Location no.
Evaluatee:	Telephone

Summary of major responsibilities:

Instructions for Page 2

1. Review the statement of objectives and priorities for 1974-1975 prepared by the person to whom you are responsible.

2. Then, based on a realistic projection of resources needed, list performance objectives that you plan to have your unit and yourself personally accomplish in the 1974-1975 school year.

3. List the key reasons for your choices, and show how others will be able to visibly determine your success in meeting these objectives.

Evaluatee Sign-off Prepared & submitted by:		Evaluator Sign-off Prepared & submitted by:	
Title	Date	Title	Date

FORM 1 - PERFORMANCE APPRAISAL - School District of Philadelphia (Jan. 1975)

The School District of Philadelphia

Performance Evaluation

Related district or office objective

Performance objective

Reasons for selecting

Performance criteria

Tasks	Target Dates	Tasks	Target Dates

Resources needed

Comments (If needed)

Evaluatee:

FORM 1 - PERFORMANCE APPRAISAL - School District of Philadelphia (Jan. 1975)

V, E-1

OBJECTIVE SETTING CONFERENCE REPORT

Penn-Harris-Madison School Corporation
Mishawaka, Indiana 46544

Superintendency Team
Appraisal System

NAME _____   POSITION _____

DATE OF CONFERENCE(S) _____   APPRAISAL TIME PERIOD _____

INSTRUCTIONS: Performance objectives developed mutually by the appraisee and his appraisal team will normally be for the purpose of enhancing or improving his performance. Unusual circumstances may dictate
that the appraisee set specific objectives to remedy an identified deficient performance area. A minimum
of three performance objectives will be established in one or more of the eight major performance area.

The Objective Setting Conference Report shall be completed in triplicate before signatures are affixed.
All three copies of the report are to be forwarded to the Superintendent for review by April 1. After
reviewing and making any notations on the report, the Superintendent forwards the original copy to the
Personnel Office for placement in the appraisee's personnel file. The two other copies are returned
to the appraisee and appraiser.

TO APPRAISEE:

STEP #1 - Compare formal job description with indicators of Administrative Performance and develop
role description.

STEP #2 - Forward role description to appraiser prior
to Objective Setting Conference.

STEP #3 - Evaluate role description in relation to
performance indicators and share with appraiser
during Objective Setting Conference.

STEP #4 - Develop performance objectives prior to
Objective Setting Conference.

STEP #5 - Schedule Objective Setting Conference
with Appraiser.

STEP #6 - Schedule Progress Conferences with
appraiser.

TO APPRAISER:

STEP #1 - Reach agreement with the appraisee's role
description of responsibilities in each of the
eight (8) performance areas.

STEP #2 - Mutually assess the appraisee's current
performance in relation to his role description.

STEP #3 - Assist the appraisee in designing a plan
for the attainment of the performance objectives
he has identified.

STEP #4 - Forward three copies of the agreed upon Objective Setting Report to the Superintendent's Office.

STEP #5 - Provide assistance, support and direction to
the appraisee during Progress Conferences.

STEP #6 - Schedule the Final Conference for the
appraisal period with the appraisee.

SIGNATURES: Signatures indicate that the appraisee and appraiser are in full agreement on the details of
of the objectives contained in this report.

APPRAISEE _____   DATE _____

APPRAISER _____   POSITION _____   DATE _____

REVIEWER _____   POSITION _____   DATE _____

20 - Osceola (Cont.)

V - E

OBJECTIVE SETTING CONFERENCE REPORT

NAME _____

PERFORMANCE AREA	ORGANIZATIONAL GOAL OR OBJECTIVE	PERFORMANCE OBJECTIVES-- STATE PRECISELY IN TERMS OF RESULTS EXPECTED	MEANS OF ACHIEVING SPECIFIC PERFORMANCE OBJECTIVES (Activities, Personnel, & Other Resources Needed)	METHODS FOR MEASURING ACHIEVEMENT (How objective Attainment will be known)	TARGET ACHIEVEMENT DATES
INSTRUCTIONAL LEADERSHIP					
PERSONNEL ADMINISTRATION					

20 - Osceola (Cont.)

NAME _____

Objective Setting Conference Report

PERFORMANCE AREA	ORGANIZATIONAL GOAL OR OBJECTIVE	PERFORMANCE OBJECTIVES-- STATE PRECISELY IN TERMS OF RESULTS EXPECTED	MEANS OF ACHIEVING SPECIFIC PERFORMANCE OBJECTIVES (Activities, Personnel, & Other Resources Needed)	METHODS FOR MEASURING ACHIEVEMENT (How Objective Attainment will be known)	TARGET ACHIEVEMENT DATES
STAFF DEVELOPMENT					
PLANNING AND EVALUATION					
BUSINESS MANAGEMENT					

20 - Osceola (Cont.)

NAME _____

Objective Setting Conference Report

PERFORMANCE AREA	ORGANIZATIONAL GOAL OR OBJECTIVE	PERFORMANCE OBJECTIVES-- STATE PRECISELY IN TERMS OF RESULTS EXPECTED	MEANS OF ACHIEVING SPECIFIC PERFORMANCE OBJECTIVES (Activities, Personnel, & Other Resources Needed)	METHODS FOR MEASURING ACHIEVEMENT (How Objective Attainment will be known)	TARGET ACHIEVEMENT DATES
AUXILIARY SERVICES					
SCHOOL- COMMUNITY RELATIONS					
ACCEPTANCE OF SCHOOL SYSTEM POLICIES, GOALS AND OBJECTIVES					

MONROE COUNTY COMMUNITY SCHOOL CORPORATION
MBO PROGRAM

PROCEDURES FOR DESIGNING & REPORTING A MANAGEMENT OBJECTIVE

1. Before leaving for the summer, each administrator will submit a statement of
   tentative objectives for the next school year. These objectives may be stated
   in broad general terms with refinement to come at a later date. The
   objectives should be submitted on the form labeled Part I, with copies going
   to the Reviewer and the Superintendent.

2. By the end of the first full week of school, but preferably prior to the first
   teacher day, each administrator will complete Part II, will confer with the
   Reviewer, and will submit a signed copy to the Superintendent. The design
   should encompass the six aspects of the A, B, C, D, E (2) format for goal
   setting:

A - AUDIENCE	To whom is the goal directed?
	Who will receive the benefit?
	Who is the audience?
B - BEHAVIOR	What will be your expected behavior?
	What, exactly, will you be doing
	that is observable and measurable?
C - CONDITION	Under what conditions or circumstances
	will your action be performed? When
	will it be done? Where will it be done?
D - DEGREE	To what degree or extent will the action
	be performed? (How much, how often)

E-1 ENABLING ACTIVITIES	What steps will you take to enable you to accomplish your goal?

E-2 EVALUATION	How will you (and others) determine that your goal has been achieved?

3. By April 30 of each year, each administrator will complete Part III, will
   confer with the Reviewer, and will submit a signed copy to the Superintendent.
   7/12/76
   To be used with the following forms:
   ADM/SPF-4   ADM/SPF-5   ADM/SPF-6

182

22 - Bloomington

MONROE COUNTY COMMUNITY SCHOOL CORPORATION
MBO PROGRAM

GUIDE FOR DESIGNING A MANAGEMENT OBJECTIVE
PART I

Administrator_____Building_____

Position_____School Year_____ _____

Statement of Tentative Objectives:

1.

2.

3.

ADM/SPF-4
Superintendent
July 1976

22 - Bloomington (Cont.)

MONROE COUNTY COMMUNITY SCHOOL CORPORATION
MBO PROGRAM

GUIDE FOR DESIGNING A MANAGEMENT OBJECTIVE
PART II

Administrator_____Building_____

Position_____School Year_____ _____

Goal: What I want to accomplish:(Refer to A, B, C, & D on the directions sheet)

Action: Procedures I will follow to accomplish this goal: (Refer to E-1 on the
                                                          direction sheet)

Evaluation: How I will determine if I have achieved this goal: (Refer to E-2 on
                                                              the direction sheet)

We have reviewed this objective and agree that is appropriate for this year.

_____   _____   _____
    Administrator's Signature   Reviewer's Signature   Date

Both sign all three copies. Reviewer keeps one copy, administrator keeps one
copy, and administrator forwards one copy to the Superintendent.

ADM/SPF-5
Superintendent
July 1976

ATTACHMENT 2

23 - Seattle

ADMINISTRATIVE GOAL SETTING

NAME: _____

GOAL: _____

OBJECTIVE (Where are you going?)	STRATEGIES (How do you get there?)	EVALUATIVE CRITERIA (How do you know when you're there?)	ESTIMATED COMPLETION DATE	REPORT OF OUTCOMES (What happened?)

ADDITIONAL AIDS FOR EVALUATION OF CERTIFICATED ADMINISTRATIVE
AND SUPPORT PERSONNEL

Appraisee _____
Appraisor _____
Location _____
Position _____
Date _____

MAJOR CONCERNS	TASKS	PERFORMANCE CRITERIA	INDICATORS
PLANNING	Establishes goals and objectives	- Formulates appropriate goals and meaningful objectives - Supports goals of District and Region or unit - Achieves goals and objectives at acceptable level	
	Organizes, assigns, schedules the use of personnel, fiscal and other resources	- Selects, organizes, assigns personnel for optimum use of professional skills and space - Plans use of available resources to support student and/or program needs	
	Involves others, as appropriate, in planning	- Seeks staff, student, community input in planning - Shares data regarding needs with staff, students, community - Develops procedures for planning and implementation	
	Develops programs	- Demonstrates initiative and creativity - Demonstrates general competency and several areas of specialized expertise - Contributes to District improvement (programs, committees....)	

MAJOR CONCERNS	TASKS	PERFORMANCE CRITERIA	INDICATORS
	Makes and implements decisions	- Allocates time to highest priority items	
		- Uses systematic procedures and alternative methods	
		- Implements needed change with appropriate support of staff, students, community	
		- Follows legal codes and demonstrates support of District policies and procedures	
	Solves problems	- Gathers data, weighs alternatives, arrives at feasible solutions promptly	
		- Deals with unique characteristics of job	
		- Overcomes obstacles, restraints with imagination; capitalizes on positive factors	
	Assures maintenance, security and safety standards	- Monitors plant, office and equipment maintenance	
		- Reports critical needs and takes appropriate follow-up action	
		- Establishes procedures and rules for safety of students and staff	

MANAGING

MAJOR CONCERNS	TASKS	PERFORMANCE CRITERIA	INDICATORS
MANAGING (Continued)	Maintains current, accurate data and records	- Maintains accurate personnel, student and fiscal records - Monitors budget and expenditures - Maintains accurate inventory of materials and equipment - Submits required reports promptly	
EVALUATING	Evaluates program(s)	- Systematically evaluates learner outcomes, and/or program operation - Uses evaluative information for program improvement	
	Evaluates staff performance	- Follows systematic plan, with documentation in evaluating staff - Reports staff performance accurately - Recommends personal/professional growth according to individual needs	
	Assesses own performance	- Monitors own performance - Solicits feedback from others - Develops and implements a self-development plan toward needed areas of expertise	

MAJOR CONCERNS	TASKS	PERFORMANCE CRITERIA	INDICATORS
I N T E R A C T I N G (PROFESSIONAL)	Develops, implements, and maintains a positive climate in school or organizational unit	- Encourages open communication, respect for differences of opinion - Deals with interpersonal problems constructively - Interacts with groups and promotes positive outcomes - Promotes improvement of self-image for students and/or staff - Models appropriate human relations skills - Promotes effective human relations - Develops and maintains high morale	
	Communicates with staff, District personnel, and agencies	- Gives and interprets to staff appropriate information from District offices - Provides District offices with staff feedback - Maintains appropriate communication with other District administrators, departments, and/or other agencies - Encourages expression of problems, criticisms and concerns	
	Responds to staff and student problems, criticisms and concerns	- Collects sufficient information for response to the concerns of staff and students - Takes appropriate action to resolve problem situations	

INTERACTING (COMMUNITY)

MAJOR CONCERNS	TASKS	PERFORMANCE CRITERIA	INDICATORS
	Promotes teacher-parent communication	- Provides meaningful information to parents regarding student progress - Encourages regular staff communication with parents	
	Communicates about school/District policy and programs with the community	- Provides information systematically to parents and community - Communicates openly with parents and community - Seeks parent/community opinion - Interacts with groups and promotes positive outcomes	
	Promotes community participation in school/District programs and activities	- Utilizes parent/community volunteers - Encourages parent/community visitations - Provides programs for parent/community audience	

EXAMPLES OF PERFORMANCE OBJECTIVES FOR EACH PERFORMANCE AREA

	Performance Objectives--State Precisely in Terms of Results Expected	Means of Achieving Specific Performance Objectives (Activity, Personnel and Other Resources Needed)	Methods for Measuring Achievement (How Objective Attainment will be known)	Target Achievement Dates
STAFF DEVELOPMENT	To assess building administrators' perception of the quality and quantity of educational services provided by my area of responsibility.	I will use a self-developed instrument based upon my job description and the roles which affect administrators, as well as an instrument from the publication The Evaluatee Evaluates the Evaluator as a means of collecting data from building administrators.	Develop and use with all building administrators a self-developed instrument to measure their perceptions of my services - as well as use the aforementioned predeveloped instrument. Data collected will be used to improve the services in my area of responsibility.	April 1
EDUCATIONAL PLANNING DEVELOPMENT EVALUATION	To conduct a Needs Assessment Survey to validate the effectiveness of the currently stated institutional mission statement and goals.	1. Study of other Needs Assessment Plans and instruments. 2. Development and field testing of a survey instrument. 3. Administer the survey instrument to a specific number of randomly selected Penn-Harris-Madison students, staff members and citizens. 4. Tabulate, interpret, report and disseminate survey results.	1. Percentage of client participation in survey. 2. To what degree clients perceive goal attainment. 3. Dissemination of Needs Assessment Survey results. 4. Modification of current mission statement and goals as needed. 5. Reallocation of human and material resources on the basis of goal priority and past record of attainment.	May 1

25 - Osceola (Cont.)

EXAMPLES OF PERFORMANCE OBJECTIVES FOR EACH AREA

Performance Objectives-- State Precisely in Terms of Results Expected	Means of Achieving Specific Performance Objectives (Activity, Personnel and Other Resources Needed)	Methods for Measuring Achievement (How Objective Attainment will be Known)	Target Achievement Dates
Explore the possibility of cooperatively purchasing supplies and equipment with neighboring school corporations	1. Confer with neighboring school system administrators to review the objectives of cooperative purchasing. 2. Compare supplies and equipment used to determine if standards which all school corporations will accept can be developed. 3. Develop a list of several supplies and types of equipment purchased frequently and compare actual prices being paid, method of delivery, storage and quantity purchased. 4. Consider time and energy factors in developing acceptable standards and coordinating purchases. 5. Analyze potential savings in regard to above factors and make a recommendation to the Superintendent accordingly.	Determine if the activities stated are happening according to target dates established	1. Feb. 28, 1973 2. Mar. 30, 1973 3. Apr. 30, 1973 4. May 15, 1973 5. June, 1973

B
U
S
I
N
E
S
S

M
A
N
A
G
E
M
E
N
T

25 - Osceola (Cont.)

V - D

EXAMPLES OF PERFORMANCE OBJECTIVES FOR EACH PERFORMANCE AREA

	Performance Objectives--State Precisely in Terms of Results Expected	Means of Achieving Specific Performance Objectives (Activities, Personnel and Other Resources Needed)	Methods for Measuring Achievement (How Objective Attainment will be Known)	Target Achievement Dates
PERSONNEL ADMINISTRATION	To design cooperatively with the Administrative Cabinet through the Superintendency Team Appraisal and Salary Advisory Committee, a Performance-Based Administrator-Supervisor-Appraisal Plan.	1. Organize a functioning Advisory Committee. 2. Formulate a framework of philosophy for an appraisal plan. 3. Obtain current research related to the mutual goal-setting approach to appraisal. 4. Study existing bi-lateral appraisal plans. 5. Committee work sessions. 6. Preparation of a rough draft by the committee for presentation to the Superintendency Team for review. 7. Board approval for proposed policy on personnel appraisal.	In-Service and implement the Performance Based Appraisal Plan for all members of the Superintendency Team.	April 1
INSTRUCTIONAL	Initiate and develop a sequential program of string instrument instruction.	1. Employ competent, enthusiastic, and experienced string specialist. 2. Secure cooperation and encouragement from entire instructional staff, students and community. 3. Secure assistance via re-assignment of current music staff. 4. Budget for background instruments. 5. Develop curricular experiences and institute program in grades 5-6. 6. Sequentially develop string ensembles and orchestra in middle schools and Penn High School.	Evaluate program annually for: 1. Verification of program objectives. 2. Record of student participation. 3. Record of adult participation. 4. Survey of student, parent, faculty and administrative attitudes of effectiveness of program.	1973-74 - Launch Program in Elementary Level 1977-78 - Middle School Program 1980-81 - High School Program

EXAMPLES OF PERFORMACE OBJECTIVES FOR EACH PERFORMACE AREA

Performance Objective-- State Precisely in Terms of Results Expected	Means of Achieving Specific Performance Objectives (Activities, Personnel and Other Resources Needed)	Method for Measuring Achievement (How Objective Attainment will be Known)	Target Achievement Dates
To develop a program intended to increase and improve among parent clientele relevant public information about the activities and curriculum of the school.	1. Organize a parent advisory council including three parents from each grade level. 2. Council to meet monthly for briefing of the on-going program, to express concerns or ask questions about the school program and to explore means of continous parent information/ involvement. 3. Issue a newsletter periodically (in addition to regular newsletter) that provides general information about the program, describes any major or minor research or evaluation studies going on within the school and important dates of meetings to be held. 4. Devise a parent volunteer program which provides a means for interested parents to volunteer their services to the school. 5. Hold an orientation session for volunteers. 6. Formulate a questionnaire-evaluation form through the parent advisory council, to be distributed to all parents in the school attendance area.	1. Observe interest emanating from parent advisory council. 2. Measure actual involvement of parents in program planning. 3. Measure increase/decrease of volunteer parent participation. 4. Analyze results of the parent opinionaires.	March 1

SCHOOL COMMUNITY RELATIONS

OBJECTIVE PLANNING PROFILE

		FOR SUPERVISOR'S USE ONLY
Manager	**Date Submitted**	RECEIVED ———————— Date
PROGRAM Language Arts	**PROJECT** Diagnostic Reading Center	REVISION RECOMMENDED———— Date Due
DEPT. OR SCHOOL Instructional Support		REJECTED ( ) APPROVED ( ) ———— Date
		SIGNED

	Tasks	Physical & Financial Resources Required	Schedule Start	Schedule Finish	(SUPERVISOR'S NOTES)
1	Arrange meeting with reading consultants of local, regional and state reading organizations to determine the "state of the art" in diagnostic reading centers.	Travel and per diem allowances – arrange for meeting facilities, etc.			OK
2	Develop time and activity sequence, cost analysis, budget, site and facilities description and organizational framework for the center's operation.	Resources of Business Services Division – secretarial support services – office supplies.			OK
3	Design and conduct local school surveys to identify potential students who would benefit from the services of the center.	Research services assistance of district reading and testing personnel – services of print Shop.			I would like to see a copy of survey form before its used
4	Develop and submit a detailed proposal to the community, administration and Board of Directors.	None			OK
5	Seek and obtain appropriate funding at local and state levels and begin program implementation including recruiting, selecting and employing qualified staff.	Services of Coordinator of federal programs			See me on this!!

OBJECTIVE A diagnostic reading center will be established within three years which will provide for the evaluation and proper placement of those students who are impaired in the regular school program because of reading disabilities.

Kent School District.

194

FORMS SHOWING VARIOUS SCALES FOR MEASUREMENT

Some forms used by school districts are void of what one normally thinks of as scaling. These forms, e.g., those of Philadelphia and Osceola, simply ask for descriptive information about the attainment of objectives. Others, such as the Montgomery County (form 30), use a three-point scale having to do with effectiveness, accompanied by a supporting statement to describe why the judgment was made. Less commonly found is the one used by the Kent school district that uses a seven-point scale that is actually an expansion of a four-point scale. The scale is used on ten factors but is not used in conjunction with specific objectives. In general, the forms used for administrators tend to be open-end descriptions of functions and accomplishment of objectives or ratings that place people in categories. The wide range of scaling techniques used (Bolton, *Selection and Evaluation of Teachers*, 1973) for measuring teacher performance was not found to be in use with administrators.

27 - Philadelphia

The School District of Philadelphia | Interim and Annual Performance Appraisal

Unit name:			Date

Evaluatee:	Title	Location	Telephone
Evaluator:	Title	Location	Telephone

Summary of major responsibilities:

Summary of Performance - Last review to current review (evaluatee)

Objectives	Results

FORM 2 - PERFORMANCE APPRAISAL - School District of Philadelphia (Jan. 1975)

27 - Philadelphia (Cont.)

Revisions and Tasks for the next Review Period

Evaluatee   Title   Date

Evaluator   Title   Date

FORM 3

28 - Osceola

V, E-2

MUTUAL OBJECTIVE SETTING SUMMARY REPORT

Penn-Harris-Madison School Corporation   Superintendency Team
    Mishawaka, Indiana 46544   Appraisal System

NAME_____ POSITION_____

APPRAISAL TIME PERIOD_____

INSTRUCTIONS: The appraiser shall state in narrative or outline
form specific results or recommendations for
categories I, II & III. After reading and discussing this report with the appraiser, the appraisee
will be given an opportunity in category IV to make
his perceptions and feelings a part of the appraisal
record.

The Mutual Objective Setting Summary Report shall be
completed in triplicate before signatures are affixed. The original copy of the report is forwarded to
the Personnel Office by the appraiser for placement
in the appraisee's personnel file. The appraisee and
appraiser each keep a copy for their record of the
self-appraisal process.

I.   Assessment of Achievement of Specific Original or Modified
Performance Objectives in the Selected Performance Areas:

II.   Record of Progress Conference(s): (Dates, Agreements
reached and Supervisory assistance provided by appraiser.)

28 - Osceola (Cont.)

III. Performance Areas Reviewed in the Final Conference
     Which are Considered by the Appraiser to be in Need
     of Improvement by the Appraisee to Meet Organizational
     Expectations: (List specific areas needing improve-
     ment, supervisory assistance to be provided and dead-
     line for achievement. Also, specify consequences of
     non-achievement of objectives.)

IV. Appraisee Comments:

V. Signatures (Signature indicates agreement with the
   facts as presented in this report)

   APPRAISEE_____

   APPRAISER_____POSITION_____

   MEMBER OF APPRAISAL TEAM_____POSITION_____

   DATE_____

29 - Montgomery County

Name Last	First	Date

□ 1st Year of Current Assignment

□ 2nd Year or □ Every 3rd Year in Same Assignment

Position Location

Position Time	Social Security No.

Evaluation Requested by _____

Grade	Step	Cert.	Issue Date	Expiration Date

A. PERFORMANCE CRITERIA EVALUATION (of Principal and Assistant Principal Services)

Performance Criteria	Effective	Needs Improvement	Not Effective	Supporting Statement
I. Demonstrates a knowledge of the needs, interests, and feelings of students.	□	□	□	
II. Directs the establishment and maintenance of a school philosophy and an educational program consistent with school community characteristics and MCPS goals and policies.	□	□	□	
III. Selects, orients, assigns, supervises, and evaluates staff in order to attain the objectives of the educational program.	□	□	□	
IV. Utilizes human and material resources available to staff in order to attain the objectives of the educational program.	□	□	□	
V. Plans and provides for an environment which supports the educational program and maintains the mental and physical health and safety of students and staff.	□	□	□	
VI. Uses administrative and management practices which promote the efficient and effective operation of the school.	□	□	□	
VII. Assures the proper evaluation of student progress and of the effectiveness of the program to determine what practices or objectives to maintain or modify.	□	□	□	

VIII. Strives to establish and maintain a school community which practices the principles of democracy, reflecting recognition of and respect for each individual.	☐ ☐ ☐	
IX. Shares responsibility for the area and total MCPS program.	☐ ☐ ☐	
X. Identifies areas for personal professional growth, acquires appropriate skills and information, and applies them.	☐ ☐ ☐	

B. Additional Job-Related Information

C. High priority objectives for following year (to be developed in detail on Worksheet)

D. Overall Evaluation (including suggestions for further training)

E.
1. Recommendation for Continuing Assignment or Reassignment (Specify)

2. Special Salary Consideration (Defer or accelerate increment)

*SIGNATURES

_____   _____
Person Evaluated   Date

_____   _____
Evaluator   Date

Conference requested with evaluator's immediate superior: Yes ☐   No ☐

*Signatures indicate completion of the evaluation process. If the person being evaluated does not agree with the contents of the evaluation, he may request a conference with the immediate superior of the evaluator.

Reviewer's Comments and Recommendation(s)

Reviewed by: _____ Date:_____

F. Date Received in Department of Professional Personnel:

PERFORMANCE FACTORS APPRAISAL

Consider each factor separately by reading the factor definition carefully and by interpreting the performance degree definitions only in the context of that factor. Appraisal on each factor should be made independently of other factors.

Indicate your appraisal on each factor by placing a check in the appropriate box. Note that there are two boxes under most of the performance degree definitions; this is to subdivide the zones of performance represented by each of these degrees.

EXCEEDS EXPECTATIONS: Results show achievements which contributed to organizational goals beyond the primary work objectives, and which exceed what is reasonably expected of a well-trained individual in this classification.

MEETS EXPECTATIONS: Results show attainment of primary work objectives in the manner reasonably expected of a well-trained individual in this classification.

NEEDS SOME IMPROVEMENT: Results are generally below satisfactory achievement. Attainment of the primary work objectives has not been reached; performance improvement is indicated.

DOES NOT MEET MINIMUM REQUIREMENTS: Results show deficiencies which seriously interfere with the attainment of primary objectives of the work.

PERFORMANCE DEGREES	1	2	3	4	5	6	7
1. **LEADERSHIP:** Applies knowledge and skills of supervision to programs and personnel and demonstrates the ability to inspire subordinates to grow and develop in a way that reflects acceptance of his leadership.							
2. **JUDGEMENT:** Demonstrates the ability to make a decision or form an opinion objectively, authoritatively and wisely, especially in matters affecting action, good sense and discretion.							
3. **PHYSICAL AND FINANCIAL RESOURCES:** Demonstrates a degree of influence on costs as evidenced by effective utilization and control of physical and financial resources.							
4. **COOPERATION:** Demonstrates responsibility for meeting with and influencing persons within the district and community toward the success of his areas of responsibility as well as the general welfare of the district.							
5. **PUBLIC RELATIONS:** Demonstrates responsibility to conduct himself in a mature, self-confident and friendly way in his personal relationships so as to contribute positively to the image of the district.							
6. **PROFESSIONAL GROWTH:** Is receptive to change and demonstrates continual development of management capabilities in a way which contributes toward meeting his goals and objectives.							
7. **COMMUNICATION:** Demonstrates responsibility in establishing an effective communicative environment which reflects openness, honesty and a high degree of mutual respect, both personal and professional.							
8. **APPRAISAL OF SUBORDINATES:** Is accurate and insightful in his appraisal of the performance of subordinates and demonstrates skill in communicating this information in a way that inspires positive reaction and improvement.							
9. **OBJECTIVES ACHIEVEMENT:** Reflects appraiser's assessment of "performance" as related to objectives and goal achievement.✱							
10. **OVERALL PERFORMANCE** during appraisal period: Place a check in the box that best reflects your appraisal of the individual's overall performance. This should be your judgement of overall performance, and not an average of the appraisals on individual performance.							

✱ Refer to district "Management by Objectives" program.

30 - Kent (Cont.)

(Note: If additional space is required for comments in Parts A through D, use plain bond paper and staple to this page.)

A. If "EXCEEDS EXPECTATIONS" or "DOES NOT MEET MINIMUM REQUIRE-MENTS" are marked, then specific supporting comments are required.

B. Describe those aspects of the individual's work performance which contribute most to his effectiveness.

C. Identify specific, prescribed steps recommended be taken to improve performance to acceptable level if "NEEDS SOME IMPROVEMENT" or "DOES NOT MEET MINIMUM REQUIREMENTS" are marked.

D. Comment on other pertinent aspects (e.g., consider the appropriateness of his current assignment), or changes that would benefit the district and the individual.

SUMMARY FORMS AND DOCUMENTS

All of the summary forms included in this section have some element that is relatively unique to the system using it. Bloomfield Hills includes a section that identifies where development is needed and what activities are needed to promote this development. Bloomington requires self-evaluation to be recorded on a summary form. Hyde Park uses a ''Target Achievement'' form that requires review of the target, summary and evaluation of achievement, written follow-up recommendations, and appraisee's comments. Kent (form 30) includes separate ratings on ten factors in addition to assessment of the individual objectives set by the administrator (form 26). Osceola (form 20) includes a summary of all progress conferences during the appraisal time period. Philadelphia (form 27) includes a summary of major responsibilities along with revisions and tasks for the next time period. Montgomery County has a detailed set of instructions along with detailed criteria for each of the items to be evaluated. (Note: the second and third pages of the evaluation (form 29) are provided in the prior section as an example of the scale used.) The success review form used in Salt Lake City requires a ''yes-no'' decision to be made in relation to attainment of objectives.

31 - Bloomfield Hills

BLOOMFIELD HILLS SCHOOLS
SECONDARY SCHOOL ADMINISTRATOR JOB PERFORMANCE REVIEW

Areas of the management job	Responsibilities--What are his responsibilities in each area?	Performance--How does he carry out his responsibilities? What is he doing well? What isn't he doing well?	What are some specific examples of what he is or isn't doing well?	What measures of performance, if any, were used, or what measures were developed from this appraisal?
Planning	His PLANNING responsibilities are: ☐ Long-range ☐ Short-range ☐ Programs ☐ Schedules ☐ Other			
Organizing	His ORGANIZING or line responsibilities involve: -people under him -people reporting directly to him -How he delegates Are the duties and responsibilities of his people in writing? __Yes __No			
Coordinating	His COORDINATING or lateral responsibilities involve: -keeping others informed by inter-departmental and inter-company communications -determing who is responsible for what			
Motivating	His MOTIVATING responsibilities involve: -How he goes about getting his job done -Inspring high performance -Appraising and talking to his people -Listening to his people -Disciplining fairly			
Controlling	His CONTROLLING responsibilities involve: -Review to see whether his methods of ORGANIZING, COORDINATING and CONTROLLING carried out his PLANNING			

32 - Bloomfield Hills

GREATEST STRENGTH ON THE JOB

WHERE DEVELOPMENT IS NEEDED

DEVELOPMENT ACTIVITIES NEEDED

_____

_____

_____

_____

_____

POTENTIAL

_____ Promotable now to _____

_____ Promotable in _____ years to _____

_____ Satisfactory. Should be able to handle greater responsibility at present level.

_____ Other _____

APPRAISAL MADE BY

Name _____ Title _____

Date of Interview _____

33 - Bloomington

MONROE COUNTY COMMUNITY SCHOOL CORPORATION
MBO PROGRAM

GUIDE FOR REPORTING THE RESULTS OF A MANAGEMENT OBJECTIVE
PART III

Administrator_____ _____ Building_____

Position_____ School Year_____-_____

Goal: What I set out to accomplish: (copy verbatim from Part II)

Results: Response to degree of completion of each step that was designed
to accomplish this goal on Part II. Attach supportive evidence,
if necessary.

Performance Rating: My personal analysis of the value and effect this goal
has had in my professional life.

We have reviewed these results and ratings and submit them to the Superintendent.

_____   _____   _____
  Administrator's Signature   Reviewer's Signature   Date

Both sign all three copies. Reviewer keeps one copy, administrator keeps
one copy, and administrator forwards one copy to the Superintendent.

ADM/SPF-6
Superintendent
July 1976

34 - Hyde Park

```
                          -SAMPLE-
              HYDE PARK ADMINISTRATIVE APPRAISAL
                      TARGET ACHIEVEMENT
```

APPRAISEE_____ POSITION_____

APPRAISAL PERIOD_____

APPRAISER_____ POSITION_____

JOB TARGET:
        (What did we hope to accomplish)

SUMMARY OF TARGET ACHIEVEMENT:
        (What was accomplished; specific
        evidence of attainment.)

EVALUATION OF TARGET ACHIEVEMENT:
        (Appraiser's judgment regarding the degree
        to which appraisee achieved job target.)

FOLLOW-UP RECOMMENDATIONS:
        (Activities which appraisee should carry out
        to reinforce gains made and/or continue
        progress toward achievement of target.)

APPRAISEE'S COMMENTS (Optional):
        (What succeeded; what failed? why?; was
        help adequate?; Is evaluation accurate?;
        next steps?)

_____

Signatures indicate completion of appraisal; not necessarily agreement.

APPRAISEE_____ DATE_____

APPRAISER_____ DATE_____

-SAMPLE-

HYDE PARK ADMINISTRATIVE APPRAISAL

<u>OVERALL APPRAISAL</u>

APPRAISEE_____POSITION_____

APPRAISAL PERIOD_____

APPRAISER_____POSITION_____

<u>APPRAISER'S EVALUATION</u>:

       (Summary evaluation of the appraisee's overall
       performance in relation to the role expectations
       for his position. Recommendation.)

<u>APPRAISEE'S COMMENTS</u> (Optional):

_____

Signatures indicate appraisee had read this report; not necessarily agreement.

APPRAISEE_____DATE_____

APPRAISER_____DATE_____

Department of Professional Personnel
MONTGOMERY COUNTY PUBLIC SCHOOLS
Rockville, Maryland

EVALUATION OF PRINCIPAL
AND ASSISTANT PRINCIPAL SERVICES

Pages 2 and 3 of this form provide the framework for the evaluation of principal and assistant principal services. The form is completed according to the instructions below. Page 4 gives the criteria for school-based administrator effectiveness and indicators.

INSTRUCTIONS

A. PERFORMANCE CRITERIA EVALUATION

Principal or assistant principal performance is evaluated in relation to the ten (10) criteria listed. Indicators for each performance criterion are provided as guides for data collection by observers and by the administrator. Additional indicators may be used.

Based on the evidence collected, the evaluator indicates the principal's or assistant principal's effectiveness in meeting each criterion as follows:

Effective—The criterion is attained and the quality ranges from acceptable through exceptional.*

Needs Improvement—The criterion is attained, but the quality is not consistently acceptable.*

Not Effective—The criterion is not attained.*

*Guides for developing Supporting Statements:

1. A supporting statement is required whenever "Needs Improvement" or "Not Effective" are checked. It should identify the recommended improvements. The criterion must also become an objective for the administrator for the following year, with the completed worksheet (MCPS Form 425-112) entered into the administrator's permanent personnel records.

2. A supporting statement is recommended to note exceptional performance when "Effective" has been checked. In noting exceptional performance, give specific facts which identify exceptional results achieved with students, faculty, or impact on the school program. A supporting statement may also be included for any other "Effective" evaluation whenever the additional information is helpful in interpreting the evaluation.

3. In addition to including supporting statements as directed under items 1 and 2 above when evaluating assistant principals, principals should also include a supporting statement for each criterion to indicate the extent to which the tasks included under each criterion have been assigned to the assistant principal evaluated. The statement should note whether the assistant principal has had a major, limited or no assignment in relation to the criterion. A major assignment means that the assistant principal was primarily responsible for the major tasks included under the criterion. A limited assignment means that the assistant principal had primary responsibility for some of the tasks and a partial or shared responsibility for others. No assignment means that the assistant principal was not ordinarily given the tasks included under the criterion.

B. ADDITIONAL JOB RELATED INFORMATION

Job related information which adds another dimension to a principal's or assistant principal's performance should be included. The evaluator lists the school and community factors which help to put the school-based administrator's performance on the ten criteria into perspective. For assistant principals, the general duties assigned may be listed here.

C. HIGH PRIORITY OBJECTIVES

One or more objectives, jointly developed by the evaluatee and the evaluator, should be identified. They will be recorded on the Worksheet for Developing Objectives for the School-Based Administrator, MCPS Form 425-112, and the completed Worksheet will be used as data for the next evaluation.

D. OVERALL EVALUATION

After a careful analysis of the information reported in A, B, and C, the evaluator develops and records a summary statement, including suggestions for further training.

E. RECOMMENDATIONS

The evaluator determines the recommendations to be made, using the following standards:

1. If the principal's or assistant principal's performance is deemed "Not Effective" on three or more of the criteria, the recommendation must be for reassignment.

2. If the principal's or assistant principal's performance is deemed "Not Effective" on one of the criteria for the second consecutive year, the recommendation must be for reassignment.

MCPS Form 430-69, Revised July 1974

SALT LAKE CITY SCHOOL DISTRICT

PRINCIPALS' SUCCESS REVIEW FORM

School_____ Date_____

Principal_____

The following items have been completed:

☐ Identification of unit objectives.

☐ Implementation of Accountability Program.

☐ Attainment of Unit Objectives:

Y ☐ N ☐ 1. _____
_____

Y ☐ N ☐ 2. _____
_____

Y ☐ N ☐ 3. _____
_____

Y ☐ N ☐ 4. _____
_____

Y ☐ N ☐ 5. _____
_____

Y ☐ N ☐ 6. _____
_____

☐ Final Evaluation of Staff members
The following will be on remediation:

_____
_____

☐ Conference with supervisor.

Superintendent _____   Principal _____

CHECKLISTS AND FORMS FOR PLANNING

The checklists, forms, and outlines provided in this section may be used as—

a. a self-study guide in preparation for Phase I, Phase II, or Phase III
b. resource material when working with practioners in continuing education activities

The materials range from an overall set of ideas to consider before initiating any activities to a checklist that can be used for assessing a Phase III conference. Since the intent of most of the materials is self-evident, very little explanation accompanies them.

38

OVERALL PERSPECTIVE FOR EVALUATION

<u>Each Person Involved in Evaluation Should</u>:

. understand the plan

. know which part of the plan he is responsible for

. know what results are expected (of him and of those for whom he is responsible)

. know how results will be measured

<u>Subordinate's Responsibility</u>:

. determine what resources will be needed

. inform supervisor what these resources are

<u>Supervisor's Responsibility</u>:

. see that needed resources are made available

ASSUMPTION: Approval of the individual proposal of goals keeps the objectives within the mainstream of the system.

39

A CHECKLIST OF INFORMATION TO CONSIDER

REGARDING THE CLIMATE OF THE GOAL-SETTING CONFERENCE

APPROPRIATE TYPES OF COMMUNICATIONS TO BE USED

- Telling

- Asking

- Exchanging

- Demanding

- Encouraging

POINT OF VIEW TO BE DEMONSTRATED

- Mutual goal setting

- Facilitating teacher reaction

- Exchanging views

- Exchanging information

- Reaching agreement on methods

- Leader/subordinate relationship

SELECTION OF APPROPRIATE SETTING

- Office of evaluator

- Office of evaluatee

- Neutral ground

40

CONSIDERATIONS FOR THE "MENTAL SET" AFFECTING CLIMATE

OF THE GOAL-SETTING CONFERENCE

DO YOU WANT TO HAVE THE EVALUATEE RESPOND TO
YOUR OBSERVATIONS?

DOES THE PARTICULAR SITUATION CALL FOR YOU TO
"TELL" THE EVALUATEEE THAT SOMETHING <u>MUST</u> BE DONE?

DO YOU WANT TO "TELL AND SELL"?

DO YOU WANT TO TRY TO REACH MUTUAL AGREEMENT
ON THINGS TO BE DONE AND WAYS TO DO THEM?

DO YOU NEED TO ESTABLISH A CLEAR LINE OF
LEADER/SUBORDINATE RELATIONSHIP?

WHAT ARE THE ADVANTAGES OF INVOLVING THE
EVALUATEEE IN SUCH DECISIONS?

SHOULD ALL GOAL-SETTING CONFERENCES BE PLANNED
THE SAME WAY?

IS THE PLANNING OF NEXT STEPS ONLY A SITUATION
INVOLVING THINGS THE EVALUATEE WILL BE DOING?

DO YOU KNOW OF ENOUGH ALTERNATIVES TO BE ABLE
TO SUGGEST MEANINGFUL DATA DATHERING AND
PLANNING STRATEGIES?

41

CRITERIA FOR JUDGING OBJECTIVES

1. TIME ASPECT -- <u>WHEN</u> is something to be finished?

2. MEASURABILITY OF OUTCOME -- <u>WHAT</u> are the current results?

    <u>WHAT</u> are the expected results?

3. WHAT IS TO BE DONE? -- <u>HOW</u> is it to be accomplished?

4. <u>WHO</u> DOES IT?

5. COST FACTOR = ? $$$$

6. <u>WHERE</u> IS TO BE DONE AND UNDER <u>WHAT CONDITIONS</u>?

(ALL OF THE ABOVE NEED TO BE CLEARLY UNDERSTOOD BY ALL PARTIES)

IN ADDITION, OBJECTIVES <u>MUST BE</u>

7. <u>WORTH DOING</u>   (COMPATIBLE WITH ORGANIZATIONAL GOALS)

42

HAVE A PLAN FOR YOUR PHASE I CONFERENCE

1. CONSIDER THE PEOPLE INVOLVED.

2. ESTABLISH CONFERENCE PURPOSES.

3. DEVELOP AN AGENDA: TOPICS, SEQUENCE, DECISIONS TO
    BE MADE.

4. OBTAIN MATERIALS NEEDED: DISTRICT HANDBOOKS,
    BUILDING HANDBOOKS, JOB DESCRIPTIONS,
    CURRICULUM GUIDES, PERSONNEL RECORDS,
    PUPIL PERSONNEL RECORDS, ETC.

5. REVIEW DATA COLLECTION DEVICES AND PROCEDURES
    (THINK ABOUT WHAT INDICATORS OF ACCOMPLISHMENTS
    MIGHT BE USED)

6. SET ASIDE TIME FOR THE CONFERENCE.

7. PROVIDE APPROPRIATE ENVIRONMENT.

8. PLAN A SUITABLE CLOSING TO THE CONFERENCE.

43

FORM FOR OUTLINE OF A PHASE I CONFERENCE*

PHASE I, PLANNING FOR EVALUATION: OUTLINE

Evaluatee's Name_____ Conference # _____

1. Climate:

2. Information available (records, recall, other):

3. Review of goals (district, unit being administered):

4. Development of evaluatee's specific objectives:

5. Ways to assist evaluateee in meeting goals and objectives:

6. Agreement on needed information and means of gathering same:

7. Timetable for next steps:

8. Bringing meeting to a suitable close:

_____

* This form may be used for making preliminary notes in
preparation for conducting a PHASE I conference.

44

THINGS YOU WANT TO KNOW ABOUT YOUR PHASE I CONFERENCE

1. Did it include all of the elements you wanted?

2. Was the format appropriate for the situation?

3. Was the desired climate achieved?

4. Was there anything that should have been added that you hadn't thought of before?

5. Was there anything which you feel should have been omitted?

6. Did you accomplish the objectives set for yourself?

7. Did you accomplish anything unintended?

8. What tasks are left undone?

9. How would you do it differently if you could do it over again?

Immediately following each conference, write some notes to yourself regarding how it went. Your own introspection will prove beneficial as you repeat the process.

45

PERSPECTIVE REGARDING PHASE II: COLLECTING INFORMATION

WHEN PLANNING FOR INFORMATION COLLECTION:

Consider total evaluation scheme.

Understand how collecting information contributes to total process of evaluation

ASK FOLLOWING QUESTIONS:

1. Will information collection procedures be compatible with goals and objectives?

2. Will information collection methods provide information needed?

3. Are better methods available for collecting information?

46

THINGS TO CHECK ABOUT COLLECTING INFORMATION

- Does the information obtained relate to the goals of the overall evaluation program?

- Is the information sufficient to make decisions?

- What are the limitations to the judgments that can be made with this evidence?

- What additional information appears to be needed to make sound judgments?

- Would the evaluatee come to the same conclusions you would based upon this evidence?

- What information should be discarded -- and why?

- Was the information collected worth the time and effort expended?

- Is the information obtained likely to be reliable?

- Is there a need for more training in information-collection techniques?

47

PERSPECTIVE REGARDING PHASE III CONFERENCE

When conducting follow-up conferences the evaluator must have the purpose(s) clearly in mind before he begins the planning of the conference. Does he wish to plan and conduct a conference that does one or more of the following things?

A. Review goals of district and/or buildings.

B. Review previously determined objectives and the means used to accomplish them.

C. Review the results produced by the objectives.

D. Analyze and interpret the information from Phase II to determine the extent to which the objectives were implemented.

E. Analyze and interpret the information from Phase II to determine the reasonableness of the previous objectives.

F. Adjust previously established objectives.

G. Make decisions about the next steps to be taken.

H. Determine strategies to be employed for the next steps.

I. Other considerations.

ASK YOURSELF: *"Why am I meeting with this person?"*

48

A CHECKLIST TO USE IN CONSIDERING WHAT THINGS ARE
IMPORTANT (TO ACCOUNT FOR) IN A FOLLOW-UP CONFERENCE
REGARDING PERSON, POSITION, TASK

LENGTH OF EVALUATEE EXPERIENCE

- -- New to district
- -- New to building
- -- New to administration
- -- Probationary
- -- Continuing service

PREVIOUSLY IDENTIFIED STRENGTHS AND WEAKNESSES

- -- Professional
- -- Environmental
- -- Personal

POSITION ANALYSIS (JOB DESCRIPTION) REVIEW

- -- Nature of position
- -- Static and dynamic features
- -- Desired administrative behaviors

SOURCES OF CONFLICT

- -- No objectives established
- -- No agreement on roles and responsibilities
- -- No assistance given
- -- No opportunity for evaluatee feedback

49

HAVE YOU THOUGHT ABOUT THE SETTING FOR THE PHASE III CONFERENCE?

1. Is your office the best place?

2. Does the setting chosen provide an atmosphere will help to accomplish your purpose(s)?

3. Will it detract in any way from what you have in mind?

4. Is there a good reason for holding the conference in the evaluatee's office?

5. Do you have the privacy you need?

6. Does this particular situation call for neutral ground?

7. Is there a reason for meeting outside the setting in which the administrator normally functions?

8. Can you get away from the phone?

50

WHO SHOULD BE INCLUDED IN A PHASE III CONFERENCE?

-- Are all conferences one evaluator, one evaluatee?

-- What about team management situations?

-- Should you ever include administrative assistants, consultants, technical specialists, staff personnel,...?

-- Is there ever a place in such a conference for teachers?

-- Would you ever include parents?

-- Under what circumstances might you consider such inclusions?

-- What purposes would this serve?

-- How would you assess the impact on the conference?

51

A CHECKLIST OF INFORMATION TO CONSIDER REGARDING
THE CLIMATE OF THE FOLLOW-UP CONFERENCE

APPROPRIATE TYPES OF COMMUNICATIONS TO BE USED

	WHERE	WHEN	HOW	WHAT CONDITIONS OR CIRCUMSTANCES
TELLING				
EXCHANGING				
ASKING				
DEMANDING				
ENCOURAGING				

POINT OF VIEW TO BE DEMONSTRATED

-- MUTUAL EVALUATION OF DATA
-- TELLING RESULTS OF EVALUATION ALREADY MADE
-- MUTUAL AGREEMENT ON NEXT STEPS
-- FACILITATING EVALUATEE REACTION

52

ANALYSIS OF DATA

I. REVIEW THE OBJECTIVES ESTABLISHED IN GOAL SETTING

    A. Discuss information indicating accomplishment of objectives.

    B. Discuss information indicating a need for changing either the implementation of the procedures or the type of procedures used.

    C. Are the objectives *still* appropriate?

II. REVIEW THE METHODS USED TO OBTAIN DATA

    A. Did the methods provide sufficient information?

    B. Were the methods easy to handle or at least within reason?

    C. Is another type of information needed?

    D. Is a better method needed?

III. REVIEW THE DATA OBTAINED

    A. What is the exact description of the procedures used by the evaluatee?

    B. What is the exact description of the results of the procedures used by the evaluatee?

    C. Can the data be displayed numerically, in tables, or on graphs?

    D. Does the display of the data lend itself to interpretation?

53

HAVE A PLAN FOR YOUR PHASE III CONFERENCE

1. Consider the people involved.

2. Establish objectives for the conference.

3. Develop an agenda (topics, sequence, decisions to be made).

4. Obtain materials (records, forms data).

5. Review data collection materials and procedures.

6. Set aside the necessary time.

7. Provide the appropriate environment.

8. Plan a suitable closing.

54

FORM FOR OUTLINE OF A PHASE III CONFERENCE*

PHASE III, USING INFORMATION: OUTLINE

Evaluatee's Name_____ Conference #_____

1. Climate:

2. Information available: (guides, records, files, data)

3. Review of objectives:

4. Review of data-collection procedures:

5. Review of data:

6. Decisions to be made:

7. Timetable for next steps:

8. Additional information for future planning:

9. Suitable closing:

_____

   * This form may be used for making preliminary notes in preparation
      for conducting a Phase III conference.

55

THINGS YOU WANT TO KNOW ABOUT YOUR PHASE III CONFERENCE *

1. Did it cover all the elements you wanted to cover?

2. Was the format appropriate for the situation?

3. Was the desired climate achieved? Were there any
    words or phrases   you used which you would
    change if you did the conference again?

4. Was there anything that should have been added that
    you hadn't thought of before? Should you still
    talk to the person about it?

5. Was there anything   you feel should have been
    omitted? How could you have done this?

6. Did you accomplish the objectives you set out to
    achieve?

7. Did you accomplish anything you hadn't intended to?

8. What tasks are left undone? Is it clear how you
    will proceed on these tasks?

9. How would you do it differently if you could do it
    over again? How will you plan for the next
    conference differently?

---

* Immediately following each conference, write some notes to
   yourself regarding how it went. Your own introspection
   will prove beneficial as you repeat the process.

Summary

Concepts presented in prior chapters have been illustrated via examples and applications collected from various school districts throughout the United States. The examples were provided to give credence to the systematic elements of evaluation described and to assist anyone who may be reluctant to initiate procedures on the basis of research results or deductive reasoning based on stated assumptions. It has been the purpose of this book to provide a sound basis for evaluation of administrators by means of research results and description of a comprehensive *system* that is flexible enough to incorporate diverse values, and to follow this with examples of how these ideas have been put into practice.

The system and the examples are intended to encourage school personnel to adopt an *ideal-approximation* approach to implementing administrator evaluation systems rather than a *problem-reduction* approach. The latter approach identifies existing problems and attempts to reduce or eliminate them; the former conceives an ideal system of evaluation, considers the constraints of the current situation, and then makes adjustments in the ideal system to implement the closest approximation to the ideal.

Examples of the following elements of an administrator evaluation system are included in this chapter:

1. a cyclical and/or continuous process
2. a systems analysis perspective
3. an interrelationship of process and product of various levels of the organization
4. a relationship of evaluation to other subsystems of management
5. a way of providing direction to the individual and to the organization
6. a planning phase that considers acquisition of needed resources
7. a means for making intermediate decisions
8. organizational support for the process of evaluation of administrators
9. a procedure for making terminal decisions
10. self-evaluation
11. involvement of external evaluators
12. common criteria for administrators
13. individualized goal setting and individualized criteria
14. a schedule for evaluation events
15. a set of purposes for evaluation

Many school districts have manuals describing procedures used in the evaluation of administrators, such as definitions of terms, examples of objectives, definitions of roles for administrators, and rules for dealing with ineffective or incompetent administrators. A listing of characteristics, along with the names of districts that included good examples of these characteristics in their manuals, has been provided in this chapter.

Responses to interviews indicate that many school districts using Management by Objectives procedures have found them beneficial but not problem free. Benefits include more productivity, self-correction, higher morale, better communication, and specific feedback; problems include too much paperwork, too complex for some people, too much variation in commitment, and difficulty in collecting data.

Written statements from several districts are included as examples of general procedures as well as examples of visual displays of schedules of activities. Various types of forms used for goal setting, collecting data, and summarizing a year's activities are provided.

Finally, a variety of checklists and forms for planning have been included for use in self-study or for designing continuing education activities for practicing administrators. The materials contain ideas for all phases of the evaluation process and should be useful for planning or initiating an evaluation process for educational administrators or supervisors.

BIBLIOGRAPHY

Arikado, Marjorie and Donald Musella. "Toward an Objective Evaluation of the School Principal." *Ontario Council for Leadership in Educational Administration* (January 1975).

Bass, Bernard. "Effective Executive Leadership Styles." In *Measuring Executive Effectiveness*, ed. Frederic R. Wickert and Dalton E. McFarland. New York: Appleton-Century-Crofts, 1967.

Beer, Michael and Robert A. Ruh. "Employee Growth Through Performance Management." *Harvard Business Review* 54:59–66 (July-August 1976).

Bentz, V. Jon. "The Sears Experience in the Investigation, Description, and Prediction of Executive Behavior." In *Measuring Executive Effectiveness*, ed. Frederic R. Wickert and Dalton E. McFarland. New York: Appleton-Century-Crofts, 1967.

Blanchard, Kenneth H. and Paul Hersey. "A Leadership Theory for Educational Administrators." *Education* 90:303–310 (April-May 1970).

Blanz, Frederich and Edwin E. Ghiselli. "The Mixed Standard Scale: A New Rating System." *Personnel Psychology* 25:185–200 (Summer 1972).

Bloom, Benjamin S. (Ed.). *Taxonomy of Educational Objectives—The Classification of Educational Goals*; Handbook I: *Cognitive Domain*. New York: Longmans Green and Co., 1956.

Bolton, Dale L. "Collecting Evaluation Data." *The National Elementary Principal* 52:77–86 (February 1973).

———. "Evaluating School Processes and Products: a Responsibility of School Principals." In *Performance Objectives for School Principals: Concepts and Instruments*, ed. Jack A. Culbertson, Curtis Henson, and Ruel Morrison. Berkeley, Calif.: McCutchan Publishing, 1974.

———. "Problems and Issues in the Evaluation of Administrative Performance." In *NSPER: The Evaluation of Administrative Performance: Parameters, Problems & Practices*, ed. William J. Gephart, Robert B. Ingle, and W. James Potter. Bloomington, Ind.: Phi Delta Kappa, 67–92, 1977.

———. *Selection and Evaluation of Teachers*. Berkeley, Calif.: McCutchan Publishing, 1973.

———. "Some Economic Concepts Pertinent to Education." *The American School Board Journal* 151:7–8 (August 1965).

————. *Variables Affecting Decision Making in the Selection of Teachers*. Seattle: University of Washington, Cooperative Research Project No. 6-1349, 1968.

———— and Daniel F. Sullivan. "Administrator Reaction to Administrator Evaluation." Mimeograph. Seattle: University of Washington, 1978.

Brown, Alan F. and Barry D. Anderson. "Faculty Consensus as a Function of Leadership: Frequency and Style." *Journal of Experimental Education* 36: 43−49 (Winter 1967).

Brumback, C. B. "A Reply to Kavanaugh's 'The Content Issue in Performance Appraisal: a Review.' " *Personnel Psychology* 25:567−572 (1972).

———— and John W. Vincent. "Jobs and Appraisal of Performance." *Personnel Administration* 33:26−30 (September−October 1970).

Campbell, John P., Marvin D. Dunnette, Edward E. Lawler, III, and Karl E. Weick, Jr. *Managerial Behavior, Performance, and Effectiveness*. New York: McGraw-Hill, 1970.

Carroll, S. J., Jr. and H. L. Tosi, Jr. *Management by Objectives: Applications and Research*. New York: Macmillan, 1973.

Carvell, James. "Case Study No. 6: Evaluating Administrative Performance." *Thrust for Education Leadership* 2:31−35 (November 1972).

Cummings, L. L. "A Field Experimental Study of the Effects of Two Performance Appraisal Systems." *Personnel Psychology* 26:489−502 (Winter 1973).

Cummins, Robert C. "Relationship of Initiating Structure and Job Performance as Moderated by Consideration." *Journal of Applied Psychology* 55:489−490 (October 1971).

Daw, Robert W. and N. L. Gage. "Effect of Feedback from Teachers to Principals." *Journal of Educational Psychology* 58:181−188 (1967).

"Dentists Pulling Too Many Teeth?" *Seattle Times* (February 22, 1973).

Drucker, Peter. *Management: Tasks, Responsibilities, Practices*. New York: Harper and Row, 1968.

Dunnette, Marvin D. "Predictors of Executive Success." In *Measuring Executive Effectiveness*, ed. Frederic R. Wickert and Dalton E. McFarland. New York: Appleton-Century-Crofts, 1967.

Dyer, William G. "Encouraging Feedback." *Personnel Administrator* 19:13−16 (June 1974).

Ellett, Chad D. "Results Oriented Management in Education." Project *R.O.M.E.* (ED 131590) Georgia State Dept. of Education, Atlanta, Georgia (1976).

Estosito, James P., Gary E. Smith and Harold J. Burbank. "A Delineation of the Supervisory Role." *Education* 96:63−67 (Fall 1975).

Etzioni, Amitai. "Human Beings Are Not Very Easy to Change After All." *Saturday Review* 45−47 (June 3, 1972).

Forehand, Garlie A. "Assessments of Innovative Behavior: Partial Criteria for the Assessment of Executive Performance." *Journal of Applied Psychology* 47:206−213 (1963).

Frederiksen, N. "Toward a Taxonomy of Situations." *American Psychologist* 27:114−123 (February 1972).

French, John R. P., Jr., Emanuel Kay, and Herbert H. Meyer. "Participation and the Appraisal System." *Human Relations* 19:3−20 (February 1966).

French, Wendell L. and Robert W. Hollman. "Management by Objectives: The Team Approach." *California Management Review* 17:13−22 (Spring 1975).

Gaslin, William L. "Evaluation of Administrative Performance by a School's Teaching Staff." *NASSP Bulletin* 58:72−71 (December 1974).

Gaynor, Alan K. "The Multidimensional World of the School Principal." A paper presented at the annual meeting of the American Educational Research Association, Washington, D.C., April 3, 1975.

———. "The Role of the School Administrator: Perspectives for a Conference on Administrator Evaluation." In *The Evaluation of Administrative Performance: Parameters, Problems and Practices*, eds. William J. Gephart, Robert B. Ingle, and W. James Potter. *Phi Delta Kappa*, (1977).

Gephart, William J., Robert B. Ingle, and W. James Potter, Eds. *NSPER.75: The Evaluation of Edministrative Performance: Parameters, Problems, and Practices. Phi Delta Kappa*, (1977).

Greller, Martin M. "Subordinate Participation and Reactions to the Appraisal Interview." *Journal of Applied Psychology* 60:544−549 (October 1975).

Griffiths, Daniel E. "The Individual in Organization: a Theoretical Perspective." *Educational Administration Quarterly* 13:1−18 (Spring 1977).

Gross, Neal and Robert Herriott. "The EPL of Elementary Principals." *The National Elementary Principal* 45:55−71 (April 1966).

Guthrie, Harold D. and Donald J. Willower. "The Ceremonial Congratulation: An Analysis of Principals' Observation Reports of Classroom Teaching." *High School Journal* 56:284−290 (March 1973).

Harkin, Roy E. "The Principal as Mediator." *The High School Journal* 53:333−343 (March 1970).

Heald, James E., and Samuel A. Moore, Jr. *The Teacher and Administrative Relationships in School Systems*. New York: Macmillan, 1968.

Hemphill, J. K. *Dimensions of Executive Positions*, Research Monograph No. 98, Columbus, Ohio: Bureau of Business Research, Ohio State University, 1960.

Heneman, Herbert G. "Comparisons of Self- and Superior Ratings of Managerial Performance." *Journal of Applied Psychology* 59:638−642 (October 1974).

Herzberg, Frederick. "One More Time: How Do You Motivate Employees?" *Harvard Business Review* (January-February 1968).

———, Bernard Mausner, and Barbara Block Snyderman. *The Motivation to Work*. New York: John Wiley, 1959.

House, Robert J., Alan C. Filley, and Damodar N. Gujarati. "Leadership Style, Hierarchical Influence, and the Satisfaction of Subordinate Role Expectations: A Test of Likert's Influence Proposition." *Journal of Applied Psychology* 55:422−432 (October 1971).

"How to Make Staff Accountable for What It Does—Not What It Is." *American School Board Journal* 161:32−36 (March 1974).

Howsam, Robert B. "Teacher Evaluation: Facts and Folklore." *National Elementary Principal* 43:7−18 (November 1963).

Hughes, Charles L. "Assessing the Performance of Key Managers." *Personnel* 38−43 (January-February 1968).

Hunaday, Ronald J., and Glenn H. Varney. "Salary Administration: A Reason for MBO!" *Training and Development Journal* 28:24−28 (September 1974).

Indik, B. P. "Superior−Subordinate Relationships and Performance." *Personnel Psychology* 14:357−374 (1961).

Ingle, Robert B. "Administrative Evaluation: A Caveat." In *The Evaluation of Administrative Performance: Parameters, Problems and Practices*, eds. William J. Gephart, Robert

B. Ingle, and W. James Potter. *Phi Delta Kappa* (1977).

Ivancevich, John M. "Changes in Performance in a Management by Objectives Program." *Administrative Science Quarterly* 19:563–574 (1974).

———— and James H. Donnelly. "Leader Influence and Performance." *Personnel Psychology* 23:539–549 (1970).

————, James H. Donnelly, and Herbert L. Lyon. "A Study of the Impact of Management by Objectives on Perceived Need Satisfaction." *Personnel Psychology* 23:139–151 (Summer 1970).

Katz, D., and R. L. Kahn. *The Social Psychology of Organizations*. New York: John Wiley, 1966.

Kavanagh, Michael J., Arthur C. MacKinney, and Leroy Wolins. "Issues in Managerial Performance: Multi-Trait-Multi-Method Analysis of Ratings." *Psychological Bulletin* 75:34–49 (January 1971).

Keegan, John J. "Performance Based Staff Evaluation: A Reality We Must Face." *Educational Technology* 15:35–38 (November 1975).

Kelber, Thomas P. "The Six Hardest Areas to Manage by Objectives." *Personnel Journal* 51:571–575 (1972).

Korman, Abraham K. "Expectancies as Determinant of Performance." *Journal of Applied Psychology* 55:218–222 (June 1971).

Landau, Martin. "On the Concept of a Self-Correcting Organization." *Public Administration Review* 33:533–542 (November-December 1973).

Latham, Gary P., Kenneth Wexley, IV, and Elliott D. Pursell. "Training Managers to Minimize Rating Errors in the Observation of Behavior." *Journal of Applied Psychology* 60:550–555 (October 1975).

Lawrence, Gordon. "Delineating and Measuring Professional Competencies." *Educational Leadership* 31:298–302 (January 1974).

Leham, H. C. "Optimum Ages for Eminent Leadership." *Science Monthly* 54:171–172 (1942).

Levinson, Harry. *The Exceptional Executive, a Psychological Conception*. New York: New American Library, 1968.

Lindemann, Bertram C. "Teacher Evaluation: Barrier to Communication?" *Educational Leadership* 28:207–208 (November 1970).

Lopez, Felix M. *Personnel Interviewing: Theory and Practice*. New York: McGraw-Hill, 1965.

McConkey, D. D. "Writing Measurable Objectives for Staff Managers." *Advanced Management Journal* 37:10–16 (January 1972).

McNeil, John D. "Concomitants of Using Behavioral Objectives in the Assessment of Teacher Effectiveness." *Journal of Experimental Education* 36:67–74 (Fall 1967).

Massey, Don J. "Narrowing the Gap Between Intended and Existing Results of Appraisal Systems." *Personnel Journal* 54:522–524 (October 1975).

Medley, Donald M. "The Language of Teacher Behavior: Communicating the Results of Structured Observation to Teachers." *Journal of Teacher Education* 22:157–165 (Summer 1971).

Meyer, H. H., Emanuel Kay, and J. R. P. French, Jr. "Split Roles in Performance Appraisal." *Harvard Business Review* 43:123–129 (January-February 1965).

———— and W. B. Walker. "A Study of Factors Relating to the Effectiveness of a Performance Appraisal Program." *Personnel Psychology* 14:291–298 (Autumn 1961).

Moffett, George McHatton. "Use of Instructional Objectives in the Supervision of Student Teachers." Unpublished Ed.D. dissertation, University of California, Los Angeles, 1966.

Niedermeyer, Fred C. "The Testing of a Prototype System for Outcomes-Based Instructional Supervision." *Educational Administration Quarterly* 13:34–50 (Spring 1977).

Noland, Robert L., and J. J. Moylan. *How to Conduct Better Performance Appraisal Interviews.* Springdale, Conn.: Motivation, Inc., 1967.

Odiorne, George S. *Management Decisions by Objectives.* Englewood Cliffs, N.J.: Prentice-Hall, 1969.

Olds, Robert. *Administrative and Supervisory Evaluation.* Arlington, Va.: AASA Executive Handbook, American Association of School Administrators, 1977.

Pambookian, Hagop S. "Initial Level of Student Evaluation of Instruction as a Source of Influence of Instructor Change after Feedback." *Journal of Educational Psychology* 66:52–56 (February 1974).

Peres, Sherwood H., and J. Robert Garcia. "Validity and Dimensions of Descriptive Adjectives Used in Reference Letters for Engineering Applicants." *Personnel Psychology* 16:279–286 (Autumn 1962).

Pfeffer, Jeffrey. "Canonical Analysis of the Relationship between an Organization's Environment and Managerial Attitudes toward Subordinates and Workers." *Human Relations* 26:325–337 (June 1973).

Pharis, W. L. "The Evaluation of School Principals." *National Elementary Principal* 52:36–38 (February 1973).

Posner, Barry Z., Allen W. Randolph, and Max S. Wortman. "A New Ethic for Work? The Worth Ethic?" *Human Resources Management* 14:15–20 (Fall 1975).

Pyron, H. Charles. *Strategies for Evaluating Employee Performance: A Summary of Theory, Research, and Practice in Oregon Firms.* University of Oregon, 1968.

Raia, Anthony P. "Goal Setting and Self-Control: An Empirical Study." *Journal of Management Studies* 34–53 (1965).

————. *Managing by Objectives.* Glenview, Ill.: Scott, Foresman, 1974.

Reddin, William J. *Managerial Effectiveness.* New York: McGraw-Hill, 1970.

Ritchie, Douglas S. "Management System—Madison Public Schools." *The Administrator* 6:33–36 (Spring 1976).

Rose, Gale W. "The Effects of Administrative Evaluation." *National Elementary Principal* 43:50–56 (November 1963).

Rosenshine, Barak. "Evaluation of Instruction." *Review of Educational Research* 40:279–300 (April 1970).

Sayan, Donald L. and W. W. Charters, Jr. "A Replication Among School Principals of the Gross Study of Role Conflict Resolution." *Educational Administration Quarterly* 6:36–45 (Spring 1970).

Silver, Paula F. "Principals' Conceptual Ability in Relation to Situation and Behavior." *Educational Administration Quarterly* 3:49–66 (Autumn 1975).

Simon, A. and E. G. Boyer (Eds.). *Mirrors for Behavior: An Anthology of Classroom Observation Instruments,* Vol. 1–6. Philadelphia: Research for Better Schools, 1967, ED 029 833.

————. *Mirrors for Behavior: An Anthology of Classroom Observation Instruments*. Vol. 7–14 and Summary. Philadelphia: Research for Better Schools, 1970, ED 031 613(a).

————. *Mirrors for Behavior: An Anthology of Classroom Observation Instruments*. 1970, ED 042 939 (b).

Skolnick, Paul. "Reactions to Personal Evaluations: A Failure to Replicate." *Journal of Personality and Social Psychology* 18:62–67 (April 1971).

Smith, Nicholas M. "A Calculus for Ethics: A Theory of the Structure of Value, Part I." *Behavioral Science* 2:111–142 (April 1956).

Smithman, Harold H. and William H. Lucio. "Supervision by Objectives: Pupil Achievement as a Measure of Teacher Performance." *Educational Leadership* 31:338–344 (January 1974).

Solem, Alan R. "Some Supervisory Problems in Appraisal Interviewing." *Personnel Administration* 23:27–35 (May-June 1960).

Streufert, Siegfried and H. M. Schroder. "Conceptual Structure, Environmental Complexity and Task Performance." *Journal of Experimental Research in Personality* 1:132–137 (1965).

Tannenbaum, Robert and Warren H. Schmidt. "How to Choose a Leadership Pattern." *Harvard Business Review* 51:162–180 (May-June 1973).

Thompson, Duane E. "Favorable Self-Perception, Perceived Supervisory Style, and Job Satisfaction." *Journal of Applied Psychology* 55:349–352 (August 1971).

Todd, Donald F., and Manning, Patrick M. "Equitable Pay for School Administrators: Job Evaluation Goes to School." *Thrust for Education Leadership*, 4(1):28–31 (October 1974).

Tosi, Henry L. and Stephen J. Carroll, Jr. "Managerial Reaction to Management by Objectives." *Academy of Management Journal* 11:415–426 (1968).

Wallace, S. Rains. "How High the Validity." *Personnel Psychology* 27:397–407 (1974).

Zand, Dale E. "Trust and Managerial Problem Solving." *Administrative Science Quarterly* 17:229–239 (June 1972).

Zimmerer, Thomas. "The Promotion Illusion, an Investigation of the Promotability of Executives Based on an Analysis of Both Self-Ratings and Superior Ratings." *Management of Personnel Quarterly* 9:8–16 (Winter 1970).

INDEX